Embracing
Judaism

Embracing Judaism

SIMCHA KLING

Revised by Carl M. Perkins

THE RABBINICAL ASSEMBLY
New York

ACKNOWLEDGMENTS

Excerpt from "The Spirit of Judaism" from *God in Search of Man: A Philoso-phy of Judaism* by Abraham Joshua Heschel. Copyright © 1951 by Abraham Joshua Heschel. Copyright renewed © 1979 by Sylvia Heschel. Reprinted by permission of Farrar, Straus & Giroux, Inc.

Excerpts from "A Place in Time," and from "Beyond Civilization" from *The Sabbath: Its Meaning for Modern Man* by Abraham Joshua Heschel. Copyright © 1955 by Abraham Joshua Heschel. Copyright renewed © 1983 by Sylvia Heschel. Reprinted by permission of Farrar, Straus & Giroux, Inc.

Translations from *Siddur Sim Shalom for Shabbat and Festivals.* Copyright © 1998 by The Rabbinical Assembly. Reprinted by permission of The Rab-binical Assembly.

Cover: From the opening page of *Pirkei Avot,* folio 139 in the Rothschild *Maḥzor,* Florence, 1492. Courtesy of the Library of the Jewish Theological Seminary.

Library of Congress Catalog Card Number: 86-63681
International Standard Book Number: 0-916219-15-1

10 9 8 7 6 5 4 3 2 1

Contents

PREFACE by Carl M. Perkins, vii
INTRODUCTION by Simcha Kling, xiii

1 *A Personal Story of Conversion*   1
   BY RACHEL COWAN

2 *Jews by Choice: Then and Now*   10

3 *Classical Jewish Sources*   23

4 *Religious Movements in Judaism*   33

5 *What Does Judaism Teach?*   44

6 *Judaism: A Way of Living*   59

7 *An Introduction to Jewish Worship*   77

8   *Congregations, Synagogues, and* Ḥavurot   99

9   *Holy Days and Festivals*   106

10 *The Jewish Life Cycle*   122

11 *History: Ancient and Medieval*   134

12 *History: Modern Times*   155

13 *American Jewish History*   173

14 *Zionism and the State of Israel*   183

AFTERWORD, 197
BIBLIOGRAPHY, 199
GLOSSARY, 211
INDEX, 223

Preface

*T*HIS book is designed to answer basic questions about the history, culture, and religious traditions of the Jewish people.

Embracing Judaism is primarily addressed to prospective Jews by choice. As Chapter 1 ("A Personal Story of Conversion") and Chapter 2 ("Jews by Choice: Then and Now") point out, the study of Judaism is critical to making an informed choice to become Jewish. If one is considering embracing a Jewish way of life, acquiring an overview of the history and practice of Judaism is a crucial step, and this book can provide just such basic knowledge.

This work is also intended to be useful to the increasing number of adult Jews who are seeking to better understand Judaism. More and more Jewish adults are realizing that, though they may have been born and raised in Jewish families, attended Hebrew school, and possibly even celebrated becoming a *bar* or *bat mitzvah*—their understanding of Judaism is inadequate. Barry Shrage, a prominent Jewish communal leader, has pointed out that many American Jews today may be "comfortable with Plato and Homer and Shakespeare, but can't name, much less understand, the five books of the Torah, or the fundamental works of Maimonides or Buber or Heschel."[1] More and more Jews are realizing the surprising fact that they are culturally deprived. They are thus seeking basic Jewish literacy, and this work can be of help in this effort.

The original edition of *Embracing Judaism* was written by Simcha Kling, *zikhrono l'vrachah* ("may his memory be a blessing"), a rabbi who devoted his life to teaching Judaism, and who inspired many others to share his passion for the Jewish way of life. I was privileged to witness that passion in person, for Rabbi Kling was my father-in-law.

Rabbi Kling loved nothing better than to share his enthusiasm for Judaism. He was gifted with the ability to speak to people with extraordinary sensitivity and caring. He knew how to listen to and intuit their innermost concerns and needs. Whether it was a mail carrier dropping by his home for a quick theological discussion between deliveries or an Israeli taxi driver in New York City who was willing to put off getting another fare, Rabbi Kling had a habit of quickly engaging people in interesting discussions about the nature of Judaism. People found themselves drawn to talk and to listen far longer than they ever intended. This book captures some of that warmth, enthusiasm, and inspiration.

Since *Embracing Judaism* was first published in 1987, the book has been popular in Introduction to Judaism and conversion courses. During these years, the number of non-Jewish men and women studying Judaism and considering conversion has grown steadily. As the Jewish community has become ever more welcom-

---

[1] Barry Shrage, "Jewish Studies, Jewish Community and Jewish Literacy: Creating a Revolution in Jewish Life" (adapted from a speech given at the Association for Jewish Studies Convention on December 17, 1995), unpublished manuscript dated July 29, 1996, p. 1.

ing and receptive to Jews by choice, rabbis in every Jewish community have found themselves devoting many hours to teaching and counseling prospective converts. The need for a book like *Embracing Judaism* has only increased since its initial publication.

Although several fine introductions to Judaism have been published during the intervening years, many of these are not specifically directed to prospective converts or are not written from the perspective of this book, which is that of Conservative Judaism. Conservative Judaism (as the reader will see described in better detail in Chapter 4) maintains that Jews share not only religious principles, but also other aspects of the heritage of a people: a particular language (Hebrew), a homeland (Israel), a sacred tradition (Torah), and norms of behavior *(mitzvot)*. All must be explored to fully embrace Judaism.

Given the increased interest in learning about Judaism and the usefulness of this volume, there was a clear need to republish it when it went out of print in the mid-1990s.

As Rabbi Kling had died in 1991, the Rabbinical Assembly asked me to revise the manuscript for a new edition. I was pleased to accept. It has been a fulfilling effort. I have been grateful for the opportunity to keep this legacy of my father-in-law in print, and thereby extend his influence.

In revising the work I have sought to preserve my father-in-law's voice and perspective wherever possible. The text and the bibliographies have been updated and several chapters have been rewritten. Rachel Cowan's personal story of conversion has been moved from the end to the very beginning of the book. Many readers of the first edition of *Embracing Judaism* had commented how inspiring and encouraging they found this first-person account of one woman's journey to a Jewish way of life; it seemed that its proper place was at the beginning of this book, inviting the reader, through study, to begin his or her own journey.

I would like to thank the leaders and professional staff of the Rabbinical Assembly who supported this effort. Rabbi Alan Silverstein, past president of the Rabbinical Assembly and co-chair of the Rabbinical Assembly/United Synagogue of Conservative Judaism Joint Commission on Intermarriage, first invited me to embark on this work. Rabbi Jan Caryl Kaufman, Director of Special Projects for the Rabbinical Assembly, provided considerable administrative help and much encouragement. Rabbi Martin Cohen, chair of the Rabbinical Assembly Publications Committee, was an intellectually inspiring colleague who read every chapter and provided many helpful suggestions. Amy Gottlieb, the managing editor of *Conservative Judaism,* skillfully guided the evolution of this edition from manuscript to finished product. Annette Botnick Muffs, Rabbinical Assembly Librarian, prepared the glossary and index to this volume. Rabbis David J. Fine, Wayne Franklin, Shira Leibowitz, Benjamin Samuels, Larry Sebert, Joel Sisenwine, and Ira Stone read portions of the manuscript. Rabbi Joel Meyers, executive vice president of the Rabbinical Assembly, demonstrated his overall support for the project.

I am grateful as well for the support of the congregation I am privileged to serve, Temple Aliyah in Needham, MA, and its many dedicated lay leaders. The indefatigable Jan Zidle, our synagogue secretary, typed portions of the manuscript and assisted me in many ways.

Every day I am grateful for the love and support of my family. My wife, Elana, read every page of the manuscript and made numerous constructive suggestions that have greatly enhanced it. She and our wonderful children, Leora and Jeremy, tolerated the many hours devoted to this project with patience and understanding.

I would like to dedicate this revised edition of *Embracing Judaism* to my mother-in-law, Edith Leeman Kling. In his preface to the first edition, Rabbi Kling thanked Edith for inspiring, assisting, and encouraging him. Indeed, Edith was the consummate *rebbetzin* (rabbi's spouse), a true *ezer k'negdo*—a fitting partner to her husband (see Genesis 2:18). Since his death, she has remained an exemplar of Jewish piety and practice, teaching Torah, visiting the elderly and the infirm, and performing many acts of lovingkindness. It is fitting that this volume should honor her warmth and *menschlikhkeit,* even as it honors her late husband's memory.

I would also, sadly, like to acknowledge the loss of my father, Morris Perkins, who died as the manuscript was nearing completion. A humble human being and a proud Jew, who greeted every human being with a cheerful countenance (*Pirkei Avot* 1:15), it would have brought him much joy to see this volume in print.

My hope is that this revised edition of *Embracing Judaism* will be as helpful a guide as was the first edition. May it assist the reader in deciding whether, when, and how to embrace a Jewish way of life.

CARL M. PERKINS
Needham, Masschcusetts
Evev Shavuot 5759

Introduction

*I*F you are thinking about conversion to Judaism, you probably have many questions. What does converting mean? What
is expected of me? Who will help me? What am I supposed to
believe? What do Jews think about converts? Will I ever feel Jewish? Most people ask these and many other questions during the
months or years that they spend making the decision to convert.

This book will answer some of your questions about the
conversion process. Technically, the procedure is straightforward. Emotionally, however, it may be more difficult. Potential
converts have to work out their own complicated family relationships while confronting attitudes in the Jewish community
that may at first be baffling to them.

This book discusses the history of conversion to Judaism,
and Jewish attitudes about conversion. It also includes a convert's description of her own conversion process, in which she
highlights some of the emotional issues which are involved. The
book, however, is more than a discussion of conversion. It is a
comprehensive introduction to Judaism, presenting the basics of
Jewish tradition, ritual, theology, worship, and history. It will
also acquaint you with some of the most important issues that
concern the Jewish community today.

xiv   *Embracing Judaism*

Each chapter of the book presents information and ideas that call for further exploration. The bibliography at the end of the book suggests further readings. One of the wondrous aspects of Judaism is that it provides such a vast and rich literature to study. Everyone, regardless of background, can find new meanings and new understanding with each reading of the Torah, of other biblical texts and commentaries, or of post-biblical literature from every era. Many Jews believe that revelation did not end when God gave the Torah to Moses on Mount Sinai. Revelation is a continuing process that unfolds at each confrontation with a Jewish text.

In the words of Dr. Abraham Joshua Heschel, "Revelation is not vicarious thinking. Its purpose is not to substitute for but to extend our understanding. . . . [We must] look for ways of translating biblical commandments into programs required by our own conditions. The full meaning of the biblical words was not disclosed once and for all. . . . The word was given once; the effort to understand it must go on forever."[1]

An ancient story tells of a non-Jew's visit to Shammai, the great teacher of the first pre-Christian century. "Teach me the whole Torah while I stand on one foot," said the non-Jew. "Then I will convert." Shammai, renowned for his short temper, was enraged by the man's mockery and drove him away. The non-Jew then went to Shammai's colleague, the gentle Hillel, to repeat the challenge. Hillel responded patiently, "'Do not unto others what you would not have them do to you.' The rest is commentary. Now go and learn."[2]

This book presents Judaism as a whole "on one foot." The rest waits for you to explore through study and experience during the rest of your life. Go and learn!

SIMCHA KLING
Louisville, Kentucky
1987

[1] Abraham Joshua Heschel, *God in Search of Man* (Philadelphia: Jewish Publication Society, 1956), p. 273.
[2] *B. Shabbat* 31a.

CHAPTER 1

A Personal Story of Conversion

RACHEL COWAN

GROWING up in Wellesley, Massachusetts, a wealthy suburban community populated largely by white Protestants, I
always assumed that I would raise my own children in a New
England colonial house such as my ancestors had built. It would
be on the side of a hill, shaded by leafy maples and apple trees in
the summer, and surrounded by brilliant foliage in the fall. At
Christmas we would cut our own tree, bake cookies, and put
two candles in each window.

I raised my children in a tenth-floor apartment on the
Upper West Side of Manhattan. My husband and I furnished it
comfortably and eclectically. Prominent on the walls are paint-
ings with Jewish themes; the bookcases house many volumes of
books on Jewish subjects. Every Friday night we lit Shabbat candles and recited *berakhot* over wine and ḥallah before dinner. At
Ḥanukkah, each of the four of us lit his own *menorah*. On the
last night, thirty-two candles would shine out toward the neighbors in the building across the street.

My children are young Jewish adults now, building their own lives and careers, celebrating their Jewishness in their own ways. We come together for the holidays, and for many Shabbat dinners. The light has passed to the next generation.

My path to Judaism has taken me far from that New England hillside, but has brought me the sense of history and the feeling for place that I longed for as a child, and much more. It took me many years to decide to convert, but now I feel deeply rooted in Judaism. History, tradition, and a growing faith in God have given more meaning to my life than I ever imagined I would find.

Looking back at the lengthy process of conversion, I see several stages of development. As a child I was deeply influenced by my parents' humanism. They taught me early that one of my responsibilities in life is to fight prejudice and discrimination. They gave me *The Diary of Anne Frank* to read, and I always felt that she was a friend to whose memory I had to be loyal. I often felt I was defending her when I argued against the ignorant, anti-Semitic ideas of my classmates. I knew no Jews in Wellesley, for there was a restrictive covenant preventing the sale of houses to them, but I had Jewish friends at summer camp and at college. They never discussed religion, however, so I knew very little about Judaism. Nevertheless, when I fell in love with Paul Cowan, I liked the fact that he was Jewish. I hoped he would be able to teach me something about Jewish traditions. He, however, had grown up in such an assimilated Jewish family that he knew nothing about any Jewish holidays.

My family attended the Unitarian Church in Wellesley, where I was active in the youth group and taught Sunday School. I agreed with the liberal ideas that the minister preached, and I loved the music and the beauty of the Christmas and Easter services. Once I met Paul, though, I thought it would be preferable to raise our children as Jews rather than as Unitarians, for they would have such a magnificent history to feel part of and such a rich culture to participate in. I also felt responsible to help maintain the chain of Jewish generations whose links had never been broken.

But it never occurred to me to convert when I married Paul. He barely knew any more about Judaism than I did, and it seemed unfair to expect *me* to convert if *he* didn't have to. Besides, nobody raised the issue with us. I knew I wanted to know more about Judaism, but that seemed like a project for us both to work on together.

If we were going to raise our children as Jews, we needed to learn many things. We didn't even know how to light a Ḥanukkah *menorah*. We asked friends to lead a Passover *seder* for us, and to teach us how to light candles on Friday night. With a group of parents we started a weekly after-school Jewish learning center for the kids (the Ḥavurah School). Working on the curriculum with the teachers, we learned a great deal.

During those years I saw myself as a fellow-traveler. I felt that our family life was enriched and strengthened by the rituals we were beginning to incorporate into our life. I was proud of what our children were learning, and glad that Paul was coming to understand more about what being Jewish means, and what it meant to him. I enjoyed the things we were doing and felt lucky to be able to participate, but I never thought I would become Jewish. It was clear to me that one was Jewish either by virtue of birth and a shared cultural history, or because of a religious commitment. But no matter how good my latkes, ḥallah, or gefilte fish tasted, I would never have Jewish genes, or know what it was like to grow up Jewish. Furthermore, I did not consider myself a religious person. Therefore, a conversion, which implied to me the taking on of a new faith, seemed to be out of the question.

It was important to me that the Jewish community we lived in regarded me as an integral part. Once, on our honeymoon, Paul and I had traveled in Israel. We met with sharp criticism from Israelis who learned that I was not Jewish. That was the first time I had been the object of prejudice, and it hurt. It made us wary of getting close to any organized Jewish group.

Several years after we started the Ḥavurah School, a group
of parents and teachers began to meet once a month to read the
Torah in English and to discuss what we read. We then began to
enclose the discussion in a very abbreviated worship service. Paul
and I also began to attend High Holy Day services conducted
by a group of young Jews in the neighborhood. They met in a
very crowded apartment and shared leadership of the service.
For several years I barely understood what was happening, but I
liked the spirit, the singing, and the English text for the medita-
tions. I began to look forward to Rosh Hashanah and joined
with Paul in fasting on Yom Kippur.

Then a terribly sad thing happened to our family. Paul's
parents were both killed in a fire in their apartment. The horror
and sadness of their death was made bearable for us by the
Ḥavurah community, who really took care of us. They brought
us food, they took care of our children, they sat and talked with
us. We had never heard of the Jewish tradition of mourning, sitting *shivah,* but they taught us what to do, and we found it comforting.

In the months after the fire, I began to look forward more
eagerly to our worship services. In trying to make sense of my
in-laws' lives and their deaths, I unexpectedly found myself
struggling with questions of faith.

Over the next two years, I took several classes—one on the
Book of Exodus, one on the Prophets, and one on *Kabbalah.* I
discovered that Jewish study was fascinating. Our family visited
Israel for six weeks. This time I felt at home there, and loved the
country despite its many problems.

One day I realized that I felt very differently about converting. What had formerly seemed impossible now seemed totally
natural. It was clear to me that Judaism would be the spiritual
path I would follow, and that the Jewish community felt like
home.

I still was troubled, however, by the question of what converting to Judaism implied about my relationship to my parents

and siblings. I did not want to participate in a procedure that implied that my family background was not adequate, or that I had to reject who I was in order to become somebody new. Some Jewish texts are very negative about converts' origins, and I didn't want to do something that subscribed to that attitude. When I married Paul, a teacher of mine once said that I did not give up my past. Rather, I brought all my strengths to the new relationship. The same would be true of becoming Jewish. I would not be bringing Christian religious beliefs into my new faith, but I would bring to my new role as a Jew the strengths I had acquired as a person, many of them taught by my parents.

As Paul and I learned more and more about Judaism, we came to observe more Jewish practices. We stopped working on the Sabbath (Saturday), stopped going out on Friday nights, stopped eating the foods that were specifically forbidden in the Bible. For me, it was important to understand something about each new law before I observed it. I couldn't take them all on at once.

As I began to look for rabbis to supervise my conversion, I reaffirmed my belief that I could take on Jewish observance only gradually. I finally realized that I felt most comfortable as a Conservative Jew, not as an Orthodox one. The attitude to women in Orthodox Judaism was also an important factor, because I had learned about Judaism from people who believed that women should participate equally in all aspects of the service, and I valued that practice highly.

It was emotionally difficult for me to meet with many rabbis, trying to find those who would accept my decision and agree to serve on a *bet din* to supervise my conversion. It was both puzzling and painful to have to knock on so many doors, only to be told that my understanding of being Jewish was not appropriate for their standards. When I finally decided that I would have a Conservative conversion, a close friend who is a rabbi found two other rabbis who readily agreed to participate in the *bet din*.

The idea of the *mikveh* made me feel anxious. For one thing, I associated it with baptism, an idea I had always resisted. Of course, I soon realized that baptism was derived from the *mikveh*, not *vice versa*, but I still felt that it would feel awkward to have to immerse myself in this strange bath under the supervision of an unknown (and, I assumed, probably judgmental) "*mikveh* lady." I asked my closest friend to come with me, as a witness who represented that part of the Jewish community with which I felt most closely identified.

The *mikveh* turned out to be a very clean, white-tiled, small pool. The "*mikveh* lady" was friendly and helpful. The water was warm and embracing, supporting, not strange. The lady made me dip twice to make sure that not even one hair went unimmersed. Then I repeated the blessings out loud so that the rabbis, who were standing outside the door, could hear.

I did not feel born again, nor did I feel cleansed. But I did feel that I had done something important, that it had helped me reach a new level in a spiritual journey that would last the rest of my life. As time passes, I appreciate the *mikveh* even more. It marked an important transition.

Rabbi Wolfe Kelman, who supervised my conversion, suggested that I invite my friends and family to an evening service at our synagogue in which I would participate. It was a wonderful idea because I could immediately do something significant to begin my life as a Jew. I had learned a passage from *K'riat Sh'ma,* which I led, and I learned to read one of the evening prayers. I also gave a short talk about my conversion. I wanted my mother and sister to hear that my decision grew out of my love for them, and I wanted my friends to understand more about my decision.

To me, this is a very important moment, a moment of passage, but one that is part of a continuum. I used to think that conversion meant that you stopped being one thing in order to become something different, and for that reason I resisted it. But Adin Steinsaltz gave me a more organic metaphor. Conversion, he said, is like marriage. You are joined to a new community, but you bring to the union the strength and values that have been your foundation throughout your life. My conversion, for me, marks officially a love that I've already experienced deeply.

That love began as the respect which my parents taught me for Jewish people, as the commitment which they instilled in me to speak out against racisim and anti-Semitism. My sisters, Connie and Peggy, and my brother Richard, have always shared that commitment. I was moved last year when my mother asked Paul and me for books to read about Israel for, she said, "I have Jewish grandchildren, and they need a country where they'll always be safe."

I fell in love with Paul seventeen years ago. Over time I have felt my identification with the Jewish people broaden from him to his parents Polly and Lou, his brother Geoff and his sisters Holly and Liza, to my friends here tonight, to the larger community and the country Israel. It became increasingly important to me not simply to identify with Judaism, but to become a Jew. I've always been proud to be a Yankee from New England. Now I'm proud to be a Jew as well.

Finally, I'd like to talk about two of my most important teachers, Lisa and Matthew. Of course, Paul and I have tried to influence their values and beliefs by sharing with them our ideas, our family histories—Midwestern Jewish and New England Protestant— and by creating places for them to learn: the Purple Circle Day Care and the Ḥavurah School. Our families and friends have also shared much with them. But we have also learned from them. They have shown us what they see as right and wrong, fair and unfair, important and trivial. I respect their opinions enormously.

Today marks an important step for me, a step in the search we all share to lead lives that are meaningful to ourselves and useful to others. I feel strengthened in that search by my children, my husband, my parents and siblings, and by my friends. I also feel strengthened by affirming publicly that an important part of the person I strive to be is being a Jew.

After the service, everyone came over to the house for a pot-luck supper. I made sure to include my non-Jewish friends, and my many Jewish friends who didn't think conversion was necessary for me to be a part of their lives, as well as my religious Jewish friends who were very happy that I had chosen to become Jewish.

It took a while after I officially became Jewish to feel Jewish. People in our synagogue were extremely accepting of me. I actually began to work there as program director a few months after my conversion. But just as born Jews often have difficulties in defining what being Jewish means to them, I, too, had a lot of growing to do. For a long time, I had been aware of not being Jewish. Now when people made remarks that I didn't look Jewish, it took months until I was comfortable saying to them that many Jews look different these days. When people referred casually to *shiksas* or to *goyim*, or said that a Jew by choice isn't really Jewish, I was not comfortable at first in pointing out the prejudice or insensitivity beneath such remarks.

That which was at first awkward for me later became a passion. I have traveled around the country, giving talks and workshops on conversion and outreach. I feel I am doing my part to help the Jewish community become more open and welcoming to those who are actively exploring the possibility of converting and to those who are just beginning to ask questions, unsure of where their journey may take them.

Looking back twenty years later, I see that my conversion, which felt so monumental at the time, was but a step on a long journey. I have trouble remembering now that I have not always been Jewish. Issues which were once difficult have receded. Dealing with Christmas was initially a problem. We would go to visit my sister on her farm each year, and share in her family's wonderful celebration. At first I needed the connection. Gradually though, the holiday lost its importance to us, and we found that Ḥanukkah met all of our needs for family, light, and celebration in winter's dark days. Thanksgiving became the big holiday with my family . . . I feel blessed by the family into which I was born. The values with which I was raised are still my core values. My sisters are my closest companions.

Over time, Judaism has become a way of life for me that incorporates daily, weekly and yearly observances, that has its own rich cycle, that meets my need for tradition, for ceremony, for community, and for God. It has become central to my identity.

After working for several years as the program director of my synagogue, coordinating a marvelous revitalization of community in a once prosperous congregation that had virtually died, I decided to apply to rabbinical school.

I so loved the richness of congregational life that I wanted to acquire the learning and the skills that would enable me to provide spiritual and educational leadership to a synagogue.

I loved the experience. But I perceived Judaism's depth and significance even more profoundly through tragedy. My husband Paul was diagnosed with leukemia in 1987 and died a year later. We both found tremendous strength during that year of his illness from the love and support of our family and community, from rituals, from prayers, and the psalms. And I was sustained through the terrible experience of loss and grief by the same community and by the spiritual wisdom I found in Judaism. As deeply as I grieved and still grieve, I felt and feel blessed that Paul and I found our home in this community and in this tradition.

I continue to work in the Jewish community as a rabbi, a teacher, and a foundation executive. As a result of Paul's illness and death, I am much more sensitive to the needs of Jews who seek healing and consolation, who want to connect with Judaism's spiritual richness. I begin each day with the traditional prayer of gratitude, thanking God for the new day, for the return of my soul, and for the opportunity to be God's partner in another day's work of creation. And I say the traditional morning blessings, including the one that thanks God for making me a Jew.

CHAPTER **2**

Jews by Choice: Then and Now

WHAT is Judaism? And what does it mean to embrace it?

Paradoxically, it is often easier for Jews to say what Judaism is *not* than what it *is*. Judaism, of course, is a religion, but there are Jews who do not claim to be religious. Jews have many national characteristics—a relationship to a specific land (Israel), to specific languages (Hebrew and in some cases Yiddish, Ladino, or another Jewish language or dialect), and a historic memory of national independence and kinship—yet Jews are citizens of many nations. Whatever they may feel about the State of Israel, they can also be loyal and active citizens of the countries in which they live, at home in the languages and cultures of those countries.

Jews are perhaps best defined as a people (*am* in Hebrew), bearers of the Jewish religious civilization. Those who are born into or choose to join the Jewish people are heirs to its teachings, beliefs, practices, and outlook. To be a Jew means to belong to a unique historical community. The community is neither racially nor genetically defined, as those born outside it may become fully accepted members. Yet it is a community in which history, culture, and tradition have been transmitted through family. Therefore, family is very important, and people not born into the community who wish to join it will want to learn about its history, culture, and traditions in order to feel fully at home.

The number of people choosing to become Jewish in the United States today is unprecedented in modern history. Although converts to Judaism have long been considered by Jewish law and tradition to be full-fledged Jews, during the past several hundred years conversion has not been widespread. To understand why, it is helpful to review briefly the history of conversion to Judaism.

During the biblical period, prior to the destruction of the Temple in Jerusalem in 586 B.C.E.,[1] the concept of formal conversion did not exist. When Israelite men married non-Israelite women, they expected their wives to leave their idols behind and worship the God of the Israelites. The wives became members of their husbands' Israelite tribes. When Israelite women married non-Israelite men, they joined their husbands' tribes. The Bible records such "mixed" or inter-ethnic marriages; for example, Moses, David, and Solomon married non-Israelite women. The biblical figure Boaz married a Moabite woman and the story of their marriage is portrayed in the biblical book that bears her name: Ruth. In the geneology that forms the coda of that book, King David appears as one of Ruth's descendants.

During the Babylonian Exile (which began in the sixth century B.C.E.), some of the people among whom the exiled Judaeans lived were attracted to the Jewish religion and became part of the Jewish people, even though they did not live in the land of Israel. The prophet Isaiah referred to them as "those

---

[1] B.C.E. is the abbreviated form of "Before the Common Era," i.e., before Christianity. Jews use it rather than B.C. ("Before Christ") as the word "Christ" means "Messiah" and Jews do not accept Jesus as the Messiah. For more on the history of the messianic idea in Judaism, see Chapter 5.

who joined themselves to the Lord" (Isaiah 56:3–7), and promised them that they would be part of the return to Zion:

> Let them rejoice in My house of prayer, . . .
> for My House shall be called
> a House of prayer for all peoples.

After the return and the rebuilding of the Temple in Jerusalem (in the late sixth and early fifth centuries, B.C.E.), Jews engaged in extensive proselytization. Several centuries later, even Roman nobility converted to Judaism. So did Queen Helena of the Mesopotamian Kingdom of Adiabene and her entire royal family.

During the first centuries of the common era, the Rabbis (Jewish scholars and sages of late antiquity) formulated laws and rituals for conversion that still remain in effect in almost the same form. The established procedure began by asking prospective converts if they understood the suffering with which the Jewish people have been continually afflicted. The prospective proselyte who still wanted to become Jewish was taught the laws, major and minor alike. A person who came "under the wings of the Divine Presence" (the traditional description of conversion to Judaism) was expected to undergo certain rituals. Conversion included circumcision for men (*brit milah*) and ritual immersion in water *(tevilah)* and the offering of a sacrifice for men and women alike. The formal proceedings that followed included a statement of commitment and had to be witnessed by a religious court *(bet din)* of three men. The only requirement that has been changed by traditional Judaism is the elimination of a sacrificial offering.

The rabbinic term for a convert to Judaism is the Hebrew word *ger* (plural: *gerim*). The word has biblical origins. In the Bible, it refers to a "resident alien," a non-Israelite who lived in the land of Israel. The Torah is filled with admonitions to the Israelites to treat the *gerim* well, for we were once *gerim* (also translated as "strangers") in Egypt and we remember our suffering there. This solicitousness toward the *ger* was carried over in the rabbinic period when the word came to refer to converts to Judaism.

The Talmud (the great collection of Jewish law and lore of late antiquity; see Chapter 3) contains many discussions about conversions and converts. One issue is whether converts to Judaism may recite certain phrases in the Jewish liturgy. Can they, for example, refer to God as "God of our ancestors" or "God who has chosen us?" Some rabbis maintained that converts may not recite these words because their biological ancestors were not Jewish and may not have worshiped God. Other rabbinic authorities, though, argued that proselytes may recite the phrases as descendants of Abraham, their spiritual ancestor. This has remained the dominant view in Jewish tradition.

According to tradition, several great rabbis, including Rabbi Meir and Rabbi Akiba, were descended from converts. Nonetheless, some rabbis were wary of converts. Following the destruction of the Temple in the first century, and the Bar Kokhba rebellion in the second century, the Jews were dispersed throughout the ancient world. Outnumbered and vulnerable, it was a risky venture for the Jewish community to accept—and even riskier to seek out—converts to Judaism. This may explain the oft-quoted rabbinic saying that, even as one should draw a prospective convert near with one hand, one should distance him or her with the other. Despite this wariness toward prospective converts, though, all authorities agreed that once a person had converted to Judaism, he or she was to be accepted as a Jew.

In the sixth and seventh centuries, after the close of the talmudic period, conversion to Judaism became a capital offense in areas under Christian domination, and thus the number of conversions declined. Nevertheless, some Christians, especially those who lived in Muslim countries where conversion was not illegal, continued to choose Judaism. Other non-Jews converted in large numbers. The fifth-century kings of Himyar (in southern Arabia) and the eighth-century rulers of a Tartar kingdom, the Khazars, converted to Judaism.

In later years a steady trickle of people became proselytes.

Some Christian clergymen, after studying what they called the Old Testament (the Hebrew Bible), came to feel that they would rather be Jewish. A priest named Vicilinus who lived in Mainz in 1012 wrote treatises on the inherent truth of Judaism. The Jews were soon expelled from Mainz, possibly as a punishment for this man's writings. Andreas, bishop of Bari, fled Italy after he was ritually circumcised, and settled in the large Jewish community in Cairo. When a young Norman nobleman named Obadiah heard of Andreas' actions in 1100, he too left the priesthood and converted.

When the First Crusade was launched in 1096, a proselyte was among the Jews who were burned at the stake in England when Christians attacked them in an early burst of zeal. People continued to convert to Judaism throughout the Middle Ages, even though the act was dangerous for both the proselyte and the teacher. Some prominent Jewish scholars maintained even then that the purpose of the dispersion of the Jews was to gain proselytes.

Maimonides, the great twelfth-century rabbinic authority, took pains to stress that converts to Judaism should consider themselves Jews in every respect. In a famous letter he wrote to a convert concerned about his status, he addressed the issue, discussed above, whether converts may refer to the Jewish patriarchs (Abraham, Isaac and Jacob) as their ancestors:

> As every Jew by birth prays and recites blessings . . . anyone who becomes a proselyte throughout the generations . . . is a pupil of our father Abraham, and all of them are members of his household. . . . Hence you may certainly say: "Our God, and God of our ancestors," for Abraham, peace be upon him, is your ancestor. . . . Since you have come beneath the wings of the Divine Presence and attached yourself to God, there is no difference between you and us. . . . Further, do not belittle your lineage; if we trace our descent to Abraham, Isaac, and Jacob, your connection is with the One by Whose word the universe came into being!

In another letter to the same convert, Maimonides declared:

Toward father and mother we are commanded honor and reverence, toward the prophets to obey them, but toward proselytes we
are bidden to love with the whole force of our heart's
affection. . . . God, in His glory, loves proselytes. . . . One who
leaves his parents and birthplace and nation at a time when they are
secure, and who attaches himself to this lowly, despised and
enslaved people; one who comes to recognize the truth and righteousness in this people's tradition, and casts aside from his heart
the matters of this world and chooses to come beneath the wings
of the Divine Presence—the Lord does not call such a person a
fool [Hebrew: *kesil*], but rather intelligent and understanding
[Hebrew: *maskil*], wise and walking correctly, a disciple of our
father Abraham.[2]

By the end of the fifteenth century, the Jews had turned
inward. There was a sense that "an impassable gulf existed
between the Jewish people and all others."[3] A strong stand was
taken by a prominent sixteenth-century Polish rabbi, Solomon
Luria:

When Israel [i.e., the Jewish People] was settled in its own
country . . . they possessed the authority to accept anyone who
came to them . . . in order to become a proselyte. But now . . . we
are in a country not our own, like slaves beneath the hands of their
owners. . . . May the seed of Israel continue to stand fast and hold
its own among the nations throughout the days of our exile without strangers joining us. This is a matter demanding the greatest
possible caution.[4]

Although proselytism was dangerous for the entire Jewish
community and rabbinic authorities had cooled to the idea of
seeking out converts, they would work with someone who insis-
tently sought them out.

---

[2] Maimonides, Letter to Obadiah (translation quoted in *Encyclopedia Judaica*,
Vol. 13, pp. 1188–1189.
[3] Jacob Katz, *From Exclusiveness to Tolerance* (West Orange, NJ: Behrman
House, 1983), p.145.
[4] *Yam shel Shlomo, Yevamot* 4:49.

When ideas of the Enlightenment became prominent in the eighteenth century, Jews were allowed back into society's mainstream. This new acceptance, though, did not diminish the Jewish community's reluctance to seek proselytes. Perhaps out of concern that it would threaten their new-found freedom, as religious tolerance became more widespread, Jews became more convinced that they should not proselytize.

Modern Judaism continued to make a virtue of refusing to seek out converts. Only gradually has that attitude begun to change in the United States. The Reform movement took the lead in reaching out to potential converts. It simplified the conversion process (in some cases dispensing with the traditional requirements of circumcision and *mikveh* immersion), and it has urged Jews to reverse the usual stand against proselytizing. Conservative rabbis throughout North America have long welcomed Jews by choice. In the past decade, Conservative outreach efforts, through courses and other opportunities to learn about Jewish life, have increased. Orthodox rabbis also teach and counsel prospective converts but, in general, prefer to focus more attention on encouraging Jews to increase their level of religiosity than on reaching beyond the Jewish community.

The Process of Conversion

For two thousand years, Jewish law has deemed the child of a Jewish mother, as well as any person who goes through a traditional, rabbinically supervised process of conversion, to be a Jew. This is the standard still accepted by the Orthodox and Conservative movements. (See Chapter 4 for a discussion of the modern Jewish religious movements.) Therefore, according to Orthodox or Conservative rabbinical authorities, if at birth a child's mother is not Jewish, the child must convert in order to be considered Jewish. (In 1983, the Reform rabbinate decided that the child of one Jewish parent, either father or mother, may be considered to be a Jew if raised as one by the parents, and therefore need not undergo a formal conversion.)

How does one go about converting to Judaism today?

The conversion process ideally involves extensive study with a rabbi or other teacher for a length of time determined by the supervising rabbi. During this period, the students learn history, theology, rituals, traditions, prayer, and Hebrew. They read widely and have a chance to make sure that the teachings of Judaism are wholly acceptable to them and they do not still cherish beliefs that are incompatible with Judaism. They also learn about the history of anti-Semitism and come to appreciate that they are choosing to join a people who have suffered intensely just because they were Jews.

When the students have completed their course of study and are deemed ready to convert, they proceed to the formal conversion ritual. Since conversion is a legal procedure in Jewish law, it must take place in the presence of a Jewish court *(bet din;* plural: *batei din).* The specific acts of the *bet din* depend on the local rabbi. There are some *batei din* whose members ask the candidate questions to ascertain the individual's knowledge and sincerity. There are others who accept the word of the rabbi (or other instructor) and act solely as formal witnesses. It should be pointed out that in some matters of Jewish jurisprudence, a *bet din* must consist of ordained rabbis; in other matters, such as conversion, it may include observant Jewish laypeople and does not require three ordained rabbis. The *bet din* may meet in the rabbi's study, a small sanctuary, or some other convenient location. If the *bet din* does not pose questions to the candidate, it may simply assemble at the site where ritual immersion is to take place. This is traditionally at a *mikveh* (although a lake or natural free-flowing source of water may also serve).

Mikveh (plural: *mikva'ot)* is Hebrew for a pool or gathering of waters. This refers to an indoor pool which is specially designed for ritual immersion *(tevilah).* Historically, wherever Jews have dwelled, they have constructed *mikva'ot.*

The primary community purpose for a *mikveh* has been in order to fulfill the *mitzvah* of *tohorat ha-mishpahah* (for women to immerse in order to resume sexual relations following their monthly menstrual cycles). Other occasions for ritual immersion apply to both men and women, i.e., in preparation for marriage or preceding Shabbat and festivals. More and more liberal Jews have discovered the appeal of making the *mikveh* part of their lives.

The *mikveh* is a square tiled pool about five feet deep. It is filled with water, the bulk of which must be from natural sources. After thoroughly cleaning oneself and removing all clothing and jewelry in order that nothing separate the water from the body, the candidate immerses. A Jewish witness (of the same gender as the convert) is present to be of help and to make sure that the immersion is ritually proper. After complete immersion the convert recites two blessings. The first praises God for the religious act of immersion:

> *Barukh atah Adonai, Eloheinu melekh ha-olam, asher kid'shanu b'mitzvotav v'tzivanu al ha-tevilah.*

> Praised Are You, Adonai our God, who rules the universe, whose *mitzvot* add holiness to our lives and who gave us the *mitzvah* of immersion.

The second blessing is one that is recited on many special occasions when people want to thank God for enabling them to experience that moment:

> *Barukh atah Adonai, Eloheinu melekh ha-olam, she-heh-kheya-nu v'keey'manu v'hee-gee-anu lazman hazeh.*

> Praised are You, Adonai our God, who rules the universe, who has kept us alive, preserved us and enabled us to reach this day.

If the convert is a boy or man, he will have to be circumcised before going to the *mikveh*. If he is already circumcised, he need only complete the ritual by a procedure in which a drop of blood is drawn from the corona of skin that surrounds the head (or glans) of the penis *(hatafat dam brit)*. One who performs ritual circumcisions is called a *mohel,* an observant Jew who is carefully trained. In Jewish tradition, circumcision is not simply a medical procedure, nor is it a ritual performed for the sake of hygiene. It is a religious act, the marking of the sign of the covenant between God and the people Israel. The covenant was first marked in this manner when Abraham circumcised himself, his children, and his servants. Ever since then it has been solemnized in the same way.

Immersion in the *mikveh* is likewise a spiritual act. Ritual immersion in the *mikveh* represents a symbolic rebirth into a new state of being, a new beginning.

Some people choose to bring a friend to the *mikveh*. Some choose to participate in a religious service after the ritual immersion or on the following Shabbat in order to celebrate publicly their becoming Jewish. Others choose to limit the participants in this process, preferring to celebrate their transformation more privately.

During the process of conversion, one chooses a Hebrew name. It may be a translation of one's English name, a name that begins with a similar sound, or an entirely different name. Some choose names of biblical or rabbinic figures (e.g., *Yitzhak/*Isaac, *Yosef/*Joseph, *Miryam/*Miriam, or Hillel or Akiva); others choose names that have specific meanings (e.g., *Asher* = "fortunate", *Penina* = "pearl", *Shoshana* = "rose"). A Jewish name dictionary can be very useful. One does not lose one's given name, but henceforth, one is known by one's Hebrew name in religious rituals.

The Challenges of Conversion

Conversion marks a profound, deliberate shift in one's state of being. It therefore poses a host of challenges for the prospective convert, which should be considered in making the decision to convert. Here are just a few of them.

A Jewish way of life is defined by certain values. Though all religious traditions have values, they may not be identical to one another. Jewish values are generally known by their Hebrew names. Some familiar examples include *tzedakah* (righteousness), *ḥesed* (lovingkindness) and *shalom* (peace). *Yirat shamayim* (reverence for the sacred) and the belief that all human beings are created *b'tzelem elohim* (in God's image) are at the core of Judaism. These values and the behaviors they inspire—such as continuous, devoted study of Torah (Jewish tradition) and the observance of traditional Jewish practices *(mitzvot)*—have long defined the piety of a Jew. A prospective convert studies Jewish values and seeks to incorporate them into his or her world view.

But this may raise serious doubts: If one wasn't born and raised a Jew, can one in fact adopt Jewish values as one's own? If so, how? Most of us think of ourselves as moral human beings. A prospective Jew by choice might wonder: "Could it be that Jewish morality is different from the moral consciousness I've acquired in the course of my life? What if I have the sense that I already believe in Jewish values, but know them by other names? If I already believe in God, how do I determine if my belief is compatible with Judaism? If I haven't thought much about God, does conversion mean that I must swear allegiance to a God in Whom I am not sure I believe?"

Beyond belief, there are additional challenges. Jews have developed specific modes of worship, life-cycle rituals, and holy days to mark the seasons of the year and recall special moments in Jewish history. Again, a prospective convert may wonder: How can I come to feel comfortable with new holidays? If I grew up observing other, non-Jewish holidays, what do I do with my affection for them? How can I get used to observing Shabbat (on Friday evening and Saturday) and learn to treat Sunday as just another day of the week? If I do not know Hebrew (and few prospective converts do, at least initially), how can I learn to read it, much less to recite prayers written in it? What does it mean to pray in a language I didn't know as a child? Will I be confused, and not know how to behave? In which community will I belong, as I face the birth of a child or the death of a loved one?

Judaism, moreover, is not just a religion or a theory of living. The Jews are a people with a unique past, a unique history and civilization. That history can pose among the greatest of quandaries for a prospective Jew by choice: How can I, really, acquire new ancestors? How can I feel myself to be part of a nation I may have known little about for most of my life? And what happens to my "other" ancestors—the ones who weren't Jewish? For that matter, what happens to my non-Jewish family members who may even today be practicing another religion? What should I do, if I have Christian relatives, on December 25th? For that matter—not to compare the two holidays—what will I expect of *them* on the 25th of *Kislev* (the first day of Ḥanukkah)? Can a Jew by choice be a fully supported and supportive member of an extended non-Jewish family?

In short—and this is the core question for the prospective convert—*How can I possibly be who I have not previously been?* How will people relate to me? Will I ever be accepted as a Jew, by Jews as well as by non-Jews? Will I ever feel competent to pass down the Jewish tradition to the next generation? Can it ever really be accomplished?

The answer is that the seemingly impossible is, in fact, achievable. And it can be enormously gratifying. In North America alone, thousands convert to Judaism each year. It used to be that the religious and ethnic identity one acquired at birth and in early life determined one's destiny. No longer. Choosing a religious identity is becoming increasingly common in America and other Western societies. With the increase in socialization between Jews and non-Jews in such societies, more and more non-Jews are learning about and considering embracing Judaism every year. Whether it is to fulfill a personal spiritual search or to create a common religious identity within a family, conversion to Judaism can be the fulfillment of deeply held yearnings.

Of course, it takes time, for conversion is a process more than an event. It takes effort and the willingness to reflect upon and to discuss one's choice with one's family and loved ones.

Most of all, it requires education. It requires courses and

books and newspapers and journals. It requires thoughtful analysis and study. It requires a good supportive student/teacher relationship with a rabbi, who can, on the one hand, challenge one to think critically about what one is doing, and, on the other hand, nurture one's evolving Jewish identity.

Also, since Judaism is more than an intellectual or spiritual stance, to become a Jew one must try out Jewish experiences. For this reason, community—a supportive Jewish community that takes Judaism seriously, within which one can grow—is essential.

Consider Shabbat as an example. One may study the theory of Shabbat. One may come to understand how devotion to Shabbat came to be characteristic of observant Jews. But reading about Shabbat is not the same as observing it. One must *experience* Shabbat—in an observant community—in order to comprehend fully what it might mean to observe it. Only then can one reflect on what it might mean to accept the *commitment* to celebrate Shabbat—not just once, but throughout one's life.

*   *   *

Becoming a Jew has always been a challenging journey for an individual to take. For this reason the Jewish tradition considers it worthy of great respect and admiration.

Jewish tradition even goes further than this. As we saw above in the excerpt from Maimonides' responsum, it is a *mitzvah* (commandment) for Jews to love those who've chosen to be Jews. By casting their lot with the God of Israel and the people of Israel, Jews by choice walk in the footsteps of Abraham and Sarah, the first Hebrews. Those heroes of the Jewish people also, for the loftiest of motives, left families and homeland to pursue a vision. They, too, were the children of non-Jewish parents. And they, too, traveled to a distant place—a place not fully revealed to them until they arrived.

CHAPTER 3

Classical Jewish Sources

WHERE do Jews turn to learn about Judaism? Where are the treasures of Jewish wisdom to be found?

The answer is found on the bookshelf. Judaism is a text-based religious civilization. The Jewish people has long had an intimate connection with texts and traditions. Intrinsic to Jewish identity has been an intimate relationship with the Bible and other sacred texts. Jewish sacred texts have always been seen as the link between the Jew and the Divine, worth studying and pondering time and again. "When I pray," noted scholar and former chancellor of the Jewish Theological Seminary, Rabbi Louis Finkelstein once said, "I speak to God. But when I study, God speaks to me." In this chapter, we briefly review the literary sources of Judaism.

The Torah

The Torah consists of the Five Books of Moses: Genesis, Exodus, Leviticus, Numbers, and Deuteronomy. In Hebrew each book is known by one of its initial words; you may hear them referred to respectively as *Bereshit, Shemot, Vayikra, Bemidbar,* and *Devarim.*

The Torah tells the story of the Jewish people. It is not a journalistic or historical account, but a poetic, theologically charged chronicle. It is best appreciated if it is read again and again, which is exactly what Jews do. The Torah is divided into 54 portions *(parshiyot;* singular: *parashah).* Each Shabbat morning a successive *parashah* is read (see Chapter 7) until the entire work is completed. Then, at the "turning of the year," on the holiday of Simḥat Torah, the Torah scroll is rolled back to the beginning and the reading begins anew.

The word *torah* literally means "instruction." It was translated into Greek as *nomos,* meaning "law," which has led to much misunderstanding concerning the essence of Judaism. The Torah does contain laws, but it also includes ethical insights and obligations *(mitzvot),* history, ritual, poetry, prayer, and many, many stories. It is a guide to Jewish religious life. Many Jews believe that it was divinely revealed, though they may differ over the definition of revelation. The Torah has been called the constitution of the Jewish people, for its teachings are the foundation of subsequent Jewish practice.

The Hebrew Bible

The Torah is the first, most sacred, part of a collection of books called the Hebrew Bible. The other books of the Bible are found in two groupings: the Prophets and the Writings. Because the Hebrew Bible is made up of these three sections—Torah, Prophets and Writings—it is referred to in Hebrew as *"TaNaKH."* The word *Tanakh* is an acronym of the three Hebrew words: *"Torah", "N'vi'im"* (Prophets), and *"K'tuvim"* (Writings).

The first six books of the Prophets—Joshua, Judges, Samuel I and II, and Kings I and II—tell the story of the Israelites from the time they entered the Promised Land under the leadership of Joshua in the thirteenth century B.C.E. until the Babylonians destroyed the First Temple in 586 B.C.E. The other books of this grouping contain the messages of the classical Hebrew prophets, e.g., Amos, Hosea, Isaiah, Jeremiah, Ezekiel, and Micah.

The Writings contain the religious poetry of the Book of Psalms, the teachings about attitudes and conduct in the Book of Proverbs, the theological speculations of Job and Ecclesiastes, the sensuous poetry of the Song of Songs, and the story of Ruth, as well as the books of Lamentations, Esther, Daniel, Ezra, Neḥemiah, and Chronicles I and II.

The Hebrew Bible is sometimes referred to as the "Old Testament." "Old Testament" is a value-laden term of Christian origin. When Christianity arose with its own collection of sacred writings, it viewed the traditions in the Hebrew Bible to be sacred, yet no longer binding in the way that Jews held them to be. The newer Christian texts were understood to supercede the older traditions. Hence, the term "Old Testament" arose to describe the older and, to Christians, less authoritative books of the Hebrew Bible, whereas the newer texts, understood to be of greater authority, became known as the "New Testament." (The word "testament" means covenant.) When Jews speak of "the Bible," they generally are referring to the Hebrew Bible exclusively (the *Tanakh*), whereas Christians may be referring to the books included in the New Testament as well.

It is difficult to study the Bible without a commentary. Throughout Jewish history, scholars have written hundreds of commentaries on the biblical texts. The most famous of these is that of the medieval French-German scholar, Rashi (Rabbi Shlomo Yitzḥaki; 1040–1105), who wrote a running commentary on the Torah and several other biblical books. A classic edition of the Bible with Rashi's commentary and a selection of other prominent rabbinical commentaries written over several centuries is known as *Mikra'ot G'dolot.*

Rabbinic Literature

As early as the biblical period, laws and traditions arose alongside the written texts we know today as the Torah. For one thing, the

Torah often states general principles without specifying how they are to be applied. For example, the Torah prohibits work on the Sabbath, yet nowhere describes what is to be considered work. "Honor thy father and thy mother" is a well-known commandment, yet the Torah does not make clear what it should mean in practice. The Torah takes marriage for granted but does not spell out marriage rites; it provides for divorce but does not specify the procedures to be followed.

Moreover, as economic, social, and political conditions change, it is natural that a society's legal norms should evolve. For example, the Torah insists that every seven years, unpaid debts should be canceled. In theory, this benefits the poor. But what if creditors refrain from lending money in the sixth year? The law then becomes self-defeating, requiring adjustment in order to achieve its objective.

It is thus natural that a body of legal interpretations, analyses, rulings, and innovations arose. This became known as "Oral Torah" *(torah she-b'al peh)* to distinguish it from the Written Torah *(torah she-bikhtav)*, i.e., the Five Books of Moses. The term "Oral Torah" came to be applied to many traditions, legal and otherwise, that were passed down over hundreds of years, from teacher to student, from generation to generation. By being called "torah," these traditions were accorded greater authority than they would otherwise have received, indeed parallel to that of the written Torah. The word *halakhah* is often used to refer to the Jewish legal tradition, which originates with the Written and Oral Torah, and includes subsequent legal developments based upon them.

For many years, the Oral Torah was transmitted by word of mouth. But in the early centuries of the common era, it came to be written down. The Rabbis authored and edited a series of texts based on the Oral Torah. It is unclear why this took place. The traditional understanding is that, as political and economic conditions in Palestine worsened under Roman oppression, it was thought that it would be safer to preserve these traditions in writing rather than to rely on the memories of scholars and sages. These traditions appeared in several varieties.

Midrash

One form of rabbinic literature is *midrash*. The Hebrew word "*midrash*" means "explication." A *midrash* (plural: *midrashim*) is a legal or literary explanation of a text in the Bible. A *midrash* may consist of a single statement explicating a verse, or a legend or story amplifying a biblical account. Over time, *midrashim* came to be collected in books, which are known as *midrashic* collections. Some of these books, such as *Bereshit Rabbah,* consist of explications of the verses in an entire biblical book. Other *midrashic* collections, such as *P'sikta Rabbati,* consist of sermons appropriate for different seasons of the year.

In the early twentieth century, Hayim Nahman Bialik and Yehoshua Hana Ravnitzky gathered together many rabbinic literary *midrashim* and published them as *Sefer Ha-Aggadah.* ("*Aggadah*" means legend or lore.) This was recently translated into English and published as *The Book of Legends.*

Midrash as a genre still exists. Although the classical rabbinic period has come to an end, men and women continue today to read and explicate the Hebrew Bible. The output of their creativity, which can take many forms (e.g., poetry, stories, plays, film), is contemporary *midrash.*

Mishnah

Another form in which rabbinic insights came to be expressed and preserved is *mishnah*. *Mishnah* is a Hebrew word meaning "teaching." A *mishnah* (plural: *mishnayot*) is a statement of Jewish law, which may or may not include a reference to a biblical antecedent. Since *mishnayot* were not necessarily tied to particular biblical texts, they came to be preserved in texts that were organized topically rather than according to the biblical order. Rabbi Judah ha-Nasi, a leading second-century sage in the Land of Israel, published a collection of Jewish law known as The *Mishnah* of Rabbi Judah ha-Nasi. As it soon became authoritative, it became known simply as *The Mishnah*. Mishnaic statements which during the editing process were excluded from Rabbi Judah ha-Nasi's compilation subsequently became known as *"baraitot"* ("excluded" [teachings]).

A unique and popular tractate of the *Mishnah* is *Avot* ("Fathers"), commonly referred to as *Pirkei Avot* ("Chapters" of the Fathers) or "Ethics of the Fathers." *Pirkei Avot* contains no law; rather it consists of a series of pithy verse sayings. Two examples are the famous aphorism of the sage, Hillel the Elder:

> If I am not for myself, who will be for me?
> But if I am only for myself, what am I?
> And if not now, when?

and that of his contemporary, Shammai: "Say little and do much, and greet everyone with a cheerful countenance." Because *Pirkei Avot* is traditionally studied on Sabbath afternoons in the spring and summer, its text can be found in many *siddurim* (prayerbooks).

Once the *Mishnah* was published (at the end of the second century), it began to be studied and analyzed by sages and scholars in the two great Jewish centers of the time: The Land of Israel and Babylonia. The explication and expatiation of the *Mishnah* was known as *gemara* or *talmud* (both words mean "teaching"). *Gemara* developed in both the Land of Israel and Babylonia.

The Babylonian and Jerusalem Talmuds

Toward the end of the fourth century, an edited arrangement of the *gemara* produced in the Land of Israel was published. This work was known as The Talmud of the Land of Israel or *Talmud Yerushalmi*—"The Jerusalem Talmud" (also referred to as the Palestinian Talmud). In Babylonia, it wasn't until the sixth century that a larger, more carefully edited work, the Babylonian Talmud *(Talmud Bavli)* was produced from the traditions which had developed there.

Each Talmud was authoritative in its own sphere of influence. When Jews from Palestine migrated to, among other places, Italy and North Africa, the *Yerushalmi* went with them. But over time, the Jews of Babylonia became far more influential. When Islam, with Baghdad as its capital, conquered much of the Mediterranean basin, the influence of the Babylonian Talmud became widespread. By the medieval period, the Babylonian was clearly the more authoritative of the two *Talmudim*. Today, when people speak of the "Talmud," they are referring to the Babylonian Talmud.

In a summary such as this, it is impossible to present the chief characteristics of the Talmud even briefly. The Talmud is difficult to describe because there is no similar work to which it can be compared. Rooted in the Bible, it is filled with biblical verses and it repeatedly cites the Bible as the authority for its decisions; yet it is neither a biblical commentary nor a legal code. It is encyclopedic in nature but it is not an encyclopedia. It is the product of many individuals and editors; yet it is not the work of any one individual or group. The Talmud contains many judicial cases, but it is more than a legal work; it contains the give-and-take of discussions and arguments as well as asides which seem to have nothing to do with the specific cases that initiated the discussions. It includes ethics, religious practices and liturgy, laws regulating personal, commercial, and agricultural life, community organization, and social welfare.

Talmudic discussions are not concise. They may include many things the Rabbis and their disciples thought to say as a result of hearing a *mishnah* cited—their reactions, explanations, and deliberations, stories that came to mind, references to other opinions or other sources. Therefore, the Talmud is not a work that can merely be read; it must be studied.

Studying Talmud is not easy, but it is an extraordinarily exhilarating, intellectually stimulating experience. The Talmud is a work which challenges and which must be probed and explored with energy, tenacity, and commitment. Until recently, the Talmud was virtually inaccessible to English speakers, but several new translations have appeared and Talmud study groups are more common than they once were. One popular English rendering of the Talmud is edited by Rabbi Adin Steinsaltz, who wrote the following description of Talmud and Talmud study:

[T]he entire Talmud is framed by questions and answers, and even when not explicitly formulated, questions constitute the background to every statement and interpretation. . . It is no coincidence that the Talmud contains so many words denoting questions, ranging from queries aimed at satisfying curiosity to questions that attempt to undermine the validity of the debated issue. Voicing doubts is not only legitimate in the Talmud, it is essential to study. No inquiry is regarded as unfair or incorrect as long as it pertains to the issue and can cast light on some aspect of it. This is true not only of the Talmud itself but also of the way in which it is studied and perused. After absorbing the basic material, the student is expected to pose questions to himself and to others and to voice doubts and reservations. From this point of view, the Talmud is perhaps the only sacred book in all of world culture that permits and even encourages the student to question it.

This characteristic leads us to another aspect of the composition and study of the Talmud. It is impossible to arrive at external knowledge of this work. Any description of its subject matter or study methods must, inevitably, be superficial because of the Talmud's unique nature. True knowledge can only be attained through spiritual communion, and the student must participate intellectually and emotionally in the talmudic debate, himself becoming, to a certain degree, a creator.[1]

The Great Codes of Jewish Law

Though the Talmud was ultimately written down, legal questions and issues continued to arise. By the ninth and tenth centuries, the Talmud was no longer sufficient to answer legal quandaries. Thus, a series of law codes developed, designed to help the scholar, or in some cases, the ordinary Jew, obtain answers to legal questions.

Law codes were produced by various *geonim* (rabbinic leaders in Babylonia after the close of the talmudic age) such as Hai Gaon

---

[1] Adin Steinsaltz, *The Essential Talmud* (New York: Bantam Books, 1976), pp. 8–9.

(939–1038) and rabbis such as Isaac Alfasi (known as the "Rif," an acronym for Rabbi Isaac alFasi), who lived in North Africa.

An important twelfth-century code is the *Mishneh Torah*, by Maimonides. Maimonides (Rabbi Moses ben Maimon, 1135–1204) organized all of Jewish law into fourteen topics. His code is unique for dispensing with the traditional practice of citing previous sources. For this reason it was roundly condemned and viewed with disfavor by many. Nonetheless, it has endured because of its clarity, lucidity, and intelligent organization.

In the fourteenth century, the *Arba'a Turim* (the "Four Rows"; its abbreviated title is "the *Tur*") by Rabbi Jacob ben Asher appeared. The *Tur* organized all of Jewish law into four domains: *Ḥoshen Mishpat* (civil and criminal law); *Oraḥ Ḥayim* (the "Way of Life"; laws of Jewish holidays and festivals); *Even Ha-Ezer* (domestic relations); and *Yoreh De'ah* (miscellaneous laws).

In the sixteenth century, Rabbi Joseph Karo (1488–1575) published the *Shulḥan Arukh* ("the set table"). Based on the organization of the *Tur,* it was a masterful, encyclopedic review of all of Jewish law which quickly became authoritative for Sephardic Jews (i.e., those of Spanish and North African origin). Once modifications for Ashkenazic (Central and Eastern European) Jews were written by Rabbi Moses Isserles (the Rama), the code became authoritative for Ashkenazim as well.

Responsa

Since the talmudic age, Jews have addressed legal questions to rabbinical authorities who have responded with written opinions. (Chapter 2 includes quotations from two of Maimonides' responsa.) The texts of such inquiries and their responses constitute what is known as responsa literature. Responsa literature takes into account the precedents found in the Bible, the Talmud, and the codes of Jewish law and often tells us a great deal about the particular cultural milieu in which it is written. Responsa are still being written today.

The *Siddur*

Jewish liturgy as we know it today arose in the rabbinic period, almost 2,000 years ago. At first, the words of the prayers were not fixed and there were no prayerbooks, but over time, communities developed *siddurim* (singular: *siddur;* prayer collections) in order to preserve prayers and to maintain uniformity and continuity in worship.

The *siddur* is a guide to the structure and themes of a Jewish worship service (see Chapter 7). The *siddur* is designed to be a meditative text. The words on the page are intended to lead the worshiper through the prayer experience, all the while serving to provoke thought and reflection, to inspire, to uplift, to comfort, and to console.

Every congregation uses a *siddur* that reflects its theology and ideology. Among those in use today are the *Daily Prayer Book* and the *Complete ArtScroll Siddur* (Orthodox); *Gates of Prayer* (Reform); the *Sabbath and Festival Prayer Book* and *Siddur Sim Shalom* (Conservative); *Kol Haneshamah* (Reconstructionist).

It is customary to use a special prayerbook known as a *maḥzor* (plural: *maḥzorim*) on the High Holidays (see Chapter 9).

Kabbalah

Although, for many years, scholars believed that mysticism was marginal to normative Judaism, this is no longer the case. The Jewish mystical tradition is increasingly recognized as fundamental to a comprehensive appreciation of Judaism. Jews have preserved mystical traditions since antiquity. Some of these are preserved in the Bible, the Talmud and the *Midrash,* but other works exclusively devoted to mystical speculation have also been produced. As a genre, these works are known as *Kabbalah* (the [mystical] tradition).

Among the best known of these works are *Sefer Yetzirah* (The Book of Creation), mystical traditions concerning the creation of the world, and the medieval work known as *The Zohar* (The Book of Splendor), written as a mystical commentary to the Torah.

CHAPTER 4

Religious Movements in Judaism

*J*UDAISM is rooted in an ancient heritage, a millennia-old civilization. Nevertheless, it is not monolithic. Jews today differ dramatically in their understanding of the Jewish tradition. Indeed, in every generation, there have been different ways of understanding and practicing Judaism.

The antecedents of the major Jewish religious movements in North America today arose in Central Europe in the eighteenth and nineteenth centuries in response to the challenges modernity posed to traditional religious faith, practice, and identity.

After the French Revolution, in 1791, Jews were emancipated in France. Thereafter, throughout Europe, Jews began to be admitted into the dominant society. Ghetto walls began to fall and Jews were permitted to share in the general European culture. Most Jews welcomed their newly acquired freedom, but their reaction to the general, non-Jewish culture around them was mixed. Some enthusiastically embraced it, while others feared it. At the same time, Jews began to understand their own culture differently. Those who were most eager to enter European society wished to reform Judaism radically so that it would not hinder their acceptance. Others sought moderate change in Jewish life, but in ways that would assure greater continuity with the Jewish people's historical experience. Still others believed that reform was heretical and, in any event, unnecessary to gain acceptance in the general society. These responses ultimately evolved into separate movements.

Reform Judaism

Some Jews argued that the essence of Judaism was a universal set of ethical principles. According to this view, any aspect of Judaism that was not of universal applicability was expendable.

These Reformers—as they became known—declared Judaism a religious faith, and rejected all of the group or national aspects of Judaism. They proclaimed the Jews a religious community rather than a people in exile. In order to de-emphasize the differences between themselves and their gentile neighbors, they introduced what were then regarded as radical ritual innovations. They began using the organ at services, which was shocking to a people who had not used instrumental music at times of prayer since the days of the Temple in Jerusalem, which had been destroyed in the year 70 C.E. They recited some prayers in German, insisted on Western standards of decorum, and introduced weekly sermons.

The Reformers eliminated whatever they deemed not "spiritually elevating," including all Jewish nationalistic practices and ideals. They dropped liturgical references to Jerusalem and prayers for the restoration of Zion. In the prayerbook, they substituted the vernacular for Hebrew. They saw Jewish law as having little contemporary relevance and declared it no longer binding. Instead, they insisted, Jews were to remain Jews because they had a mission: to teach the moral principles of the Prophets to humanity. They saw everything else as particularistic; tribal customs that were no longer relevant. Although the majority refused to go to such extremes, some rabbis even shifted the

Sabbath from Saturday to Sunday, and advised eliminating circumcision as a sign of the covenant. The ambiance of many Reform synagogues (or "temples") resembled that of liberal churches; traditional Jewish practice disappeared from many Reform homes.

When Reform came to America, its leaders followed in the footsteps of the German reformers. They conducted dignified and decorous services. They eliminated whatever struck them as archaic. They were indifferent and sometimes antagonistic to folk celebrations and ritual observances. They emphasized the prophetic demand for social justice and morality.

Reform became a movement in America when its rabbis organized themselves and their congregations and established a rabbinical school in the latter part of the nineteenth century. The movement possessed a great strength: it allowed for self-criticism and change when deemed desirable. When several Reform thinkers concluded, for example, that the break with the past had gone too far, they set about bringing Reform Judaism closer to the tradition.

Originally, Reform rejected the principle of Jewish peoplehood. All parochial aspects of Judaism were eschewed. This began to change in the middle third of the twentieth century. With the rise of Hitler in the mid-1930s, many Reform Jews began to rethink the nature of Jewish peoplehood. Whereas most of the early Reformers had been bitter anti-Zionists, the majority increasingly accepted the need for a Jewish state. With the birth of the State of Israel, only a very small minority remained hostile, and by now the entire movement has become wholly committed to Israel's survival and to Zionism as a religious value. Other aspects of Jewish peoplehood are also becoming increasingly important in Reform.

Personal autonomy—the freedom to interpret Jewish tradition from the perspective of individual conscience—has always been a key element in Reform Judaism. Originally it served as the rationale for the rejection of many traditional practices. During the past twenty years (its "postclassical" period), that same freedom has allowed Reform to become much more open to traditional Jewish practice. For example, although early Reformers rejected the dietary laws *(kashrut)*, today some Reform Jews choose to observe some of them. Similarly, although until recently *kippot* (head coverings, sometimes referred to, in Yiddish, as *yarmulkes*) or *tallitot* (prayer shawls) were not worn in Reform synagogues, now they can be seen with increased frequency. Reform liturgy also reflects increased openness to tradition. Originally, most prayers were recited in the vernacular at a service which often included organ music and a choir; today, services include much more Hebrew and recently published Reform prayerbooks include traditional texts among other liturgical options.

Another key feature of Reform today is its inclusivity. Reform has long been an egalitarian movement in which women have participated fully, and Reform was in the forefront in reaching out to gays and lesbians, ordaining gay and lesbian rabbis, and developing Jewish commitment ceremonies for gay couples. Reform has also aggressively promoted outreach to interfaith couples and in 1983 decided to accept as a Jew without conversion the child of any intermarried couple, provided that he or she was to be raised and educated as a Jew.

Reform today remains committed to a strong social action agenda. Under the banner of "*Tikkun Olam*"—"Repairing the World," Reform congregations enthusiastically participate in a variety of social action projects. The Reform movement maintains the Religious Action Center in Washington to promote these goals on a national level.

Orthodox Judaism

Other Western and Central European Jews who were attracted to the European culture opening up before them had a different point of view. They also wanted to participate in cultural life (e.g., attend universities, go to the theater, read secular literature), but not at the price of relinquishing the observance of Jewish law. They adhered to their traditional belief that the Torah had been revealed to Moses by God on Mount Sinai and that all of its instructions are eternally binding. They also believed that all of the subsequent religious law developed by the rabbis was an expression of divine will, not subject to change by any modern interpretation not authoritative for them.

The foremost proponent of this school of thought, known as Neo-Orthodoxy, was Rabbi Samson Raphael Hirsch (1808–1888). His book, *The Nineteen Letters of Ben Uzziel,* is the best popular presentation of this philosophy, which sought to remain steadfastly loyal to traditional Judaism while remaining open to the ideas and insights of western culture. Neo-Orthodoxy, later known as Modern Orthodoxy, grew in America during the twentieth century.

Modern Orthodoxy is not the only expression of orthodoxy. Eastern European Orthodoxy always shared a deep commitment to Jewish law, but never took an interest in active involvement in any part of secular culture. Eastern European religious authorities refused to countenance any adaptation of traditional practice or outlook on life. They dismissed the university as an outpost of secular values, and promoted traditional education in *yeshivot* (singular: *"yeshiva,"* a talmudic academy of higher learning). Hence, such Orthodoxy is sometimes referred to as Yeshiva Orthodoxy. Today, rigorously Orthodox Jews (known in Hebrew as *"haredim"*—those who "tremble" in the presence of the Almighty) wear the kind of garb worn by their ancestors for centuries. They frown on secular education and teach only those subjects required by the government.

The recent growth of Yeshiva Orthodoxy in America and Israel has put pressure on Modern Orthodox communities, forcing them to defend their integration into secular culture. Many Modern Orthodox now refer to themselves by a new name: "Centrist Orthodox," lest they be accused of being too closely aligned with Western, non-Jewish culture. As a result of such pressure from the right, many accounts suggest that religious observance in Orthodox communities has grown much more stringent during the past twenty years.

Services in Orthodox congregations are in Hebrew. If there is a sermon, it is usually given in the vernacular. The liturgy is the traditional text of the *siddur*. There may be slight variations from congregation to congregation, but these generally stem from local practices developed in different parts of Europe, not from ideological differences. Men and married women keep their heads covered at all times. Men and women sit in separate sections of the synagogue. Although women are encouraged to pray, they do not participate in the conduct of the service in any way other than by following the service from their seats.

This may be changing—at least within Modern Orthodox communities. Within some congregations, women have organized their own "women's *tefillot*" (prayer services). Upon reaching the age of majority, more and more young Orthodox women are celebrating, within the limits imposed by their community's interpretation of Jewish law, a *bat mitzvah*. Generally, this consists of a party at which the young woman delivers a learned talk (known as a *d'var Torah*) but it may also include an all-women's service in which the *bat mitzvah* takes a leadership role.

In general, despite their differences, the various strands of Orthodoxy are punctilious about observing all aspects of Jewish law, and adhere strictly to rabbinic law as it is interpreted by their authorities.

Conservative Judaism

A third interpretation of the Jewish religion also emerged in Germany and developed in the United States. The adherents of Conservative Judaism (originally known as Positive-Historical Judaism) agreed with some of the theses of both Reform and Neo-Orthodox Judaism and disagreed with others.

From its inception, Conservative Judaism was characterized

by its loyalty to tradition and openness to change based on a rigorous examination of Jewish sources and historical developments. On the one hand, the Conservative movement insisted that *halakhah* (the Jewish legal tradition) is binding. On the other hand, the Conservative movement found within Jewish history a process of evolution in response to new realities, new ideas, and new perceptions of the world. It tried to walk the fine line between two less desirable options: on the right, an uncritical acceptance of the Jewish past and, on the left, a radical rejection of that past. The position of the movement was that "Jewish piety can be fully at home in minds open to the best of modern thought."[1] Thus, modest changes in Jewish practice, rooted in and consistent with Jewish legal principles, were made by the early leaders of the movement.

This process of slow, methodical change continued during the rapid expansion of Conservative Judaism in America in the middle of the twentieth century. For example, in the 1950s, the movement's Committee on Jewish Law and Standards (the CJLS) issued a ruling permitting the use of electricity on Shabbat. That ruling distinguishes electricity from fire, which may not be kindled on Shabbat. The same ruling permitted riding in an automobile on Shabbat, but solely for the purpose of attending synagogue services and returning home.

One of the more prominent recent developments within Conservative Judaism has involved the role of women. Traditional Jewish law does not permit women to lead public worship services at which men are present. (Women are even forbidden from sitting together with men during worship.) Relying on a combination of arguments, and responding to the widespread perception within the movement that change was halakhically possible (i.e., consistent with Jewish law) and ethically warranted, the CJLS published a series of responsa permitting con-

---

[1] Louis Jacobs, *The Jewish Religion: A Companion* (Oxford: Oxford University Press, 1995), p. 93.

gregations to adopt egalitarian practices. During the past few decades, most Conservative congregations have become fully egalitarian. That is, in these congregations women are counted in a *minyan* and are as free as men to assume the ritual responsibilities of Jewish life: to pray wearing *tallit* and *tefillin,* and to lead others in prayer.

Throughout its history, despite the movement's commitment to *halakhah,* the levels of observance on the part of Conservative Jews have varied widely. Whereas some Conservative Jews are devoted to Jewish practice, others are less observant. While the movement promotes standards of Jewish practice, one may find a diversity of halakhic expressions within the Conservative Jewish community.

But, as Rabbi Louis Jacobs has written, "Despite [their] wide divergencies and pluralistic tendencies, all Conservative congregations agree in affirming the basic institutions of traditional Judaism—observance of the Sabbath and the festivals, the dietary laws, circumcision, daily prayer, marriage and divorce, conversion in accordance with Jewish law, the centrality of Hebrew in the synagogue service, and, above all, the study of the Torah as a high religious obligation."[2]

These and other commitments were detailed in a monograph published in 1988, entitled *Emet Ve-Emunah,* the first statement of principles published by the movement.

Rabbi Ismar Schorsch, chancellor of the Jewish Theological Seminary, has suggested that seven elements of a "sacred cluster" of Jewish values are at the core of Conservative Judaism. These are the quest for the sacred (faith in God), loyalty to the Torah, commitment to *halakhah* (Jewish law and tradition), love of the Hebrew language, devotion to Torah study, responsibility for the welfare of the Jewish community, and support for the State of Israel.

More North American Jews today are affiliated with Con-

[2] Ibid., p. 95.

servative synagogues than with those of any other religious movement. It remains a pluralistic movement of men and women striving to live Jewish lives, fulfill *mitzvot,* support the Jewish community, transmit Jewish values, and pursue justice (see Deuteronomy 16:20).

Reconstructionist Judaism

A fourth movement in Judaism emerged in the United States from within the Conservative movement in 1934. Reconstructionism is the fruit of the thinking of Rabbi Mordecai M. Kaplan, who, though long identified with the Conservative movement and professor at its Jewish Theological Seminary for more than half a century, found the other three approaches wanting. In his vision of the totality of Judaism, he defined Judaism as "the evolving religious civilization" of the Jewish people. "Evolving" implies that Judaism is not static; it has always developed and grown. "Religious" implies that the main emphasis of Jewish civilization has been religious in that it has been concerned primarily with God and spiritual living. "Civilization" implies that Judaism is more than a religion; it is a total way of life encompassing folkways and mores, a common history and common aspirations, a language and a relationship to a special land, a religion and a legal system.

Rabbi Kaplan rejected supernaturalism; his position was that of "religious humanism." He conceived of God as a Power, not as a person. He even dared to define God as "the Power that makes for salvation" and "the Power that drives man to make the most of himself." He accordingly removed from the prayerbook all supernaturalist expressions as well as those deemed *passe.* Nevertheless, Reconstructionist liturgy follows the traditional pattern and reflects the traditional intertwining of peoplehood and religion, although it does introduce basic changes and reinterpretations into the text of the prayerbook. Reconstructionists do not necessarily accept *halakhah* as binding, but they observe traditional practices which they consider to be expressions of the Jewish religious civilization.

For many years, the Reconstructionists were considered the left wing of the Conservative movement, and those who accepted Rabbi Kaplan's philosophy belonged to either the Conservative or the Reform movements. Some continue to do so even though there are now Reconstructionist congregations and *ḥavurot* (see Chapter 8), and the movement has established its own rabbinical school, the Reconstructionist Rabbinical College. Many American Jewish leaders do not accept Rabbi Kaplan's theology, but all have been affected deeply by his analysis of contemporary Jewish life and his prescriptions for curing its ills. The impact of Reconstructionism is far greater than its numbers would imply.

Movements, Not Denominations

The Reform, Orthodox, Conservative, and Reconstructionist movements are not parallel to the various groupings within Protestantism; they are not separate denominations. There are differences among them, but all Jews, including secularists, are deemed by Jewish law and by the vast majority of Jewish leaders to be members of one Jewish people.

The liturgical and ritual differences among these groups center principally on their interpretation of Jewish law and stem from the fact that both Reform and Reconstructionism maintain that *halakhah* is no longer binding, while Orthodox and Conservative Jews insist that it is. Doctrinal differences stem from the greater openness of those in the more liberal movements to rethink traditionalist assumptions concerning the historicity and authority of the Bible and other sacred Jewish texts.

Although many Jews today are affiliated with one or another of the four major religious movements, some are not. Some Jews define themselves as "just Jewish," and profess no particular loyalty to any movement. Some Jews may belong to more than one synagogue, or feel attracted to aspects of several different movements. Some Jews express their religiosity within small Jewish groups (i.e., *minyanim* or *ḥavurot;* see Chapter 8) not affiliated with any of the national movements. It may be that we are moving toward a time of increasingly individualistic Jewish religious expression when the familiar labels described in this chapter ("Orthodox," "Reform," etc.) will be less helpful than previously to distinguish one vision of Jewish life and practice from another.

CHAPTER 5

What Does Judaism Teach?

A Jew is a person who was born into the Jewish people or a person who has chosen to become part of the Jewish people. A Jew is neither required nor expected to articulate a particular credo. At the moment of ordination, rabbis make no confession of faith; they are ordained because they have acquired enough knowledge to be recognized religious authorities. A young person upon becoming a *bar mitzvah* or a *bat mitzvah* does not vow allegiance to a formulated dogma but rather leads and/or participates in part of a synagogue service, thus demonstrating the ability to join the congregation as a regular participant.

Judaism, however, has always made affirmations, has always taken stands. Certain beliefs have been normative, and there have been boundaries beyond which one could not go and still remain within the Jewish fold. Nonetheless, the most prominent boundaries have generally been those of behavior rather than of thought or belief. The reason for this is that Jews have tradition-

ally understood their faith as a covenant, an agreement. They
have understood their duty under the covenant to be the performance of certain prescribed behaviors (known as "*mitzvot*"—
"commandments"). This is why it may be more accurate to
describe Jews who are serious about Judaism as "observant"
rather than "religious."

Halakhah (Jewish law) prescribes behaviors in all areas of
human life, from the most personal and intimate, to the most
universal. Traditionally, a commitment to *halakhah* has been a
significant measure of religiosity. More than common belief,
shared behavorial expectations have served to define a given
Jewish community.

Nonetheless, from time to time, authorities have attempted
to set down what they felt to be the basic principles of Judaism.
One of the greatest rabbinic authorities of all time, Moses Maimonides of twelfth-century Spain and Egypt, composed Thirteen Principles of Faith. They were later adapted as a hymn (the
Yigdal) which is widely sung in synagogue services.[1] Although
these principles were accepted for hundreds of years, they never
became binding. Other authorities disagreed with some of them.
Succeeding writers tried reducing them to five or to three principles, or even to one principle. Each effort remained the personal
statement of its author.

From its very beginnings, Judaism has not been monolithic
in its theology or philosophy. Within the same general framework
Jewish thinkers have viewed society and God from differing perspectives. The authors of the Psalms did not look at God and
mortals in the same way that the authors of Judges, Job, or Ecclesiastes did. One writer might express his or her faith in a very sim-

---

[1] The thirteen principles are: God is eternal, unique, formless. Only God is to be
worshiped, God is the sole creator, the words of the prophets are true; Moses
was the greatest of the prophets; the Torah is of divine origin; the Torah is
immutable; God understands our innermost thoughts; God rewards and punishes; the Messiah will come; God will resurrect the dead. See *Siddur Sim Shalom
for Shabbat and Festivals,* p. 53.

ple manner, another in a much more sophisticated way; one person might emphasize emotional, another intellectual, aspects of life; one book might be an outpouring of piety, another a philosophic inquiry.

The classic text of Jewish law, the third-century *Mishnah*, records both majority and minority opinions of the ancient rabbis. The *Gemara*, the sixth-century collection of rabbinic discussions and analyses of the *Mishnah*, does the same. It reflects the wide variety of the theological understandings of the many great rabbis of several centuries. The tradition of encouraging debate and diversity has remained essential to Jewish religious thinking ever since.

Though there has always been room for theological diversity within Judaism, there has been much less diversity regarding proper conduct. Throughout the centuries, rabbis debated the interpretation of various details within the system of law, called *halakhah*, but once they reached a decision, the ruling was binding. (At the same time, one must realize that there are differences of opinion on matters of Jewish law as well. Different groups within the Jewish community often look to their own specific authorities for interpretations on matters of Jewish law.) Observant Jews, however they conceive of God, accept that it is a duty for Jews to pray, and praiseworthy to do so together with others in the Jewish community; to observe the Sabbath in a special way; to eat in accordance with regulations of dietary laws *(kashrut);* and to fulfill additional commandments *(mitzvot).*

Judaism, a religion with specific laws and with various conceptions of God, immortality, and the Messiah, embraces all types: mystics and rationalists, the unsophisticated and the highly educated, the followers of one sage and the disciples of another.

From these many strands of Jewish thought, one can weave some major teachings on basic theological issues. In this chapter, we will review several of these, and hopefully give the reader a good sense of the range of Jewish concerns. The bibliography at the end of the book should be consulted for the names of works in which these ideas are discussed more fully and in much greater depth.

Teachings on God

Every morning and evening the observant Jew at prayer recites the biblical verse that contains the essence of Jewish belief. No observant Jew would have any hesitation in affirming: *Shema yisrael Adonai eloheinu Adonai ehad* ("Hear, O Israel: *Adonai* is our God, *Adonai* is One"). This proclamation of pure monotheism insists that God is not plural and that God is not a divine being in human form.

From its very inception, Judaism has never compromised on the oneness of God. There is only one God, and this one God is indivisible. Other ancient religions saw many powers at work in the universe, some in conflict with others. Some contemporary faiths maintain as much today. The Bible taught that God is the unique Supreme Ruler who governs all and that the various deities that are worshiped simply do not exist. In ancient Persia, people believed in the religion of Zoroaster, which taught that two rival powers, Light and Darkness, continually struggle for supremacy. Judaism could not accept this dualism, for in Judaism God is the sole Master of all. For similar reasons, Judaism rejected the trinitarian doctrine as it developed within Christianity. As Christianity developed, it insisted that the one God was made up of three parts (the Trinity); Judaism considered this doctrine as diluted monotheism and rejected it.

Although Jews have always proclaimed God's oneness and uniqueness, they never defined God's nature precisely. They have believed that finite, mortal human beings cannot define God, who is infinite and immortal. As Rabbi Saadia Gaon of tenth-century Egypt said, "If I understood God, I would be God."

Even Moses, who is depicted in the Torah as having come closer to God than any other human being, could not fully comprehend Him. "No one can see Me" [i.e., fully understand my essence], God is described as saying in the Bible, "and still live" (Exodus 33:20). Maimonides insisted that we can assert only what God is not, for any positive attributes are inescapably human and therefore metaphorical. In other words, when we say that "God is just," what we really mean is "God is not unjust." Similarly, we can assert that God is not unkind, or that God is not untruthful.

Despite Maimonides' doctrine of God's "negative attributes," he believed that some of the characteristics of God can be asserted. For example, God is wholly spiritual. Much as we might imagine God to exist as do other substances in the world, this is incorrect. As formulated in the hymn *Yigdal*, "He has no physical substance, nor does He have the appearance of a physical substance." Though Jewish folklore often pictures God as a king sitting on a heavenly throne, Jewish religious tradition does not take literally the image of God as king. The anthropomorphic terms that ascribe human characteristics to God were understood by the rabbis as a technique for explaining certain divine attributes to people unable to grasp abstractions.

Traditionally, God has been referred to with masculine pronouns and adjectives, but these simply reflect the inadequacies of human language. Today, more and more prayerbooks are striving to translate traditional appellations for God using gender-neutral language (e.g., recent editions of *Gates of Prayer* (Reform), *Kol Haneshamah* (Reconstructionist), and *Siddur Sim Shalom* (Conservative). Orthodox prayerbooks continue to translate traditional, masculine, divine attributes literally, without intending to imply, however, that God in fact has a gender.

It is difficult for human beings to grasp the reality of pure spirit. Many peoples have resorted to creating idols. They could see or touch an image or a statue; they could feel the reality of a god of wood or stone. Judaism, however, has always defined itself in opposition to idolatry, whether it be the worship of graven images or the elevation of science, politics, or the ego above the worship of God. Throughout the Bible, God, Moses, and the prophets exhort the Israelites to smash idols, to shun mere "gods." They constantly warn the people about the dangers of succumbing to idolatry.

Central to Jewish theology is the conception that God is ethical: both just and loving, both righteous and compassionate. The corollary is that we must be ethical as well. God is neither indifferent to human needs nor aloof from human affairs; rather, God insists that people live moral lives and fashion an ethical society. The Rabbis explained the verse, "You must walk in God's ways" (Deuteronomy 11:22) to mean, "Just as God is merciful, we must be merciful; just as God is gracious, we must be gracious; just as God is truthful, we must be truthful; just as God is righteous, we must be righteous."[2]

Morality is not simply an attribute that enables people to get along without destroying themselves. It is a divine imperative. Jewish monotheism is an "ethical monotheism." It goes beyond faith in the existence of God, beyond the conviction that God is One. Its premise is that the One God is moral, demanding that we, God's creatures, act morally, too.

Teachings on the Afterlife

What happens if a people or a person refuses to act morally? Throughout the generations, Jewish thinkers have asserted that God rewards and punishes human actions. Jewish teachings on the nature of reward and punishment, however, have changed greatly over the ages. In biblical days the emphasis was on group reward and group punishment (although the concept of individual reward and punishment also existed). A nation that disobeyed the divine commandments would suffer drought or famine or exile, but one that adhered to them would benefit from the bounties of nature and would prosper.

It has always been a challenge to apply the doctrine of divine reward and punishment to individuals, for in every age wicked have prospered and righteous have suffered.[3] In the post-biblical period (there are hints in Daniel, a late biblical book), the notion

---

[2] See *Sifre Deuteronomy*, Piska 49.
[3] See the Book of Job for the classic biblical presentation of this crux.

that evil would be punished and good rewarded in an afterlife was developed. If there seemed to be no reward and punishment in this world, they surely would be meted out in the next.

It is important to keep in mind that together with this concern about reward and punishment, which led to the doctrine of *ha-olam ha-ba* ("the world to come") in which the unfairnesses and inequities of *ha-olam ha-zeh* ("this world") would be addressed, Jewish tradition has always emphasized the obligation to live a worthy life for its own sake, free of the expectation of reward or the fear of punishment. As it is said in *Pirkei Avot,* "Do not be like servants who serve their master in order to receive a reward; be like servants who serve their master unconditionally, with no thought of reward."[4] Nonetheless, speculation regarding the afterlife has persisted.

Different views regarding the afterlife are reflected in the divergent views of the schools of Shammai and Hillel, the two great masters of the first pre-Christian century. The school of Shammai taught that upon death, the good dwell with God, the evil go to *gehinnom* (Gehenna), and those in between first go down and then come up to be healed after a time. The school of Hillel disagreed, insisting that God's mercy would not permit any but the truly evil to be sent to *gehinnom.*

The Rabbis envisioned *ha-olam ha-ba* as a reality in which people would be free of all physical needs and therefore able to spend eternity in study. The third-century sage Rav taught: "*Ha-olam ha-ba* is not like *ha-olam ha-zeh* ['this world']. There is no eating or drinking, no procreation, no bargaining, no jealousy, hatred or strife. The righteous sit with their crowns on their heads. What then will they eat and drink? The presence of God is food and drink to them."[5]

Immortality (of the soul) also became a Jewish concept, but

[4] *Pirkei Avot* 1:3.
[5] *B. Berakhot* 17a.

attempts to describe the specifics remained in the realm of legend. "To borrow an analogy from Maimonides," Rabbi Robert Gordis wrote, "for us to conceive of life after death, an existence necessarily free from physical traits and attributes, is as impossible as for a color-blind person to grasp the colors of a sunset."[6] Others have reinterpreted the concept naturalistically. As stated by Rabbi Milton Steinberg:

> Death cannot be and is not the end of life. Man transcends death in many altogether naturalistic fashions. He may be immortal biologically, through his children; in thought, through the survival of his memory; in influence, by virtue of the continuance of his personality as a force among those who come after him; and ideally, through his identification with the timeless things of the spirit.[7]

Teachings on Sin, Repentance, and Free Will

Within classical Jewish writings, the concept of Original Sin, the idea that human beings are inherently tainted, is generally dismissed. On the other hand, the contrasting theological notion that people are born inherently good, becoming corrupted solely because of external social forces, is also rarely encountered. Rather, for the most part, Jewish sources recognize both good and evil drives in the human makeup: *yetzer ha-tov,* the good inclination, and *yetzer ra* or *yetzer ha-ra,* the evil inclination.

Which inclination will dominate a person, the *yetzer ha-tov* or the *yetzer ha-ra*? These inclinations exist in constant tension within each of us. God gave us the freedom to choose between them. Each person is responsible for his or her own conduct. The Book of Deuteronomy (30:19) declares: "Behold, I set before you this day life and death, good and evil. Therefore,

---

[6] Robert Gordis, *A Faith for Moderns* (New York: Bloch Publishing Company, 1960), p. 239.
[7] Milton Steinberg, *Basic Judaism* (New York: Harcourt Brace, 1986), p. 160.

choose life." According to this formulation, God wants us to choose life, but leaves the decision to do so in our hands. What happens when we do not make the proper choice, when, to use religious terminology, we sin? If our actions are the result of free will, each of us must be held personally accountable.

This does not, however, imply hopeless resignation in the face of sin. Judaism teaches that we can atone for our transgressions. We must do this as individuals. We cannot rely on intermediaries to make atonement for us. We cannot, for example, confess to a rabbi and expect to receive absolution. Rabbis cannot perform that function because they are no closer to God than any other Jew.

Instead, we must face God directly and atone for our own sins. We begin by recognizing our error. We admit it, we confess it, and we resolve never to repeat it. This process, called repentance *(teshuvah)*, is the central theme and task of the High Holy Days (Rosh Hashanah and Yom Kippur).

Teachings on Ethics

THE SANCTITY OF LIFE AND THE PURSUIT OF PEACE

A key concept in Judaism is that every human being is created in the divine image, that every life is inviolate and holy. The *Mishnah* (the third-century Jewish code) records:

> Humanity began with a single human being, to teach us that to destroy a single life is to destroy a whole world, even as to save a single life is to save a whole world. That all people have a common ancestor should make for peace, since no one can say to anyone else: "My father was greater than your father." That humanity began with a single human being is an answer to heretics who could claim the existence of more than one Creator. That humanity began with a single human being proclaims forever the greatness of the Holy One. For human beings stamp many coins with one die and they all look alike, but the Holy One stamped every

human being with the die of the first human being, yet no person is like any other. Therefore, every human being must declare, "It is for my sake that the world was created."[8]

According to Jewish tradition, life is precious. Therefore, everything possible must be done to protect and to improve life. Both individuals and the community have a responsibility to care for the sick, the aged, and the vulnerable. They should never be abandoned.

Even animal life is precious. Jewish law forbids hunting for sport. Animals may be killed only for food (and then only according to specific laws designed to minimize fear and pain).

Although the *mitzvot* are of utmost importance, all but three may be waived if death would be the consequence of obedience. (The three which may never be transgressed are the prohibitions against the denial of God, sexual immorality, and murder.)

As important as life is, it is not an absolute. Indeed, the sixth commandment states, "You shall not *murder*"; it does not state, "You shall not *kill*." Jewish tradition permits people to defend themselves when attacked. Judaism contains pacifist strains, but it teaches that some battles are not evil. At times it would be a greater evil not to fight than to fight. Allowing terrorists to kill people would be a greater wrong than fighting to prevent or to counter their attacks. When acquiescence means death, people are obliged to fight to save lives, though always with painful resignation. In the absence of alternatives, the inevitable is performed with sadness. Even in self-defense, killing diminished God's image in the world.

The Jewish tradition has never gloried in military victories. At the Pesaḥ *seder,* when Jews celebrate their delivery from ancient Egyptian slavery, we always pour out a few drops of wine from the cup to symbolize our sadness over the loss of Egyptian lives. King David, from whom, tradition tells us, the Messiah will

[8] *Mishnah Sanhedrin* 4:5.

be descended, was not permitted to build the Temple of the
Lord in Jerusalem because he was a soldier with bloodstained
hands. Judah the Maccabee led a small band of men in victori-
ous attacks against superior forces and saved the Temple from
the Hellenists, yet his military exploits do not dominate the religious ritual commemorating Ḥanukkah.

When the Israeli troops returned home after their brilliant triumph in the Six Day War of 1967, there were no victory parades,
no cheering throngs. Israeli Commander (later Prime Minister)
Yitzhak Rabin eloquently described the people's reaction:

> The joy of our soldiers is incomplete and their celebrations are
> marred by sorrow and shock. There are some who abstain from all
> celebration. The men in the front lines were witness not only to
> the glory of victory, but the price of victory: their comrades who
> fell beside them bleeding. The terrible price which our enemies
> paid touched the hearts of many of our men as well. It may be that
> the Jewish people never learned and never accustomed itself to feel
> the triumph of conquest and victory, and therefore we receive it
> with mixed feelings.[9]

The prophet Isaiah describes a Jewish vision of peace:

> He will judge among the nations and arbitrate for many people;
> And they shall beat their swords into plowshares;
> And their spears into pruning hooks.
> Nation shall not take up sword against nation;
> They shall never again know war. (Isaiah 2:4)

The Rabbis further developed the idea. They declared that
the universe rests on three pillars: truth, justice, and peace. The
last passage of the *Amidah*, the central prayer of the three daily
services, asks God for the blessing of peace *(shalom)*. The *Mish-*

---

[9] Yitzhak Rabin, quoted in *The Israel-Arab Reader, 2nd edition*, ed. Walter
Laqueur (New York: Bantam Books, 1971), pp. 231–232.

nah closes with the statement that God has chosen peace as the best instrument with which to bless the people Israel.

TZEDEK/TZEDAKAH (JUSTICE)

Peace alone, precious as it is, cannot maintain a good society. The Hebrew word for peace, *shalom,* connotes more than the absence of warfare. It means fullness, completeness, the presence of well-being. Peace cannot exist in a society that is not just.

The passion for justice permeates Jewish tradition. The Bible commands: "Justice, justice shall you pursue" (Deuteronomy 16:20), making social justice a religious requirement. A huge proportion of the Talmud deals with civil and criminal law whose purpose is the implementation of this ideal throughout society. The Jewish legal system protects the rights of the individual; the ethical system teaches that a society which permits exploitation, poverty, and ignorance defies God's teachings and will suffer God's wrath.

The passion for justice is expressed in the concept of *tzedakah.* The word means much more than charity; it means justice. Charity is something given by someone to another who has less. *Tzedakah* is more than a gift; it is an act of justice. Helping others is fulfilling one's duty, not simply an act of kindness. Everything on earth belongs to God. We are obliged to share with others whatever portion of it we happen to control.

In Jewish tradition, being poor is not considered an expression of piety; nor is being wealthy a sign of virtue. Jews regard poverty as a cause of suffering which should be eradicated. Jewish teachings about social justice implant a sense of responsibility in everyone.

A rabbinic passage that is read daily during morning prayer states:

> These are the deeds which yield immediate fruit and continue to yield fruit in time to come: honoring parents, doing deeds of lovingkindness, attending the house of study punctually, morning and

evening, providing hospitality, visiting the sick, helping the needy
bride, providing a funeral for the dead, probing the meaning of
prayer, and making peace between one person and another.[10]

Note the prominence on this list of responsibilities to help
those unable to help themselves. In talmudic times, everyone
had to contribute to a common fund that was used to maintain a
free soup kitchen, provide lodging for travelers, and help the
unfortunate. Special organizations provided poor brides with
dowries, tended the sick, lent money without interest, and took
care of the dead. Employers were expected to pay their workers
on time and were not to take advantage of them. That emphasis
on social justice was translated into communal institutions which
functioned in all Jewish communities. Taking care of the needy
has always thus been understood to be a sacred obligation. Even
in Western democracies, where participation in Jewish life is vol-
untary rather than obligatory, *tzedakah* has remained a prime
concern of affiliated Jews. Jewish federations in every community raise and distribute tremendous sums for local and national
needs as well as for Israel and for other Jews throughout the
world. In addition to the federations, there are an increasing
number of alternatives. Jewish organizations such as Mazon
(which combats hunger in America), the New Israel Fund
(which targets humanitarian and other needs in Israel) and Ziv
(which funds specific, underfunded *tzedakah* initiatives in Israel
and in America) are steadily growing. Jews who may not look
upon themselves as "religious" and who may know little of Jewish law or lore nevertheless often faithfully carry out the responsibility of *tzedakah*.

ḤESED (LOVINGKINDNESS)

According to Jewish understanding, a society cannot exist without justice, but justice alone can be dispatched heartlessly unless

---

[10] Based on *B. Shabbat* 127a.

it is tempered with lovingkindness and mercy. The Hebrew term for lovingkindness is *ḥesed*. God, extolled as just, is also praised as merciful. In the Torah we are commanded to walk in God's ways (eg., Deuteronomy 11:22). One interpretation of this concept is given in the following *midrash:*

> Is it possible for a mortal to follow God's presence?
> Rather, this comes to teach us that we should pattern
> ourselves after the Holy One. Just as God clothes the
> naked, you must clothe the naked; just as God visits
> the sick, so too must you visit the sick; just as
> God comforts mourners, so too must you comfort
> mourners.[11]

By living a life imbued by *ḥesed*, we realize the full implications of our theology.

TIKKUN OLAM (PERFECTING THE WORLD)

Judaism has been described as an optimistic religion. It teaches that we are capable of being just and merciful, of improving ourselves and our society. One of the best-known prayers, *Aleinu*, which is recited at the end of every service, expresses the yearning—and the sense of duty to act—to perfect this world [*tikkun olam*] through God's kingship.[12]

There have, of course, been desperate periods in Jewish history when Jews passively awaited divine intervention, through a Messiah, to bring them a just society. For the most part, however, they have felt impelled to take action themselves, refusing to be frozen into despair that their dream might not be realized.

Nor did they relegate their vision of perfection to the after-

[11] *B. Sotah* 14a.

[12] "And so we hope in You, Adonai our God, soon to see your splendor, that You will . . . perfect the world by Your sovereignty so that all humanity will invoke Your name, bringing all the earth's wicked back to You, repentant." (*Siddur Sim Shalom for Shabbat and Festivals,* p. 183).

life. Judaism has remained focused on *this* world. It did not minimize social problems by looking to the world to come. It did
not seek escape from this world, as some Eastern religions did.
Even Jewish mystics who could find religious ecstasy only in soli-
tude, married, raised families, prayed in a synagogue with others,
and took some active role in the life of the community.

Judaism insists that every person assume the obligations of
being a responsible member of society. By adhering to God's
laws, and by correcting social wrongs rather than acquiescing to
them, Jews can make the future better than the present.

This optimism may seem utopian, but Jewish tradition has
constantly devised ways of giving concrete expression to abstract
ideals. It has embodied them in a way of life guided by law
(halakhah). The myriad details which are part of the *halakhah*
reflect the wisdom of the sages who understood that words
mean little if they are not translated into deeds. If people profess
love and practice cruelty, their profession is meaningless; if they
preach charity and act miserly, their sincerity is questionable. As
Rabbi Simeon ben Gamliel taught: "It is not the preaching that
counts, but the deed."[13]

Although they could not legislate emotions or sincerity, the
Rabbis did work out rules of conduct which concretize principles and translate ideals into a way of life. They relied on a deep
faith that God's spirit is at work in the world, inspiring men and
women to become their best possible selves.

Not everyone succeeds; Judaism has always recognized that
human beings are not perfect. But we must never stop striving to
attain the ideal. As Rabbi Tarfon taught, "You are not obliged to
complete the task, but neither are you free to desist from it."[14]

---

[13] *"Lo ha-midrash ha-ikkar elah ha-ma'aseh," Pirkei Avot* 1:17.
[14] Rabbi Tarfon, *Pirkei Avot* 2:21.

CHAPTER 6

Judaism: A Way of Living

*I*N the previous chapter we looked at several basic Jewish values. As we pointed out there, values by themselves can be abstract and lifeless. Judaism tries to put values into practice, to incorporate basic commitments into a way of life. Jewish tradition presents a system of *mitzvot*—obligatory ritual practices and moral behaviors—to be incorporated into the daily lives of its adherents.

What is the goal of *mitzvot*? This is a challenging question which has long been debated by Jewish philosophers and thinkers. Some have argued that, ultimately, the search for justifications for *mitzvot* is futile: *mitzvot* should, instead, be accepted on faith. Others, though, have seen several prominent religious goals.

One of these is *l'tzaref et ha-briyot*—to refine the human being. Understood in this way, fulfilling *mitzvot* is the Jewish way to pursue a life of holiness. *Mitzvot* can elevate a human being to a high moral and religious level. The nineteenth chapter of the Book of Leviticus, which contains a very large number of *mitzvot* (e.g., "Do not gossip," "Revere the Sabbath," and "Do not place a stumbling block before the blind") contains as well a sublime statement which can be understood to be the organizing theme of the entire chapter: "You shall be holy, for I, the LORD your God, am holy." Jewish tradition maintains that a holy life is an attainable goal for every individual. The details of Jewish practice can lead us to that goal.

The range of *mitzvot* is all-encompassing and as such, defines parameters affecting all aspects of personal and communal life. For example, Jewish law addresses how we use speech in order to avoid gossip and slander. There are *mitzvot* that address how we conduct business. Intimate relations and family life are shaped by specific *mitzvot* and prescribed norms of behavior. Mutual respect, honesty, and integrity inform all of these.

Many *mitzvot* seem to be universal; for example, as we saw in Chapter 5, Jews must not stand idly by while others suffer; they must care for the poor and the aged; they must visit the sick and comfort the bereaved. Other *mitzvot,* however, clearly distinguish the Jew from the gentile. Adopting *mitzvot,* therefore, is an important aspect of one's Jewish identity formation. Whether one is a Jew by birth or by choice, behaving as a Jew—i.e., fulfilling characteristically Jewish *mitzvot*—alters not only one's relationship with God, but also one's relationship with others.

In this chapter we present a survey of several important distinguishing *mitzvot* which can play a significant role in developing one's Jewish identity.

Distinctive Clothing

The Jewish tradition has long recognized that clothing can be an instrument of religious identity and group cohesion. A visitor to a morning service in a synagogue may be struck by the sight of a sea of *tallitot* (large prayer shawls worn over one's clothing) on the shoulders of worshipers. Wearing a *tallit* during morning worship is a very old practice that has its origins in the Bible.

The Hebrew word *tzitzit* (pronounced *tzitzis* in Ashkenazic Hebrew) means a fringe or fringes. The commandment to wear *tzitzit* on garments is found in Numbers 15:37–39. One of these verses explains the purpose of this *mitzvah* concisely: "Looking upon [these fringes] you will be reminded of all the commandments of the Lord and fulfill them, and not be seduced by your heart or led astray by your eyes."

This biblical command has generally been interpreted to mean that one should wear fringes all day. Observant male Jews wear a small garment (called a *tallit katan*) under the shirt. It is a square cloth with an opening for the head, with *tzitzit* attached at the corners. Some people allow the *tzitzit* to show. Most non-Orthodox Jews generally encounter *tzitzit* on the four corners of a *tallit*, worn during morning service.

Traditionally, women (even those who took upon themselves the obligation to pray every day) did not wear *tallitot*. Some women today, however, have begun to take this obligation upon themselves. Special *tallitot* designed especially for women are becoming increasingly popular.

An observant Jew also puts on *tefillin* every morning except on Shabbat or holidays. *Tefillin* consist of two small leather boxes with attached leather straps. One box is placed on the left arm (unless the person is left-handed, when it is placed on the right) and tightened just above the elbow. The single strap is then wound around the forearm seven times. The other box is placed upon the head, with one of its attached straps falling to the left and the other to the right. Next, the strap on the arm is wrapped around the fingers in a prescribed way. The boxes contain small parchment scrolls on which a scribe has written the following four passages: Exodus 13:1–10 and 13:11–16 and Deuteronomy 6:4–9 and 11:13–21. These passages remind us to love, serve, and obey God fully. They also contain the biblical verses commanding us to "bind" God's words on our arms and place them as symbols on our foreheads—which we fulfill by wearing *tefillin*.

Although it is not understood to be a *mitzvah*, it is a firmly rooted Jewish custom—traditionally practiced by men only—to cover the head to inspire reverence and humility. Generally this is done by wearing a cap known as a *kippah* or *yarmulke,* but in some communities, hats are worn instead of or in addition to *kippot*. Some Jews cover their heads all the time; others while reciting prayers or while eating; others only in synagogue.

Jewish women have traditionally worn headcoverings for a different reason: modesty. Following marriage, Jewish women were obliged to cover their heads with either a kerchief or a wig. This is still the practice in traditional communities. In liberal communities in which women are beginning to accept upon themselves the duty to wear a *tallit* (and/or *tefillin* during weekday prayers), women (irrespective of their marital status) are experimenting with the wearing of *kippot* and other head coverings.

The Jewish Home

A Jewish home is distinguished in a number of ways. Even before entering, one should be able to see a *mezuzah*, a small case attached to the doorframe of the home. Each *mezuzah* contains a piece of parchment on which a scribe has written the verses of Deuteronomy 6:4–9 and 11:13–21. These two passages contain the biblical verses that declare our duty to "inscribe" words of Torah upon the doorposts of our homes.

A *mezuzah* should also be attached to the doorway of every room in the house, except the bathroom. It is attached to the doorway diagonally with the top leaning toward the inside and the bottom toward the outside. It is placed on the upper third of the doorpost, on the right side as one enters.

On the outside casing of the *mezuzah* the Hebrew letter

שׁ (pronounced *"shin"*) often appears. *"Shin"* is the first letter of one of the biblical names of God, *"Shaddai,"* and thus draws our attention to God. The presence of the *mezuzah* then suggests that God is revered in the home. *Shaddai* is also understood to be an acronym for the phrase, *"Shomer D'latot Yisrael,"* meaning, "Guardian of the Doorways of Israel (the Jewish People)." Thus, for some, the *mezuzah* provides assurance and comfort, suggesting that God is watching over the home and its inhabitants.

A *mezuzah* is a powerful Jewish symbol. In the same way that words of Torah, written on parchment, fill the little *mezuzah* box, so too can spoken words of Torah fill the home. The *mezuzah* is a constant reminder of the values, such as *shalom bayit* (family harmony) which should inform the behavior of those who enter through the doorway of the home to which it is attached.

Berakhot (Blessings)

The practice of reciting *berakhot* is fundamental in Jewish life. In the Talmud it is stated that anyone who experiences anything in the world without expressing appreciation to God is a thief. For this reason, *berakhot* are recited not only prior to eating but on many other occasions as well. The prayerbook contains many texts of *berakhot* for various occasions, such as seeing the first buds in spring, hearing thunder, smelling spices, and upon receiving good or bad news.

Before and after eating, observant Jews remind themselves of God's gifts as they express gratitude with various appropriate blessings. These *berakhot* also remind us not to take food for granted. For example, the following *berakhah* is recited before eating bread (by itself or at the start of a meal):

Barukh atah Adonai Eloheinu melekh ha-olam ha-motzi leḥem min ha-aretz.

Praised are You, Adonai our God, who rules the universe, bringing forth bread from the earth.

This *berakhah* is recited before one drinks wine (or grape juice):

> *Barukh atah Adonai Eloheinu melekh ha-olam borei pri ha-gafen.*
>
> Praised are You Adonai our God, who rules the Universe, creating the fruit of the vine.

After meals, *birkat ha-mazon* (Grace after Meals) is recited. The first paragraph of this collection of blessings furnishes a fine example of the universal dimension of Jewish tradition:

> Praised are You, Adonai our God who rules the universe, graciously sustaining the whole world with kindness and compassion, providing food for every creature, for God's love endures forever. God, abounding in kindness, has never failed us; may our nourishment be assured forever. God sustains all life and is good to all, providing every creature with food and sustenance. Praised are You, Adonai, who sustains all life.

Kashrut (Jewish Dietary Laws)

Among the most distinguishing of Jewish *mitzvot* is the system of dietary rules, known as *kashrut*. Our earlier comments regarding the difficulty of determining particular purposes for fulfilling the *mitzvot* are particularly apt with respect to *kashrut*. People who accept the Torah as divine need no rationale for *kashrut*, a discipline they understand to be commanded by God. Those who consider the Torah to be holy but not necessarily literally revealed can accept *kashrut* as a part of the Jewish way of life which can add meaning to their lives.

The word "kosher" means "proper, correct"; it is applied to religious objects or religious behavior. For example, a Torah scroll that meets all the ritual requirements is referred to as "kosher"; one that does not is spoken of as "not kosher." The term, however, is most often used in connection with the dietary laws. Those who observe the rules of *kashrut* are spoken of as people who "keep kosher."

There are those who, throughout history, have believed the purpose of the dietary laws to be a safeguard of good health. Most scholars today agree, however, that whatever hygienic advantages may have accrued to Jews from observing *kashrut,* they are secondary.

To the extent that we can point to an organizing principle to explain the rules of *kashrut,* the one which appears to have the firmest grounding is, in the words of Rabbi Samuel Dresner, not health, but *holiness.*[1] The biblical passages which present the basis of the laws of *kashrut* are often followed by statements that imply that these laws are part of the discipline expected of a holy people. For example, in chapter eleven of the Book of Leviticus, forty-four verses of instruction about dietary laws are followed by the statement: "I am the Lord your God; sanctify yourselves therefore and be holy, for I am holy" (a restatement of the passage quoted earlier in this chapter).

Kashrut is, then, a dietary discipline undertaken not in order to lose weight, not in order to become more attractive, not even to promote health, but to help infuse all of life with a sense of holiness.

One way in which it can achieve this goal is through refining the practice of making distinctions. *Kashrut* can help us shape a way of life that is marked by distinctions: between the permitted and the forbidden, the sacred and the profane, the good and the bad. Distinguishing between permitted and prohibited foods can be part of a total way of life that constantly helps us refine our sense of control over our passions and desires.

Although only a few teachers of Judaism ever went so far as to promote vegetarianism, the Torah implies that it is an ideal.

[1] See Samuel H. Dresner, Seymour Siegel and David Pollack, *The Jewish Dietary Laws* (New York: The Rabbinical Assembly and the United Synagogue Commission on Jewish Education, 1982), pp. 12-13.

In the Garden of Eden, Adam and Eve ate no meat. After the Flood, the permission granted Noah to eat meat seems to be a concession to human weakness. Animals are also creatures of God. If we take their lives for the sake of our own sustenance, we are obliged to do so in a restricted way, one in which the animal experiences a minimum of pain. This is one of the ways in which Jewish tradition teaches reverence for all life.

If an animal is to be slaughtered, this must be done in the manner prescribed by Jewish law. The slaughterer is called a *shoḥet*. The *shoḥet* must be knowledgeable as well as pious. The sharp knife he uses must be tested periodically for nicks and dullness. He must know enough about anatomy to insure a minimum of pain to the animal, as well as to detect the slightest malfunctioning of an organ, because the flesh of an animal that was diseased or had certain types of blemishes may not be eaten. If there is any question, a rabbinic authority must be consulted to decide whether or not the meat may be used. Forbidden food is designated *taref* or *tereifah*, often pronounced *treif*. (The word literally means "torn to pieces," and originally referred to the flesh of animals which had died as the result of an attack, the eating of which the *kashrut* laws forbid.)

Eating blood is forbidden. Blood is blood, whether it comes from a human being or an animal. In prohibiting the consumption of blood, the Torah seems to be concerned that it can excite a blood-lust in human beings and may desensitize us to the suffering of human beings when their blood is spilled. In the passage in which the prohibition against eating "flesh with its life-blood in it" is first found we also see the prohibition against murder: "Whoever sheds the blood of man/By man shall his blood be shed" (Genesis 9:6). Because life—even an animal life—is sacred and "the life of the flesh is in the blood" (Leviticus 17:11), the blood of animals must not be eaten; it must be disposed of carefully.

Meat is rid of blood by soaking it in cold water for half an hour in a utensil used only for this purpose. It then is sprinkled liberally with salt and drained on an inclined, perforated board for an hour. After it is rinsed with cold running water, it is free of blood. This may be done at home, though generally today it is done at the butcher shop. Liver or steaks that are to be broiled need not be salted; they need only be rinsed with cold water and placed over or under an open fire.

As stated in the Torah, the meat of certain animals may not be eaten. Land animals must have cloven hooves and chew their cud; this eliminates the flesh of pigs and rabbits, for example. Birds of prey and certain other kinds of fowl are prohibited. Fish must have fins and scales. Other seafood, such as eels and shellfish, are *treif*.

Kashrut requires the separation of meat from milk. The basis for this is a passage in the Bible (repeated three times) that prohibits the boiling of a calf in its mother's milk. The rabbinic tradition expanded this prohibition to forbid cooking or eating milk or milk products together with meat or meat products. All dishes, utensils, serving dishes, sponges, and dish towels used for meat must be totally different and separate from those used for milk. Meat and meat derivatives are commonly referred to by the Yiddish word *fleishig*. Milk and milk products are commonly referred to as *milkhig*. In kosher homes, different colors or different markings help to differentiate the two sets, often red for *fleishig*, and blue for *milkhig*.

Some foods are neither *fleishig* nor *milkhig*. They are called *pareve*. Fruit, vegetables, grains, fish, and eggs are *pareve*. They may be eaten with either *milkhig* or *fleishig* foods.

Although it is permissible to use one set of glass dishes for both *milkhig* and *fleishig* (because they can be thoroughly cleaned and are not porous), the practice is not encouraged as it does away with the idea of separation which is an important aspect of *kashrut*.

Keeping a kosher home appears complicated to the uninitiated. One soon, though, becomes accustomed to reading labels in the supermarket to make sure that packaged goods that appear to be kosher really are. This may seem difficult. How can one be sure, for example, that baked goods were not cooked with lard or beef suet? How does one determine which products have milk or milk derivatives in them? How does one know which products are truly *pareve*?

The answer, though, is really quite simple. One determines whether a product is kosher, and if so whether it is *pareve, milkhig* or *fleishig*, by looking for a rabbinic certification on the product's label. Such a certification is known as a *hekhsher*. Several well-known national certifications can be found on literally millions of products produced today. As recently as twenty years ago, one would be forced to examine ingredients on labels; today, this is generally no longer necessary.

Kosher meat is more expensive than non-kosher meat, among other reasons because more people are involved in producing and inspecting it than is the case for other meat. Those who keep kosher believe the observance to be so important that it is worth the expense.

Eating out in non-kosher restaurants or in the homes of people who do not keep kosher causes some difficulties and challenges. Some Jews will not eat anything from plates in homes or restaurants which serve non-kosher food. This standard renders it unlikely that one will consume non-kosher food, though it does limit one's ability to interact socially with those who do not keep kosher. Others, in order to participate more fully in the general community, adopt a more lenient legal position. Some will eat only cold fruit, vegetables, or salad in non-kosher homes or restaurants. Others will eat even hot, cooked food, but will insist upon non-meat products, such as pasta, broiled fish, or vegetarian dishes. Such a standard of *kashrut* observance requires, though, considerable vigilance. Not everyone, for example, has the same understanding of the term "vegetarian." One might need to inquire, say, that a so-called vegetarian soup is not made with chicken stock, or that a seemingly innocuous salad does not contain shrimp or other non-kosher products.

This suggests that adopting a commitment to keep a kosher home and eat only kosher food requires one to discuss it with family, friends, and acquaintances. It does distinguish one from others. It does make one different.

A commitment to eat only kosher food provides a constant reminder of the covenantal nature of Judaism. Every time a choice must be made whether or not to eat certain foods, one is reminded that one is a Jew. Sometimes one must remind others that one is a Jew. One has the opportunity to think about one's faith, one's identity, and one's character several times a day.

Shabbat

Shabbat (pronounced *Shabbos* in Ashkenazic Hebrew and in Yiddish) is the climax of the week. It is the day associated with peace, as reflected in the greeting *Shabbat Shalom (shalom* means peace). Another common greeting, derived from the Yiddish, is "Good *Shabbos.*"

Jewish tradition considers Shabbat to be a foretaste of Paradise. Poets speak of this day as a bride and as a queen. In the Ten Commandments Shabbat is referred to as a reminder of both Creation and the Exodus from Egypt. The centrality of Shabbat is reflected in the Hebrew names for the days of the week, which are all related to Shabbat. Sunday, for example, is "the first day," Monday is "the second day," and so forth.

Many descriptions of Shabbat have attempted to capture its purpose and mood. Perhaps the most eloquent words written in modern times about Shabbat have been those of Rabbi Abraham Joshua Heschel in *The Sabbath:*

> The seventh day is the armistice in man's cruel struggle for existence, a truce in all conflicts, personal and social . . . a day on which handling money is considered a desecration, on which man avows his independence of that which is the world's chief idol. The seventh day is the exodus from tension . . . the installation of man as a sovereign in the world of time.[2]

---

[2] Abraham Joshua Heschel, *The Sabbath: Its Meaning for Modern Man* (New York: Farrar, Straus & Giroux, 1983), p. 29.

Six days a week we live under the tyranny of things of space; on the
Sabbath we try to become attuned to *holiness in time*. It is a day on
which we are called upon to share what is eternal in time, to turn
from the results of creation to the mystery of creation; from the
world of creation to the creation of the world.[3]

and in *God in Search of Man:*

The Sabbath is an assurance that the spirit is greater than the universe, that beyond the good is the holy. The universe was created
in six days, but the climax of creation was the seventh day. Things
that came into being in the six days are good, but the seventh day
is holy. The Sabbath is holiness in time.

What is the Sabbath? The presence of eternity, a moment of
majesty, the radiance of joy. The soul is enhanced, time is a delight,
and inwardness a supreme reward. Indignation is felt to be a dese-
cration of the day, and strife the suicide of one's additional soul.
Man does not stand alone, he lives in the presence of the day.[4]

The Sabbath begins on Friday night before dusk (*erev* Shabbat). At synagogue, it is introduced with *Kabbalat Shabbat* (see
Chapter 7). At home it is introduced with lighting candles, accompanied by a *berakhah*. Candlelighting—the time set aside on Friday
afternoon for the lighting of the Shabbat candles—is about twenty
minutes before sunset, though the candles may be lit earlier. Traditionally, women light the candles, but in the absence of a woman, a
man should light the candles and recite the *berakhah*. One need
not be married to fulfill this *mitzvah;* indeed, it has traditionally
been performed by unmarried men as well as women. Today some
couples take turns lighting them. Children sometimes join in saying the *berakhah*. Many people, after reciting the Hebrew
berakhah, add their own personal silent prayer or meditation.

Following candlelighting, parents bless their children. For
boys, a verse from Genesis is recited: "May God make you as

[3] Abraham Joshua Heschel, *The Sabbath*, p. 10.
[4] Abraham Joshua Heschel, *God in Search of Man: A Philosophy of Judaism* (New
York: Farrar, Straus & Giroux) 1955, p. 417.

Ephraim and Manasseh"; for girls the following is said: "May God make you as Sarah, Rebecca, Rachel, and Leah." Both forms of blessing conclude with the words of the priestly blessing (Numbers 6:22–24):

> May God bless you and keep you.
> May God show you favor and be gracious to you.
> May God show you kindness and grant you peace.

All present then gather around the Sabbath table for the recitation of *kiddush*. *Kiddush*, which means sanctification, is a prayer expressing gratitude to God for the gift of Shabbat. It is chanted over a cup of wine, symbol of joy. Men have traditionally recited *kiddush*, but in some households today women share this obligation and honor. After *kiddush*, everyone drinks some wine or grape juice.

The table is set with a fresh cloth and the best dishes and wine cups in honor of Shabbat. Fresh flowers often adorn the home as well. In a place of honor on the table are two covered whole loaves. Hallah (plural: hallot) is braided egg bread, traditionally associated with the Sabbath. The two loaves recall the double portion of manna that God gave the Israelites in the wilderness before Shabbat (so that they would not have to gather manna on Shabbat itself).

As is appropriate before all meals at which bread is eaten, but particularly observed by many on Shabbat and holidays, there is a ritual washing of the hands. Water is poured over each hand from a pitcher or cup and a *berakhah* is recited. Then *ha-motzi* is recited over the hallah, and pieces are distributed to all. Salt is sprinkled on the hallah as a reminder of the Temple ritual during which salt was sprinkled on some of the offerings.

There is no required menu, but certain dishes have come to be associated with the warmth and uniqueness of Shabbat dining. Among Ashkenazi Jews (Jews of Central or Eastern European background), gefilte fish, chicken soup with knaidlakh (matzoh balls), roast chicken and kugel (noodle pudding) are often on the menu. Whatever the food may be, Shabbat is an occasion for a festive, leisurely meal at which we can be enriched by special food and a special spirit. Following the meal, many sing Sabbath songs (*z'mirot*) before chanting the *birkat ha-mazon*.

Shabbat morning is the time for communal prayer and study. A portion of the Torah is publically read and discussed, and the community gathers for a communal *kiddush*. (See Chapter 7 for a more complete description.)

As on Friday evening, it is customary to invite guests for Shabbat lunch, which also begins with *kiddush* over a cup of wine and with *ha-motzi* recited over two ḥallot. As on Friday, *z'mirot* are sung following the meal. The afternoon is devoted to relaxing pursuits, such as leisurely walks, reading and study, companionship of family and friends, and naps. Some congregations hold classes in the late afternoon. The mood throughout is one of *oneg* ("enjoyment"), and for this reason outward signs of mourning are not permitted on Shabbat. Neither is fasting (unless Yom Kippur happens to be on Saturday; it is the only day whose ritual takes precedence over that of Shabbat).

Since eating is considered essential to the enjoyment of the Sabbath, three meals are to be eaten. The first is on Friday evening, the second is at midday on Saturday, and the third is to be eaten before dark. This last meal does not have to be elaborate, but it should include bread so that *ha-motzi* may be recited before it and *birkat ha-mazon* afterwards. This meal is known by its Hebrew name: *seudah shlishit* (literally, "third meal") or *shalosh seudos*. In some synagogues, *seudah shlishit* is served to those who gather for the late afternoon and evening services.

The Sabbath concludes each week about one hour after candlelighting time the previous evening. (Shabbat is thus at least twenty-five hours long.) Just as the Sabbath was ushered in with a religious ceremony, it is escorted out with one. This ceremony is called *havdalah* (literally "distinction"). It affirms the distinction between the holy and the secular, between the Sabbath and the weekday. At *havdalah* a braided candle is lit and held. The person chanting the *berakhot* and other passages holds a cup of wine. A container of spices *(besamim)* is passed around for all to sniff; spices symbolically restore vitality to us, as we are each diminished by the departure of Shabbat.

One of the prominent features of Shabbat and other holy days is the prohibition of work. Working is not defined solely as expenditure of energy or earning a livelihood. It is a religious-legal concept worked out by the Rabbis in the post-biblical era. It includes acts which most people do not ordinarily think of as labor—for example, it is prohibited to write, sew, cut, or use money. Carrying in the public domain is defined as "work" on Shabbat. (Observant communities often erect and maintain an *eruv,* a *halakhically* defined boundary within which carrying is permitted on the Sabbath.) As no fire may be kindled, cooking, baking, and smoking are not permitted on the Sabbath.

There is a long-standing prohibition against riding on the Sabbath and the holy days. In the 1950s, though, with the rise of suburban communities in which people came to live great distances from the synagogue, the Conservative movement's Committee on Jewish Law and Standards ruled that it is permitted to ride to the synagogue and back home if one would not otherwise be able to participate in public worship. This permission to ride was not extended to riding for other purposes.

When electricity became available for domestic use in the nineteenth century, rabbinic authorities extended the prohibition of kindling a fire to electricity. Some Conservative authorities today, however, do not regard electricity as fire and therefore permit its use.

The fact that certain acts are forbidden does not make the Sabbath or holy days austere or gloomy. To the contrary, they are designed to be days of joy and of great spiritual delight, distinct from ordinary days. People who observe them through prayer, study, and companionship can find themselves physically and spiritually renewed.

As Rabbi Heschel wrote, observing the Sabbath is ideally

more than the fulfillment of one's obligation or duty; it can and should be an opportunity to elevate ourselves to a higher spiritual plane:

> The art of keeping the seventh day is the art of painting on the canvas of time the mysterious grandeur of the climax of creation. . . . The love of the Sabbath is the love of man for what he and God have in common.[5]

Talmud Torah (Study)

Study is a basic religious obligation in Jewish tradition. People who seek to shape committed religious lives establish a fixed period of study every day. The Bible, especially the Torah, and the Talmud are their obvious choices, but they study other texts as well.

Religious fulfillment requires more than the performance of ritual or ethical obligations; it must include dedication to Torah study. The Rabbis long ago asserted that ignorant people cannot be truly pious. Judaism cannot survive without learning. A well-known talmudic story dramatically illustrates this conviction.

The great Rabbi Akiba lived in the second century, when the Empire of Rome was determined to put an end to the Jewish faith, which it considered heretical. Realizing that physical force had failed to achieve the goal, the emperor issued a decree forbidding Jews to practice ritual circumcision, to observe Shabbat, or to teach Torah. Jews who wanted to survive as Jews had no choice but to defy such decrees. Accordingly, the sages continued to meet with their disciples to pursue the path of Torah.

A noted teacher and scholar, the revered Rabbi Akiba, refused to teach surreptitiously. He met his students openly. One of his friends, aware of the consequences of this act, urged him to desist. Rabbi Akiba responded with this fable:

"A fox on a river bank noticed the frantic movement of fish

---

[5] Abraham Joshua Heschel, *The Sabbath,* p. 16.

in the water. He asked them why they were so agitated, and was told that fishermen had come to the river intent upon catching fish. Thereupon the fox invited the fish to leave the water to join him on dry land where they would be safe. The fish replied to the fox, 'And they call you the wisest of creatures? If we cannot survive in water, which is our natural habitat, we surely cannot survive *outside* it!'"

"Thus it is with us," concluded Rabbi Akiba. "If we cannot survive *with* Torah, which is 'our life and the length of our days,' we surely cannot survive *without* it." He continued to teach until he was arrested, imprisoned, and put to a martyr's death.

Throughout the centuries, Jews have always insisted that learning is an obligation. Jewish life has been guided by the rabbinic maxim, "If you possess knowledge, what can you lack? If you lack knowledge, what can you possess?" Mothers sang lullabies to infants in cradles praising Torah as the most valuable of all acquisitions. Moses, the greatest figure of Jewish history, is extolled as liberator and lawgiver, but he is known primarily as *Moshe Rabbeinu*, "Moses, Our Teacher." Classically, the heroes of the Jewish people have been students of Torah. In the European community, the ideal husband was a scholar. The rich man who was ignorant was not as honored or respected as the impoverished man whose life was dedicated to study.

Unfortunately, with the massive migration of Jews to North America came the loss of devotion to Jewish learning and Jewish culture. In North America:

> . . . the traditional values of Jewish existence were marginalized or ignored by the mainstream institutions that dominated American Jewish life. Serious Jewish learning [and] Jewish literacy . . . became marginal goals for American Jewry and the preoccupation of a small minority of American Jews.[6]

[6] Barry Shrage, "Jewish Studies, Jewish Community and Jewish Literacy: Creating a Revolution in Jewish Life" (adapted from a speech given at the Association for Jewish Studies Convention on December 17, 1995), unpublished manuscript dated July 29, 1996, p. 2.

The traditional Jewish passion for learning was transferred to secular studies, while Jewish learning was neglected. The resulting unfamiliarity with and alienation from the sources weakened the quality of Jewish life and threatened the very future of the Jewish community. In response to this, Rabbi Heschel urged:

> We must create a climate of elucidation, of pronouncing our people's waiting for meaning, by discovering and teaching the intellectual relevance of Judaism, by fostering *reverence for learning and the learning of reverence.* . . .[7]

Many Jewish leaders have been striving to revive the traditional emphasis on Jewish education and are developing creative approaches to Jewish learning.

It is only through a renewed and consistent involvement with learning that Jews as a community will continue to be what Muhammed once called us: "The People of the Book."

[7] Abraham Joshua Heschel, Speech before the 34th General Assembly of the Council of Jewish Federations, 1965.

CHAPTER 7

An Introduction to Jewish Worship

*P*RAYER is a fundamentally spontaneous activity. It may take place at any time of the day. It may be inspired by a natural phenomenon, such as a sunset, or by a perception which arises in one's consciousness while sitting alone. It may consist of words or it may be soundless. It may be lengthy or it may be brief.

Throughout its history, the Jewish tradition has encouraged spontaneous prayer. In addition to spontaneous prayer, formal, fixed prayer services were developed by the Rabbis as a means of heightening one's spiritual consciousness and in order to more fully serve God. Time is thus set aside, throughout each and every day, for prayer to take place. A common liturgy and a common choreography of worship have served to unify the Jewish people. To a great extent, the words recited by Jews today in Jewish worship services are identical to those which have been recited for thousands of years. This reinforces our links with the past and future, and with fellow Jews around the world.

In order for Jewish worship to achieve its goals, however, it must be understood. In order to participate fully, one must have a sense of its overall structure. Otherwise, one may feel lost.

How do you get to feel at home in the world of Jewish prayer? It might seem simple at first—just go to a synagogue, pick up the prayerbook, and follow the service! That, however, is easier said than done. Not that it is difficult to find a prayerbook. Most synagogues have copies available. But following the service and understanding the prayers are another matter. In traditional congregations, all or most of the prayers are recited in Hebrew. Many words and phrases, chants and melodies may seem strange at first. Few, if any, translations are able to convey the true meaning and emotional impact of the original Hebrew.

The best way to learn to feel comfortable with Jewish worship begins with getting to know the prayerbook, the *siddur*. To understand it, you will need to study it, not just glance through it.

Understanding the *siddur* can bring you to the heart of Judaism. More than any other single volume, the *siddur* expresses the yearnings of the Jew and the Jewish tradition. It conveys the historic hopes, the religious longings, and the spiritual ideals of the Jewish people.

The *siddur* is not the product of any one person or of any one age. It records the religious creativity of an entire people throughout the ages. It contains passages from the Bible and the Talmud, from medieval poets, and, in some editions, from modern and contemporary thinkers. All Jews have followed the same basic core of the service, but different communities have supplemented this core with liturgical poems and other selections, often modifying and adding to the text. (For more on the *siddur*, see Chapter 3).

According to Jewish law, people may pray in any language they understand, although praying in Hebrew, even if imperfectly understood, is considered preferable. The primary reason for this is that Hebrew is a holy language for Jews. Since antiquity, Hebrew letters and words have been considered to possess sacred qualities. For thousands of years—long before it became the language of modern Israel—Hebrew was the language of Jewish poets, prophets, and teachers, and Hebrew prayers reverberate with deep, classical associations. Jews, for the most part, have found that Jewish values and ideals are most fully expressed in Hebrew. Moreover, because Hebrew is undeniably Jewish, its use not only binds Jews to past generations but to Jews throughout the world today. Hence, the use of Hebrew persists in services, and virtually every *siddur* contains all or part of the service in Hebrew, even though not all worshipers know the meaning of all of the words. Most prayerbooks printed in the West have translations on the pages facing the Hebrew; many contain transliterations of selected prayers as well in order to aid those unfamiliar with the Hebrew alphabet.

Although at first glance it may not be apparent, the liturgy for each prayer service is intricately organized. In this chapter we will seek to describe that organization. Although we will not describe every prayer, we will review the highlights of the daily prayer services so that structure and flow can be appreciated.

Before doing so, though, a caveat: a prayer service is more than its liturgy, and praying is more than saying words—even words that are clearly understood. Studying the *siddur* may enhance prayer, but the study of prayer is no substitute for praying. In a prayer service, choreography and melody play important roles. In a public service, moreover, others are present and one's relationship to them is also a factor. All of these contribute to the phenomenon we call prayer, which is highly subjective and emotional and must be experienced to be fully appreciated.

The Berakhah/Blessing: The Building Block of Jewish Prayer

The *siddur* is filled with blessings, known in Hebrew as *berakhot* (singular: *berakhah*). These are exclamations which express appreciation to God. One talmudic sage, Rabbi Meir, suggested that we should recite one hundred blessings each day—testifying to our constant appreciation of the sacred dimension of the world.

Blessings are said at key moments throughout the day: before eating, before performing a *mitzvah,* upon experiencing something new (see Chapter 6). Pausing to recite a blessing is a critical religious act: it stops the flow of time and heightens the significance of a moment. Blessings are therefore an important feature of the spiritual life of the individual Jew.

Blessings are found throughout the liturgy. These serve to synchronize the thoughts and feelings of the entire congregation, creating a communal focus at particular points in the service. They thus serve, particularly for the novice, as helpful markers to define the various sections of the service.

A familiar sequence of words found in rabbinic *berakhot* is: *Barukh atah Adonai, Eloheinu melekh ha-olam . . .*—"Blessed (or Praised) are You, *Adonai,* Our God, Sovereign (or King) of the Universe . . ." This sequence is generally followed by a predicate, such as ". . . the Creator of Peace."

A *berakhah* may be short, consisting only of a simple statement. Such blessings as the *ha-motzi* (said before eating bread) or the *she-heḥeyanu* (said upon experiencing something new) are short *berakhot.*

Generally, though, in the liturgy a *berakhah* consists of one or more paragraphs. The first *berakhah* in a series usually begins with the traditional formula, *"Barukh atah Adonai, Eloheinu melekh ha-olam . . ."* All blessings conclude with the phrase *Barukh atah Adonai . . .* followed by a predicate.

Weekday Services

THE EVENING SERVICE—*MA'ARIV,* OR *ARVIT*

We begin by studying the evening service because it is the first service of the Jewish day, which begins at sundown. It is called *ma'ariv,* or *arvit.* (Both words are related to the Hebrew word for evening, *erev.*)

The service begins with the leader chanting the *Bar'khu*—a formal call to prayer: *Bar'khu et Adonai ha-m'vorakh*—"Praise Adonai, the Exalted One."

The congregation responds: "Praised be Adonai, the Exalted One, throughout all time."

It should be noted at the outset that different prayerbooks translate these and other passages differently. Some prayerbook translations are more faithful to the original Hebrew; others are more poetic. Increasingly, liberal prayerbooks are becoming sensitive to gendered and hierarchical language in the traditional prayerbook and are suitably modifying the translations. For example, in some prayerbooks, such as *Siddur Sim Shalom for Shabbat and Festivals* (from which the above translations are taken), the proper Hebrew name for God, *"Adonai,"* is left untranslated. (The traditional translation, "Lord," is now deemed by some to convey an unattractive image of God.) In other prayerbooks, non-gendered and/or non-hierarchical English words are used to refer to the deity. Hebrew is inherently gendered, yet few prayerbooks are willing to alter the original Hebrew text because of the Jewish people's deep-seated veneration of the core of the traditional liturgy, which was fixed almost two thousand years ago. Nevertheless, some revisions of the traditional prayers which reflect contemporary concerns have been made. Because the effectiveness of a prayerbook depends on harmony between its language and the theological ideas of those reciting the prayers, there will undoubtedly continue to be much discussion of, and development of, new translations in the years ahead.

The Shema and its Blessings.   The service proceeds to the recitation of the *Shema* and its blessings (known in Hebrew as *"k'riat shema uvirkhoteha"*). This section consists of two introductory *berakhot,* three passages from the Bible, and two concluding *berakhot.*

The first *berakhah* praises God for the divine act of Creation and heightens our awareness of the grandeur and mystery of dusk:

> Praised are You Adonai our God, who rules the universe, Your word bringing the evening dusk. . . . You create day and night, rolling light away from darkness and darkness away from light. . . .
>
> Praised are You Adonai, for each evening's dusk.

The second *berakhah* expresses our appreciation for God's gift of the Torah, an expression of God's love for us:

> With constancy You have loved Your people Israel, teaching us Torah and *mitzvot,* statutes and laws. Therefore, Adonai our God, when we lie down to sleep and when we rise, we shall think of Your laws and speak of them, rejoicing always in Your Torah and *mitzvot.* For they are our life and the length of our days; we will meditate on them day and night. Never take Your love from us.
>
> Praised are You Adonai, who loves the people Israel.

These two *berakhot* set the stage for the recitation of the *Shema.*

The *Shema* consists of three biblical passages; the first of these (Deuteronomy 6:4–9) begins with the Hebrew word *"Shema!"* which means, "Hear!" or *"Listen!"* The first, and most famous, verse of the *Shema* is a call for awareness, alertness and allegiance:

> *Shema Yisrael Adonai Eloheinu Adonai Eḥad.*
> Hear, O Israel: Adonai is our God, Adonai alone.

The *Shema* proclaims the oneness of God and is the central declaration of Jewish faith. This is often the first biblical verse that children learn and it is the passage prescribed by tradition to be among the last words uttered before death. But the *Shema* is more than a simple declaration of a belief in one God. It is also a way of looking at the universe. Several deep religious notions can be understood to flow from the *Shema*. If God is one—that is, if all conceptions of the divine are in fact pointing to the same source—then all human beings are God's children, united in one family. If God is one, then history is not a series of isolated episodes, but a series of events related to each other with meaning and purpose. Moreover, if God is one, then the forces of nature are part of a whole, not random. By proclaiming "God is one," the Jew can be understood to be asserting faith in the unity of all people, the importance of human history, and the harmony of a natural world which is hospitable to human beings.

It is customary to whisper a response immediately after reciting the first verse of the *Shema:* "Praised be God's glorious sovereignty throughout all time." After whispering this, *k'riat shema* continues with Deuteronomy 6:5–9.

> You shall love Adonai your God with all your heart, with all your soul, with all your might. And these words which I command you this day, you shall take to heart. Teach them, diligently, to your children, and recite them at home and away, night and day. Bind them as a sign upon your hand, and as a reminder above your eyes. Inscribe them upon the doorposts of your homes and upon your gates.

This paragraph instructs us to perform several important *mitzvot:* to teach Torah, to recite the *Shema* before we go to sleep and upon awakening, to wear *tefillin* and to place a *mezuzah* on the doorposts of our homes (*Tefillin* and *mezuzah* are reviewed in Chapter 6.) The fact that this paragraph is to be recited twice daily reinforces the importance of these *mitzvot*.

The second passage of the *Shema* (Deuteronomy 11:13–21) suggests that consequences follow our choices: If we, the Jewish people, *do* fulfill our charge expressed in the first verses of the *Shema* (to "listen" to and to "love" God and to observe God's *mitzvot*), we will be blessed; if we fail to hearken to God's will, we will suffer the consequences. The third passage of the *Shema,* Numbers 15:37–41, instructs us to wear *tzitzit* (discussed in

Chapter 6) on the four corners of our garments in order to remember to fulfill all of God's *mitzvot*.

K'riat Shema is followed by two *berakhot*. The first, *Ga'al Yisrael,* praises God for redeeming us from Egyptian bondage. The Exodus from Egypt is often recalled in the liturgy because that momentous event has been taken as evidence that God was, is, and will be the Redeemer of the people Israel. The second concluding *berakhah, Hashkiveinu,* praises God for His peace and protection. It is a prayer which can calm our souls as we prepare to go to sleep for the night.

The Amidah. The other major section of the evening service is a silent prayer, so basic that in Hebrew it is called, *"ha-tefillah,"* meaning, *"the* prayer." Recited at every service, it is today generally known by two Hebrew names. One is *Amidah,* which means "standing," for it is always recited while standing. (The *Shema,* on the other hand, is traditionally recited while seated. Note, though, that in some Reform congregations, it has become customary to rise to recite the *Shema* while standing.) The other name for the *Amidah* is *Sh'moneh Esreh,* a Hebrew word meaning "eighteen," since when it was originally composed it consisted of eighteen *berakhot.* (A nineteenth *berakhah* was added later.)

The first three and the last three *berakhot* of the *Amidah* are the same for weekday, Sabbath, and Festival services, and so we will review these first.

The first *berakhah* is called *Avot* ("ancestors") because it refers to our God as the God of Abraham, Isaac, and Jacob— that is, the God of history. *Avot* is worth focusing on because, when one converts to Judaism, one acquires Jewish ancestors. As discussed earlier, Maimonides and other authorities emphasized the privilege all Jews possess to affirm that Abraham is their spiritual ancestor.

> Praised are You Adonai, our God and God of our ancestors, God of Abraham, God of Isaac, and God of Jacob, great, mighty, awesome, exalted God who bestows lovingkindness. . . . You remem-

ber the pious deeds of our ancestors . . . Praised are You Adonai,
Shield of Abraham.

Though each generation may conceive of God in a different
way, God remains the same throughout all time. It has been
noted that the text reads "God of Abraham, God of Isaac, and
God of Jacob," rather than "God of Abraham, Isaac, and
Jacob." God is related directly to each patriarch, since each
emphasized a different aspect of the same God. Each brought
God into his life in his own way.

Our patriarchs were not alone on their journeys, spiritual
and otherwise. They were accompanied by the four matriarchs:
Sarah, Rebecca, Rachel, and Leah. In the past several decades,
many Jews, both male and female, seeking to create an inclusive
liturgy, have begun to include the names of the matriarchs in the
text of *Avot,* in order to remind us of the female role models in
our tradition as well. Despite the traditional reluctance (described
earlier) to revise the texts of the ancient statutory *berakhot,* several texts of an inclusive *Avot berakhah* have been composed. The
following is a translation of a version found in the newly revised
edition of the Conservative movement's *Siddur Sim Shalom.*

> Praised are You Adonai, our God and God of our ancestors, God
> of Abraham, God of Isaac, and Jacob, Sarah, Rebecca, Rachel, and
> Leah . . . Praised are You, Adonai, Shield of Abraham and
> Guardian of Sarah.

Just as each of the patriarchs and matriarchs may have recognized a different aspect of God, this may be true of us as well.

The second *berakhah* of the *Amidah* is known as *Gevurot*
("Powers"), and it refers to God's mighty deeds.

> Your might, Adonai, is boundless. You give life to the dead; great
> is Your saving power. Your love sustains the living. Your great mer-
> cies give life to the dead. . . . You keep Your faith with those who
> sleep in dust. . . . Praised are You Adonai, Master of Life and
> death.

This *berakhah* appears to refer to bodily resurrection, a doctrine adopted by Jews toward the end of the biblical period. Yet not all Jews have accepted this doctrine literally. Hence, without changing the time-honored words of the Hebrew *berakhah,* some modern authorities have taken liberties with the translation of the *berakhah.* Others have changed the wording of the original Hebrew text. For example, in the Reform prayerbook, *The Gates of Prayer,* the concluding phrase reads, "Who Gives Life to All."

The third *berakhah* of the *Amidah* is called *Kedushah,* "holiness":

> Holy are You and holy is Your name. Holy are those who praise You each day. Praised are You Adonai, holy God.

We will skip the intermediate section of *berakhot* now, to present the three concluding *berakhot* of the *Amidah.* The first of these is called *Avodah* (worship):

> Accept the prayer of Your people Israel as lovingly as it is offered. Restore worship to Your sanctuary, and may the worship of Your people Israel always be acceptable to You. May we witness Your merciful return to Zion. Praised are You Adonai, who restores the Divine Presence to Zion.

Ever since the Romans destroyed the Temple in the year 70 C.E., the Jewish tradition has expressed the yearning of Jews to return to Zion and Jerusalem. This prayer kept alive in the hearts of Jewry the passionate longing for a reborn Jewish Commonwealth in which Jews would be free to worship God in their own manner.

The next passage is referred to as *Hodayah* (grateful acknowledgement):

> We proclaim that You are Adonai our God and God of our ancestors throughout all time. . . . We thank You and praise You for our lives that are in Your hand, for our souls that are in Your charge. . . . May every living creature thank You and praise You

faithfully . . . Praised are You Adonai, the essence of goodness,
worthy of acclaim.

The last *berakhah* is called *Shalom* because it is a prayer for
true peace, which Judaism has always regarded as the greatest
blessing.

Grant true and lasting peace to Your people Israel and to all who
dwell on earth, for You are the supreme Sovereign of peace. May it
please You to bless Your people Israel in every season and at all
times with Your gift of peace. Praised are You Adonai, who blesses
the people Israel with peace.

We now introduce the interior *berakhot* of the *Amidah*.
These vary considerably depending on whether the day is an
ordinary weekday or a Sabbath or Festival.

On weekdays, thirteen petitionary *berakhot* are recited.
Space does not permit a full exposition of these *berakhot*.
Nonetheless, it is helpful to review briefly their themes, for they
are intended to be in the minds and hearts of the worshiper during the recitation of the *Amidah*. As is the case with all of the
berakhot in the *Amidah*—indeed, virtually all *berakhot* in the *siddur*—these are phrased in the plural: when we recite even the
petitionary section of the *Amidah*, our focus is not on the personal but on the collective.

The first of the petitionary *berakhot* focuses on knowledge
and understanding:

You graciously endow mortals with intelligence, teaching us wisdom. Grant us knowledge, wisdom, and discernment. Praised are
You Adonai, who graciously grants us intelligence.

This is followed by *berakhot* with the themes of repentance, forgiveness, redemption, healing, the earth's bounty, ingathering of
the dispersed, justice, humbling the arrogant, and sustaining the
righteous.

The *Amidah* continues with petitions for the rebuilding of Jerusalem, the advent of the Messianic Era, and for the answering of prayer. It concludes with:

> Hear our voice Adonai our God. Have compassion upon us, pity us. Accept our prayer with loving favor. . . . Praised are You Adonai, who listens to prayer.

Articulating the words of the *Amidah* in silent reverence focuses one's attention away from the self and toward the needs, goals, and aspirations of the Jewish people. If one thinks about the lofty ideals which are its themes (eg., repentence, justice, redemption, peace), one cannot but be drawn to reflect on one's own duty to take part in addressing them. The *Amidah* can thus serve as the basis for personal meditation and determined resolution.

Reciting the *Amidah* should never become rote; "do not make your prayer a routine activity, but a heartfelt yearning in the presence of God."[1]

Aleinu. Every service concludes with a prayer known as *Aleinu* ("We rise to our duty . . ."). The first paragraph of *Aleinu* expresses the duty to praise the Lord of all, who fashioned the Jews as a distinct people. The second half of the *Aleinu* proclaims the universality of God and looks forward to the time when all humanity will ultimately pledge allegiance to God alone.

The Mourner's Kaddish. *Kaddish* (an Aramaic word meaning "holy") is a publically recited prayer that appears throughout the service. It generally serves to divide one section of the service from another. One form of the *Kaddish* is traditionally recited by mourners and is referred to as the Mourner's *Kaddish,* which concludes the evening service. By reciting it, the

---

[1] *Pirkei Avot* 2:18.

mourner affirms faith in God and the possibility of a peaceful, just world at moments of greatest trial and doubt.

> May God's name be exalted and hallowed throughout the world that He created, as is God's wish. May God's sovereignty soon be accepted, during our life and the life of all Israel. And let us say: Amen.

> May God's great name be praised throughout all time.

> Glorified and celebrated, lauded and worshiped, exalted and honored, extolled and acclaimed may the Holy One be, praised beyond all song and psalm, beyond all tributes that mortals can utter. And let us say: Amen.

> Let there be abundant peace from heaven, with life's goodness for us and for all Israel. And let us say: Amen.

> May the One who brings peace to His universe bring peace to us and to all Israel. And let us say: Amen.

Traditionally, because the Mourner's *Kaddish* is a personal affirmation made by those individuals who have suffered a loss, only mourners and those observing the anniversary of a death (*yahrzeit*) rise to recite it. In most Reform congregations, though, as an expression of solidarity with the mourners, everyone rises to recite the Mourner's *Kaddish*.

THE MORNING SERVICE—*SHAHARIT*

The core of this service is similar to that of *Ma'ariv*. It is a longer service, however, and includes two introductory sections. The first of these is known as *Birkhot Ha-Shahar* ("morning blessings"), a section which celebrates the renewal of life each day. These blessings express gratitude and praise for God's gifts of body and soul, as well as for God's compassion, for our covenant with God, and for the Torah. Passages from the Torah and from rabbinic literature are included to fulfill the minimal obligation for daily study.

The next section, known as *P'sukei D'zimra* ("passages of praise"), contains psalms and passages from throughout the Bible which seek to direct our attention to God's presence in the world. *Birkhot Ha-shaḥar* and *P'sukei D'zimra* precede the morning service because the authors of the *siddur* recognized that prayer requires preparation. In order to pray with full intentionality and commitment, one's heart, mind, and spirit must be freed from distractions and properly directed. These sections can help the worshiper approach the core of the morning prayer service in the proper spirit.

The core of the service is similar to *Ma'ariv*. It begins with the formal call to worship *(Ba'rkhu)*, and *K'riat Shema* and its *berakhot*. As at *Ma'ariv*, *K'riat Shema* is preceded by two *berakhot* which express gratitude to God for Creation and for Revelation, but it is followed by only one *berakhah*, with the theme of Redemption.

When reciting the *Amidah* in the presence of a *minyan*, it is customary for the prayer leader to repeat the *Amidah* aloud. When this is done, a responsive prayer known as the *Kedushah* ("sanctification") is chanted. This responsive recititation is structured around biblical verses understood to express mystical visions of the diety.

The *Amidah* is followed by a short reading from the Torah on Mondays and Thursdays (these were the market days in ancient Israel, appropriate times for teaching the Torah in public). The reading is taken from the portion to be read on the following Shabbat morning. On certain days, in some congregations, private prayers of petition known as *Taḥanun* are then recited. *Aleinu* and the Mourner's *Kaddish* conclude the service.

THE AFTERNOON SERVICE—*MINḤAH*

This is the briefest service of the day. The word *minḥah* means "gift." This service recalls the late afternoon sacrifice (the *minḥah* offering) offered in the ancient Temple. The *Minḥah* service generally is held just before *Ma'ariv*, although it can be recited earlier in the afternoon.

This modest service opens with the *Ashrei,* a selection of verses from the book of psalms. Three times the word *ashrei,* meaning "happy" or "fortunate" appears in the opening verses. The repetition of this word seems designed to induce in the worshiper the proper mood for prayer: thankfulness and appreciation. The *Amidah* follows. *Aleinu* and the Mourner's *Kaddish* conclude *Minḥah.* As at *Shaḥarit,* the petitionary prayers of *Taḥanun* may be recited.

Shabbat Services

KABBALAT SHABBAT—FRIDAY EVENING

Shabbat, which begins at sundown Friday night, is devoted to prayer, study, time with family and friends, and rest. Shabbat services are longer than those on weekdays. *Ma'ariv* on Friday evening is preceded by a brief special service of Welcoming Shabbat *(Kabbalat Shabbat). Kabbalat Shabbat* begins with six psalms (corresponding to the six days of creation) and a liturgical poem, *Lekha Dodi,* which was composed by a sixteenth-century mystic who personified the Sabbath as a beloved bride. The poet, Shlomo ha-Levi Alkabetz, lived in the city of Safed, which is nestled in the Galilean hills of the Land of Israel. Many mystics resided in Safed. It was their custom to leave the city on Friday afternoon, dressed in white, to welcome the Sabbath, and to usher her into their community as one would royalty. The author of *Lekha Dodi* urged his colleagues (as indeed he urges all of us):

> Beloved friend, come greet the bride;
> Let the Sabbath presence among us abide.[2]

Many melodies have been composed for this prayer and congregations generally sing all or most of it in unison. Following *Lekha Dodi,* the psalm for Shabbat (psalm 92) is recited. Psalm 93 and the Mourner's *Kaddish* conclude *Kabbalat Shabbat.*

---

[2] Translation from *Ḥadesh Yameinu: Renew Our Days,* edited and translated by Ronald Aigen (Montreal: Congregation Dorshei Emet, 1996).

The *Ma'ariv* service is similar to that of weekdays, but several prayers which have a weekday quality to them are deleted and other prayers are added in honor of the Sabbath. During the *Amidah*, the thirteen intermediate petitionary *berakhot* are not recited, for the concerns over such requests are not felt to be appropriate on a day devoted to joy and celebration. The intermediate section of the *Amidah* consists of a single *berakhah*, extolling the special sanctity of the Sabbath day.

Before *Aleinu*, the prayer known as *kiddush* is recited over a cup of wine. (*Kiddush*, like *Kaddish*, is related to the Hebrew word *kadosh*, which means "holy.") It is important to stress that one does not bless or in any way transform wine by reciting *kiddush*. One praises God, not the wine, and the day is thereby sanctified. The wine plays a part in the sanctification because it is a traditional symbol of joy and well-being. Traditionally, *kiddush* is recited at the table at home before the Sabbath meal (see Chapter 6), but because it is such an important part of Shabbat observance, it is also recited during *Ma'ariv* in case anyone present will not be partaking of a Sabbath meal where *kiddush* will be recited. Chanting the words of *kiddush*, we proclaim the sanctity of the Sabbath and thank God for the gift of the holy seventh day which commemorates Creation and the Exodus from Egypt.

Something should be said here about the late Friday evening services which can still be found in some American congregations. Traditionally, men came to the synagogue late Friday afternoon for *Minḥah, Kabbalat Shabbat,* and *Ma'ariv.* They then went home to their Shabbat meal and spent the evening with their families. The principal Sabbath service was on Saturday (Shabbat) morning. In the United States, however, particularly during and soon after the wave of Eastern European immigration during the early part of the twentieth century, a new pattern developed. It was difficult to get to a Friday afternoon service before dusk. Stores could not be closed early, and traveling took longer than it had in the tiny villages of Eastern

Europe. Even if Jews could leave work early on Friday after-noons, they were reluctant to do so, lest this mark them as dif-ferent from the average Americans they were striving to become. The Reform movement and some Conservative congregations replaced the traditional *Kabbalat Shabbat* and Sabbath *Ma'ariv* with a late Friday evening service for the entire family. This ful-filled a need on the American scene in the early and middle decades of the twentieth century.

Increasingly, Friday evening services are being restored to the traditionally appropriate time of dusk, so that worshipers can then return to their homes for Shabbat dinner. Each of the American Jewish religious movements is stressing the impor-tance and beauty of home-based celebrations to welcome Shab-bat on Friday evenings, and seeking to restore them to their sacred status. The economic and social pressures of a generation ago which motivated the creation of the late Friday evening ser-vice are now less intense. Simultaneously, American Jews are increasingly willing to engage in practices which distinguish them from their non-Jewish neighbors, friends and colleagues. Feeling less need to conform, and greater appreciation of the traditional celebration of Shabbat, Jews have been reclaiming more and more of the Sabbath Day.

SHABBAT *SHAḤARIT*—SATURDAY MORNING

The Saturday morning service *(Shaḥarit)* also includes special features not present on weekdays. For example, poetic passages extolling creation and the joy and beauty of Shabbat are added to the service and the middle *berakhah* of the *Amidah* is devoted to the theme of Shabbat. The most significant and prominent insertion into the Shabbat morning service, though, is the Torah service, during which a Torah scroll is ceremoniously removed from the Ark and read aloud.

The Torah Service. In the absence of weekday routine, there is more time on Shabbat for the reading of the Torah and for the study of its sacred words. This is an important aspect of the spiritual regeneration of Shabbat.

The Torah scroll *(sefer torah;* plural: *sifrei torah)* is removed from the special ark *(aron ha-kodesh)* where the Torah scrolls are kept. The curtain *(parokhet)* is pulled back, the doors are parted, and the Torah is taken out. A formal procession through the congregation allows people to express love and respect for the Torah by kissing the mantle covering it. (People generally do this indirectly, by first touching the mantle with a *siddur* or one of the fringes of a *tallit,* and then kissing the *siddur* or *tallit.)* The crown, breastplate, and mantle of the *sefer torah* are removed, and then the Torah scroll is placed on a reading desk and opened to the place where the reading is to begin.

Each week a different section *(parashah* or *sidrah)* of the Torah is read. Generally, it is the continuation of the verses that were read the previous Sabbath morning. The Torah is divided into sections that allow for the complete reading of all five books each year. The cycle begins with the first words of the Book of Genesis each fall, after the holidays which initiate the new year of the Jewish calendar. The practice of completing the reading of the Torah in one year arose in Babylonia; during the medieval period, the practice became widespread. Many congregations today follow this annual cycle of readings.

In the Land of Israel, it was the custom to read smaller portions from the Torah each week, so it took three years to complete a reading of the entire Torah. (Hence the term "triennial cycle.") In recent decades, some congregations (mostly Conservative) have returned to reading about a third of a *parashah* each week. They have not reintroduced the precise form of the old Palestinian triennial system, because they want to preserve the unity of Jewry's religious expression by reading from the same portion from which all other Jewish communities are reading. Therefore, they read one-third of the weekly *parashah* (i.e., one-third of the portion read in its entirety by other congregations on the same morning). Each year, a different third of the weekly *parashah* is read. Thus the entire Torah is completed every three years.

Who reads the Torah in the synagogue? Anyone who has mastered the art. And indeed it is an art! The Torah scroll does not contain a printed text. It is painstakingly written by hand on parchment by a scribe, who must follow the exact procedures used throughout the centuries. Modern Hebrew books may be printed with vowels. A Torah scroll contains no vowels. Moreover, it contains no punctuation. Further, as the division of the Bible into verses and chapters did not exist until late antiquity, no verses or chapters are indicated in the Torah scroll. The Torah reader (called a *ba'al korei*) must prepare most carefully in order to read correctly and to know where to pause or stop.

Actually, the Torah is usually not read, but chanted. (The exception is in Reform congregations, where it is customary for the Torah to be read.) Each word has a specific assigned cantillation, indicated in printed bibles by certain markings called trope. The *ba'al korei* must learn the proper chant from a printed text and then transfer it mentally to the reading from the Torah scroll.

Each *parashah* is divided into subsections, before and after which someone recites a *berakhah* thanking God for the gift of the Torah. It is an honor to be asked to recite this blessing. This honor is known as an *aliyah* (literally, "a going up"). Traditionally, the first person called is a *kohen*, a descendant of the priests *(kohanim)* who functioned in the ancient Temple. The second *aliyah* is customarily given to a *levi*, a descendant of the Levites who also served in the ancient Temple in Jerusalem. The remaining *aliyot* (plural of *aliyah*) are given to those who are in neither category. Each one of them is known, generally, as an "Israelite" *(yisrael)*. Some congregations have dispensed with the practice of distinguishing among *kohen, levi,* and *yisrael* and call up any Jews, whatever their lineage, for any of the *aliyot*.

On Shabbat, seven people are called to the Torah. Each individual with an *aliyah* kisses the Torah scroll with a *tallit* or some other appropriate object and recites the *berakhah*. Then the *ba'al korei* reads from the Torah, after which the honoree again kisses the Torah and recites the concluding *berakhah*.

On Shabbat an additional person is called for an *aliyah:* the *maftir* (which means "additional"). This portion usually is a rep-etition of the last few verses of the section read. (On festivals and certain *Shabbatot*, this portion is read from a second *sefer torah*.) Two more people are then called to the Torah. One (called *ha-magbiah*) raises the Torah scroll and sits with it, hold-ing it in an upright position. The second (called *ha-gollel*) ties a sash around the middle of the rolled scroll and slips the mantle over it.

The *maftir* then chants a designated passage from one of the prophetic books of the Bible. This selection is called a *haf-tarah* (a "concluding reading"). It often bears some relationship to the *parashah* (or, on a festival, to the festival reading)—a simi-larity of ideas or an association with a theme, personality, or spe-cific words mentioned in the Torah reading. It may focus atten-tion on an upcoming holiday. The *haftarah* is ordinarily chanted from a printed text rather than from a scroll. The symbols indi-cating the proper chanting for the *haftarah* are the same as those for the Torah reading, yet they indicate a different musical mode. Being asked to chant the *haftarah* is regarded as a great honor.

When the Torah scroll is returned to the ark, the congrega-tion chants several passages, concluding with the singing of *"Etz Ḥayim Hi,"* a passage which expresses our commitment to Torah study and our faith in its rewards:

> It is a tree of life for those who hold fast to it, and those who sup-port it are blessed. Its ways are ways of pleasantness, and all its paths are peace . . .

The ark is then closed. At this point, there may be a ser-mon, a *d'var torah* (a discourse on the Torah portion), or a Torah discussion.

The Musaf Service. Musaf means "addition" or "supple-ment." It is a term for the additional sacrifice (along with the daily one) which was offered every Sabbath, festival and *Rosh Ḥodesh* in the days of the ancient Temple. Following the destruction of the Temple, it became the practice to recite an additional *Amidah* on Shabbat, festivals and *Rosh Ḥodesh*, in place of that offering. Although the middle *berakhah* of this *Amidah* includes a petition for the restoration of the ancient Temple service, many Jews do not wish for or anticipate a return to animal sacrifice. They find other themes in this *Amidah* to which they can relate, such as the love and yearning for Zion. Some *siddurim* have modified the middle *berakhah* so that it articulates reverence for our ancestors' mode of worship without asking for a return to that worship.

After the *Musaf Amidah*, the congregation sings one of the most popular liturgical poems: *Ein Keloheinu*. It proclaims the uniqueness of God, asserting that there is none like our God, our Ruler, our Sovereign, our Deliverer. This hymn is followed by *Aleinu*, the Mourner's *Kaddish*, and usually the hymn *Adon Olam*.

Following services, it is customary for the congregation to join in a brief reception. This is called a *kiddush* because the Shabbat midday *kiddush* is recited over a cup of wine. (The *kiddush* is repeated in the home prior to the midday meal; see Chapter 6.) In many congregations, the congregational *kiddush* is an important communal experience: it is an opportunity to connect with friends, exchange greetings, and gather as a community.

SHABBAT *MINḤAH*

All services feature a distinctive chanting of the liturgy, but that of the Shabbat *Minḥah* service is particularly melancholy. Usually held late in the afternoon, the music reflects the collective sadness of anticipating the end of the holy day of rest. As on weekdays, the service begins with *Ashrei*. Several prayers are added in honor of Shabbat. The most distinctive feature of the service is a short reading from the portion of the Torah which will be read on the following Shabbat.

THE CONCLUSION OF SHABBAT

It is traditional to eat a communal light meal after the *Minḥah* service, the so-called "third meal" of Shabbat (known in Hebrew as *seudah shlishit* or *shalosh seudos*), following which, at day's end, the *Ma'ariv* service and *Havdalah* are recited. This may take place either in the synagogue or in the home. *Havdalah* ("separation" or "distinction") is a recitation of blessings over wine, spices and light, marking the separation between the holy day of Shabbat and the ordinary weekday to follow. Following *Havdalah,* the new week has begun; we greet one another with the words, *"Shavuah Tov!"* ("A Good Week!").

Festivals and Other Holy Days

Just as the liturgy of Shabbat reflects the distinctive character of the day, so too does the liturgy of the other holy days. On the High Holy Days, many, many additional prayers are recited (see Chapter 9). On the festivals and *Rosh Ḥodesh* (the semi-holiday at the beginning of each new month), services are similar to that of Shabbat, with insertions reflecting the themes of the day. To add to the spirit of rejoicing, the *Hallel,* a collection of psalms of praise, is recited.

It has not been possible in this brief introduction to describe all Jewish worship services in detail. (Several fine introductions to the liturgy have recently been published; see the bibliography.) The best way, though, to proceed in learning to participate in these services with conviction and understanding is to take part in them. Entering a synagogue, picking up a *siddur,* asking someone to help you find the place can achieve wonders. Remember that the liturgy is enormously rich; even those who've been *davening* (reciting the traditional prayers) for years are constantly learning. Do not be discouraged. The potential for comfort, support, and spiritual uplift is great.

CHAPTER 8

Congregations, Synagogues, and Ḥavurot

*T*HE community has always been a significant feature of Jewish life. As the great sage Hillel once said, "Don't separate yourself from the community."[1] The community was the primary instrument by which, throughout their long history of dispersion and persecution, Jews took care of their common needs. In the Middle Ages, local Jewish communities became known as *kehillot kodesh* (singular: *kahal kadosh* or *kehillah k'doshah*)—"holy congregations." The *kehillah* had the power to tax individuals and to allocate funds for the good of all. In addition to providing a place for communal worship and communal study, the community took care of its poor, its sick, and its elderly. In essence, it provided virtually all of a community's social services. It provided the dowry when poor brides married and handled funeral rituals for all its members.

Today, many local Jewish institutions in North American communities provide for Jewish communal needs: there are Jewish hospitals, Jewish social service agencies, and bureaus of Jew-

---

[1] *Pirkei Avot* 2:5.

ish education; there are Jewish schools and Jewish cemeteries. Among all of these institutions, though, there is one that has remained the pre-eminent local Jewish institution with which the greatest number of Jews affiliate and identify, and that is the synagogue.

The Synagogue

The institution we today call the synagogue may be over 2,500 years old. The Jews who were exiled to Babylonia following the destruction of the first Temple in Jerusalem are thought to have begun gathering in community centers there for communal worship, study, and fellowship. When some of the exiles returned to the Land of Israel, they may have brought these centers back with them. Some scholars believe that these evolved into what later became known as synagogues.

In any event, the synagogue is at least 2,000 years old. Its name, which is Greek, dates from the Hellenistic period. It means "a place of assembly."

The functions those Babylonian community centers served remain at the core of the synagogue today. Three distinct Hebrew terms are used to refer to the synagogue. It is a house of worship *(beit tefillah)*, a house of study *(beit midrash)*, as well as a house of assembly *(beit k'nesset)*. Jews thus turn to the synagogue for educational and social needs as well as purely spiritual ones.

The word "synagogue" is used throughout the world. When the early Reform movement rejected the traditional prayer for the rebuilding of the Temple in Jerusalem and declared synagogues to be its equivalent, they began referring to the latter as "temples," a term which is still sometimes used.

For many observant Ashkenazi Jews, the synagogue is referred to as *shul*. The Yiddish word for "school," the term reflects the educational role of the synagogue. In Israel, the synagogue goes by the classical Hebrew term, *beit k'nesset*.

Jews may pray anywhere, and may fulfill many of their religious obligations even if there is no synagogue in a community. Moreover, faithful attendance at synagogue services does not automatically confer special religious status. (As we have seen, the obligations of an observant Jew extend far beyond the walls of a synagogue.) Nonetheless, although Jews do not need a synagogue in order to be religious, they have created and sustained synagogues wherever they have migrated, and virtually all observant Jews belong to synagogues. This is so because of the considerable value of belonging to a community. A community devoted to the fulfillment of *mitzvot* is a community of caring and of shared values. It seeks to nurture the needs of its members, while reaching beyond itself to help others as well. It is also true that people can derive greater strength and inspiration from praying at fixed times with others who share their faith and tradition.

The Minyan

This preference for worship by and within a group is enshrined in Jewish law. Although Jews may always pray as individuals, communal prayers may only be recited in the presence of a quorum of ten or more Jewish adults. Such a quorum of ten is known as a *minyan* (the Hebrew word *"minyan"* means "count").

The requirement for ten is based upon a passage in the Torah which refers to ten men as constituting a "congregation," and traditionally, the ten worshipers have had to be males. This is still so in all Orthodox and in some Conservative congregations, though some of these allow groups of women to organize and conduct their own services. In 1973, the Conservative movement's Committee on Jewish Law and Standards ruled that women may be counted as part of the required *minyan*. More and more Conservative congregations are following that ruling. Reform and Reconstructionist authorities have long allowed for the full participation of women as well as men in services.

Because a public worship service can only be conducted in the presence of ten, a regularly scheduled weekday service in a synagogue may be commonly referred to as "the *minyan*." At a synagogue, one often hears such remarks as "We need one more for a *minyan!*" or "Thanks for coming! You've made the *minyan* for us!"

The Rabbi

Congregations eventually choose a rabbi (the word means "teacher") to provide religious leadership and to teach them. Having earned the title after years of study, culminating in ordination, the rabbi is an authority on interpreting and deciding matters of Jewish law and practice. In contemporary America, rabbis may serve as congregational spiritual leaders, as well as teachers, scholars, administrators, chaplains, and communal leaders. Congregational rabbis preach, teach, and counsel within the congregation and the general community, lead synagogue services, and officiate at life-cycle events such as weddings and funerals.

In recent years, in response to the opening up of other professional avenues previously closed to women, the rabbinate has become open to women as well as men. The Reform, Reconstructionist, and Conservative rabbinical schools now ordain women as well as men. Although the subject of women's ordination has been broached within Orthodoxy, and several Modern Orthodox congregations permit women to serve as para-rabbinic pastors, most Orthodox authorities do not seriously consider the possibility of women rabbis.

Each congregation selects its own rabbi, turning to the national body with which it is affiliated for acceptable candidates. The recommended candidates are interviewed by a congregational committee which makes a recommendation to be acted upon by the membership who have the authority to elect a rabbi.

The Ḥazzan

A congregation often chooses another religious leader: the *ḥazzan,* or cantor, whose area of expertise is music. An elaborate musical tradition is associated with the liturgy of the synagogue. The different public worship services are each chanted according to their own unique musical mode. Whenever the Torah or other books of the Bible are read publicly, they are chanted according to an ancient system of cantillation. The *ḥazzan* chants the service, is responsible for all of its musical aspects, and often serves as teacher and as a musical resource within the community. Although congregations are free to elect anyone without formal training to the position of *ḥazzan*, contemporary synagogues have increasingly required that cantors be professionally trained at recognized institutions. Cantorial schools have been established to provide professional training. All of the liberal cantorial schools now accept women students as well as men.

Music was used to accompany worship in the ancient Temple. Following the destruction of the Temple, as a sign of mourning, synagogue services were conducted without instrumental accompaniment. (In any event, the use of musical instruments was forbidden on the Sabbath.) With the rise of the Reform movement in Germany in the nineteenth century, the use of the organ was introduced into synagogue services, and during the following century, many Reform and some Conservative congregations in this country permitted the use of musical instruments in the synagogue service, even on the Sabbath. Today, rules vary, but fewer congregations employ a choir and organ to accompany their worship services. This reflects both a changing aesthetic as well as a desire by many Jews today for a more traditional service.

Synagogue Architecture

There is no standard synagogue architecture. Structures vary from community to community and within the same community. Synagogue architecture traditionally has been influenced by the architecture of its environment. Yet there are certain features common to all synagogues.

The first of these may be surprising. It is traditional for a synagogue to have windows. In the Book of Daniel, we read that Daniel looked out of a window and prayed facing the city of Jerusalem. Windows thus allow us to orient ourselves toward the Land of Israel. But windows serve another function as well. They allow us to see the world outside of the synagogue and to reflect upon it. Our focus is broadened and prayer thus becomes enhanced.

In the center of the wall facing the congregants (usually, in North America, the eastern wall) is an ark *(aron kodesh)* containing at least one Torah scroll. Usually there are several scrolls because there are occasions when it is necessary during a service to read from two or three different books of the Torah, and it is easier and considered more proper to do so from different scrolls prepared in advance than to require the congregation to wait while a single scroll is rolled. People may donate a Torah scroll to a congregation in honor of a special (i.e., once-in-life-time) occasion. They're quite expensive, usually far more expensive than the silver ornaments with which they are adorned.

The parchment scroll, wrapped around two wooden staves called *atzei ḥayim* ("trees of life;" singular: *etz ḥayim*) is covered by a mantle of velvet or silk. Often it is crowned with a silver crown, symbolizing the sovereignty of Torah in Jewish life, or with silver handle covers known as *rimmonim* ("pomegran-ates"—an allusion to the tradition that a pomegranate is said to contain 613 seeds, equal in number to the *mitzvot* in the Torah). Most Torah mantles are adorned with silver breastplates. A pointer known as a *yad,* meaning "hand," used when the Torah is read, usually hangs near the breastplate.

Above the ark is an Eternal Light *(ner tamid).* It symbolizes God's eternal presence as well as the eternal truth of the Torah. It is a reminder of the *menorah* (seven-branched candelabrum) that once stood in the ancient Jewish shrines, the tabernacle and the Temple, and was lit each day.

In most Western synagogues the ark is on a raised platform resembling a stage. This is referred to as the "pulpit" or *bimah.* Traditionally, the *bimah* was in the center of the synagogue away from the ark, and was where people gathered to read from the Torah.

Other symbols may be present in the synagogue. In some congregations, a *menorah* is placed on or near the pulpit, though it is not required by Jewish law. Very often, two tablets representing the tablets of the Ten Commandments are placed above the Ark. Sometimes the figure of a lion, the symbol of the tribe of Judah, is placed alongside each tablet. Scriptural verses or rabbinic statements often adorn the ark. One of the most popular, taken from the Talmud, is: *Da lifnei mi atah omed* ("Know before whom you stand"). Another, taken from the Book of Psalms, reads, *Shiviti Adonai l'negdi tamid* ("I set Adonai before me always").

The Ḥavurah

In the late 1960s, a new Jewish worship community arose: the *ḥavurah*. "*Ḥavurah*" (plural: "*ḥavurot*") means "fellowship." The early *ḥavurot* were independent, communal, loosely organized fellowship circles. Some met in members' homes; others purchased buildings for communal worship, study, and living. The original *ḥavurot* were the product of the 1960s. They were designed to provide intense, participatory, religious experiences for their members.

Today, there are *ḥavurot* and *minyanim* (another term used for a group of Jews who gather for periodic worship) in every major American metropolitan area. Although many have affiliated with the Federation of Reconstructionist Congregations and Havurot, some have remained independent.

There are also *ḥavurot* and *minyanim* within synagogues. As synagogues grow larger, community feeling may diminish. Members of large congregations are increasingly expressing the desire for small, intimate, fellowship circles within them. (In some metropolitan areas, congregations may number 1,500 or more households.) In response, many large congregations have spawned their own intra-congregational *ḥavurot* and *minyanim*.

CHAPTER 9

Holy Days and Festivals

O NE of the most noticeable features of Jewish holy days for
those accustomed to determining the date by looking at
an ordinary, secular (Gregorian) calendar is that they fall on different dates each year. The reason is that, unlike the Gregorian
calendar, which is based solely on the sun, the Jewish calendar is
based as well on the cycles of the moon.

The Jewish year consists of twelve months, each of which
begins on the day on which a new moon appears. It takes the
moon approximately twenty-nine and a half days to revolve
around the earth. Therefore, lunar months do not correspond
precisely to the months of the Gregorian calendar. In fact,
because a lunar year is only 354 days long, every few years
(seven times every nineteen years) a leap year is necessary: the
twelfth month of the year must be doubled in order to keep the
calendar roughly in alignment with the solar year.

Therefore, although Jewish holy days fall on different secular
dates each year, they fall in the same season and on the same Jew-

ish date each year. Moreover, the phase of the moon on which a holiday falls is identical from year to year. The recurring cycle of holidays gives the year spiritual meaning and ritual texture. Each holiday is known as a *yom tov* (plural: *yamin tovim*) in Hebrew, a *yontif* in Yiddish. You will often hear Jews whose families came from Europe saying, *"gut yontif!"* to each other on these days. The Hebrew *yom tov* is often translated as "holiday," but its meaning is really "holy day." (Literally it means a "good day.")

Aside from Shabbat, the most important days of the Jewish calendar are Rosh Hashanah and Yom Kippur, Sukkot, Pesaḥ, and Shavuot. The week-long holidays of Sukkot and Pesaḥ begin and end with *yamin tovim.*

Outside of the land of Israel, each *yom tov* (except for Yom Kippur) is observed for two days by all but some liberal (mainly Reform and Reconstructionist) congregations. The two-day observances date from the time before a fixed calendar was established. People living far from Jerusalem, where the first day of each new lunar month was declared, could never be certain about the exact date of a *yom tov* because communications were so poor. They observed the *yom tov* for two days to make sure they were observing one on the correct date. This practice became a fixed tradition outside the Land of Israel and it persisted even after the calendar became established in the fourth century. It continues today everywhere but in Israel. (The only exception is Rosh Hashanah, which is observed for two days even within Israel.)

Some liberal congregations believe that, given the establishment of the fixed calendar, there is no longer any practical need for the duplication of each *yom tov.* Others point to the rebirth of the Jewish State in the Land of Israel as a reason for diaspora communities to adopt its practice of observing only one day of *yom tov.* Nonetheless, the observance of the second day of *yom tov* has continued.

As on Shabbat, each *yom tov* begins at nightfall of the preceding evening (known as *erev*). This is marked with candle-lighting and appropriate *berakhot,* and is followed by *kiddush, motzi,* and a festive meal. (There are also evening services). The next day follows the pattern of Shabbat as well, with synagogue services and a festive meal. As on Shabbat, work is prohibited (see Chapter 6), but cooking is permitted, as is carrying to and from a public domain.

The High Holy Days

The religious cycle of the year begins with the month of *Elul,* which ushers in a season of spiritual preparation for the year. It is traditional to recite petitionary prayers known as *seliḥot* during this month; many congregations schedule midnight or early-morning *seliḥot* services shortly before Rosh Hashanah. Rosh Hashanah (literally, "head of the year") falls on the first and second days of *Tishri,* and Yom Kippur, the Day of Atonement, falls ten days thereafter. They are often called the *Yamim Noraim* (High Holy Days or the Days of Awe). Rosh Hashanah is also known as the Day of Judgment. These Holy Days and the days between them are known as the Ten Days of Repentance.

Rosh Hashanah and Yom Kippur are days set aside wholly for the spirit. They do not commemorate a specific historical event or any cyclical change in nature (though Rosh Hashanah is referred to as the "Birthday of the World" and is understood to be the date on which the world was created). They are devoted to critical self-examination, introspection, and spiritual evaluation. On these days Jews are called upon to ponder carefully their conduct of the past year, to acknowledge their faults and sins, to repent of them, to ask forgiveness of those whom they have offended, and to resolve not to repeat their sins.

Within Judaism, repentance is not simply a ritual act which wipes the slate clean. The Hebrew word for repentance *(teshuvah)* means "return." It implies returning to the point where one went astray and then proceeding on a new path which avoids the errors of the old. It connotes a return to God and to God's ways.

ROSH HASHANAH

The Rosh Hashanah liturgy focuses our attention on the need to live a moral life and helps us articulate ways to achieve this. Judaism teaches that all of us have the power to choose good and reject evil. Even though the liturgy declares that our destiny is determined by our previous conduct, it also states that it can always be altered by repentance, prayer, and moral living.

On Rosh Hashanah, the services are chanted with distinctive, majestic melodies. The services are longer than on all other holidays (except for Yom Kippur) and they often include many *piyyutim* (medieval hymns) devoted to the themes of the day.

One of the few ritual obligations of Rosh Hashanah is to listen to the sounding of *shofar*, the ram's horn. A ram's horn is mentioned in the Book of Genesis, in the narrative known as the Binding of Isaac (the *Akedah;* Genesis 22), which is the Torah reading for the second day of Rosh Hashanah. The patriarch Abraham, at God's command, bound his son Isaac upon an altar on a mountaintop, in preparation for offering him as a sacrifice. Abraham was stopped at the last moment by an angel of God and commanded to substitute a ram for Isaac. The ram's horn recalls this climactic moment.

The *shofar* was sounded in ancient times at the coronation of kings. The metaphor of God's kingship is prominent in the liturgy of Rosh Hashanah and Yom Kippur. On the High Holy Days we proclaim our faith that no human being or human institution is supreme, that God alone is our Sovereign.

The *shofar,* also sounded at Mount Sinai when the Ten Commandments were given, calls us to renew our dedication to the moral law. Tradition has it that the *shofar* will be sounded to announce the advent of the Messianic age.

In the words of Maimonides, the sounding of the *shofar* is also an insistent call to arouse us from moral lethargy:

> The *shofar* exclaims: Wake up from your slumber! Examine your deeds, turn in repentance, remember your Creator! You sleepers

who forget the truth while caught up in the fads and follies of the
time, frittering away your years in vanity and emptiness: take a
good look at yourselves! Improve your ways![1]

As is Shabbat, Rosh Hashanah is ushered in at home with the
recitation of *berakhot*. The candles are lit and a special *kiddush*,
enhanced by a distinctive melody and additions in honor of the
holy day, is chanted over wine. At the dinner table, after the
washing of the hands, *ha-motzi* is recited over ḥallah. At Rosh
Hashanah it is traditional to use a round rather than a braided
ḥallah, symbolizing the completion of one year and the beginning of another. It is customary for those at the table to dip
sliced apples in honey while wishing each other a sweet new year.

An interesting custom practiced on the afternoon of the
first day of Rosh Hashanah is called *tashlikh*. (If the first day is
on Shabbat, *tashlikh* takes place on the second day.) The word
tashlikh is found in a verse in the Book of Micah (7:19): "You
will cast *(tashlikh)* all our sins into the depths of the sea." We
symbolically cast our sins into a sea, river, stream, or any other
body of water. At the edge of the water, the verse from Micah
and other passages are recited, and crumbs are taken out of
pockets and cast into the water as a symbolic statement that we
can remove sin from our lives.

YOM KIPPUR

Yom Kippur is the most solemn day of the Jewish year. It is a
day of fasting, prayer and introspection. It is also called the
Day of Atonement, as on this day we seek purification, forgiveness, and reconciliation.

We often are more aware of physical desires than of spiritual
needs. Physical desires also seem to be more easily satisfied. Yom
Kippur emphasizes proper priorities. By not eating or drinking,
by not satisfying physical demands, we focus on the importance
of the spiritual dimension of our life.

---

[1] *Mishneh Torah, Hilkhot Teshuvah* 3:4.

In the late afternoon before Yom Kippur begins, people gather for a pre-fast meal. The evening service commences with the chanting of *Kol Nidrei,* which begins before sundown. *Kol Nidrei* is a moving liturgical highlight of the year, although it is not actually a prayer. It is a legal formula which emphasizes that all the words which we utter are serious commitments. The formula releases worshipers from promises made to God that they might not fulfill, removing the guilt of unfulfilled commitments. The formula cannot and does not absolve us of vows made to other human beings. The traditional chant and its associations are deeply moving. The slow, somber, thrice-repeated chant, recited as the sky is darkening, conveys the mood of Yom Kippur. Many people speak of Yom Kippur evening as *Kol Nidrei* Eve. The evening service is filled with many special hymns. Some of these poetically express the many ways in which human beings can fail in their pursuit of the moral life. Others emphasize God's forgiving nature.

The entire next day is spent in the synagogue. The prayerbook marks four distinct services, but the congregation often regards them as one day-long service. (In some congregations, there is a break between the morning and afternoon prayers.) The liturgy elaborates the themes that are of prime concern on Yom Kippur: sin, forgiveness, atonement. *Yizkor,* a memorial service for relatives and loved ones, is recited. Five times on Yom Kippur the congregation rises to ask forgiveness for a variety of sins, accepting the concept of corporate responsibility. The *ashamnu* confession, which is chanted in unison by the congregation, is not couched in the singular ("I have sinned") but in the plural ("*We* have sinned"). Together we recognize the evil of immoral acts, together we seek to atone for them.

The Book of Jonah is chanted as the *haftarah* during the afternoon Torah service. It emphasizes God's compassion for all creatures, and the ever-present possibility of, and desirability to engage in, *teshuvah.*

The awesome day comes to a close as the sun sets. The final service of *Neilah* (literally, "closing") is followed by a final sounding of the *shofar.* A weekday *Ma'ariv* service and a *hav-*

dalah ceremony conclude the long day. After services, family and friends gather to break the fast together.

The Pilgrimage Festivals

In ancient times, it was customary for Jews to go up to Jerusalem with offerings three times during the year: on Pesaḥ (Passover), Shavuot, and Sukkot. These holidays are associated with different phases of the agricultural cycle of the year. Over time, they also became associated with different events in the history of the Jewish people. Since the year 70 C.E. there has been no Temple in Jerusalem, but the term "Pilgrimage Festivals" has been retained for these three festivals.

SUKKOT

Five days after the intensely spiritual, introspective and triumphant close of Yom Kippur, Sukkot begins. It is the great festival of thanksgiving. Originally a harvest festival, it came to be seen as a reminder of the period during which the Children of Israel wandered in the wilderness.

The most elaborate and complex act associated with the holiday is completed before the holday even begins: the construction of a *sukkah,* a temporary, makeshift shelter, in which Jews eat, drink, and socialize during the festival.

Many begin building their *sukkah* right after the close of Yom Kippur services. Sukkot lasts eight days. Holy days *(yamim tovim),* with special synagogue services, begin and end the festival. On the other days, known as "intermediate days" *(ḥol ha-mo'ed),* there are special additions to the weekday service but most normal work patterns are permitted.

Many Sukkot observances remind us that we have much for which to be thankful. A major focus of observance is the *sukkah,* built next to the home and the synagogue, and which ranges from the simple to the elaborate. The *sukkah* has walls but no solid roof. Green boughs attached to the rafters serve as the roof, through which the stars should be visible. People hang fruits and vegetables from the top and on the walls of the *sukkah* to symbolize the bounty of the harvest and to remind us of our gratitude to God for creation and sustenance. Some families eat all their meals in the *sukkah*. It is considered praiseworthy to spend as much time as possible in the *sukkah;* some even sleep there. People without their own *sukkah* go to a neighbor's or to the synagogue's for *kiddush* in order to fulfill the commandment to say the special *berakhot* and to eat some food in the *sukkah*.

The *sukkah* recalls the temporary shelters in which the Israelites lived on their wilderness journey from the slavery of Egypt toward the freedom of the Promised Land. It also evokes the insecurity of the Jews throughout history, and of life itself, and symbolizes God's sheltering presence.

Another prominent ritual of Sukkot is the waving of the *lulav* (a cluster of palm, myrtle and willow branches) and *etrog* (a citron). On every day of Sukkot except for Shabbat, people lift the *lulav* and *etrog* and recite blessings over them. This is generally done at home and also in synagogue during the morning service. The date palm, from which the long stem of the *lulav* is taken, is a majestic tree found throughout the Middle East. The citron is a lemon-like fruit with a lovely aroma. The fruit and the branches represent the bounty of the earth.

As one would expect, the liturgy reflects the emphasis on thanksgiving. On Sukkot, as on every festival, psalms known liturgically as *Hallel* are added to the service. *The lulav* and *etrog* (plural: *lulavim* and *etrogim*) are held while *Hallel* is chanted. Special Sukkot prayers called *hoshanot* are recited as worshipers march around the synagogue in a procession while holding their *lulavim* and *etrogim*. Five people are called up to the Torah. It is customary to read the Book of Ecclesiastes *(Kohelet)* during this holiday.

The eighth day of Sukkot is distinct. It is called Shemini Atzeret (the Eighth Day of Assembly). People stop using their *lulavim* and *etrogim,* and no longer eat in the *sukkah*. The memorial service known as *Yizkor,* also said on the last days of Pesaḥ and Shavuot as well as on Yom Kippur, is recited.

For the past thousand years, Jews have celebrated another *yom tov* at the end of the week of Sukkot. Simḥat Torah (Rejoicing over the Torah) is the day on which the reading of the Torah is completed and its rereading is begun. The synagogue reverberates with exuberance. During both the evening and morning services all the Torah scrolls owned by the synagogue are carried in a festive procession throughout the sanctuary. People sing and dance in the aisles. Everyone is given the opportunity to carry a Torah scroll. Children follow in the parade with flags that are sometimes topped with apples.

At the morning service everyone, including each child, receives the honor of being called to the Torah. The two greatest honors are reserved for the individuals who are called before the last verses of Deuteronomy and before the first verses of Genesis are read.

Those congregations which no longer observe the second day of *yom tov* follow the Israeli practice of combining Shemini Atzeret and Simḥat Torah on one day.

PESAḤ (PASSOVER)

As Sukkot celebrates the Fall harvest, Pesaḥ celebrates Spring. As Sukkot recalls the journey through the desert, Pesaḥ recalls the redemption from Egypt. Pesaḥ is the great Festival of Freedom. It obliges each of us to consider himself or herself as personally having been redeemed from bondage. In commemorating the Exodus of the Israelites from slavery, Pesaḥ teaches that the God of Israel desires all people to be free. Because the Exodus marked the transition of the Jews from a family of tribes to a people, Pesaḥ celebrates the birth of a nation.

The festival is marked by a strict prohibition (found in the Torah) against eating leavened bread or any foods with ingredients that might contain leavening. Pesaḥ preparations begin with a thorough housecleaning to rid the home of any trace of leavening *(ḥametz)*. Matzah, unleavened bread, is also known as the bread of affliction. It should remind us of our ancestors' hardships in Egyptian slavery, as well as the haste of their departure.

Before Pesaḥ, Jews clean out closets, reline shelves, and store the cookware and dishes they use during the rest of the year. Then they bring out the special Pesaḥ dishes, silverware, and pots and pans. Metal and glass dishes used throughout the year can be kashered for Pesaḥ. For many people, these preparations heighten the anticipation of the *yom tov.*

Any foods considered *ḥametz* are sealed away in a closet. Many follow the custom of giving unopened boxes and cans of food to the non-Jewish poor. Ashkenazic Jews refrain from eating rice and legumes on Pesaḥ, though Sephardic Jews do not have this custom. Packaged goods must be certified as permissible for consumption on Pesaḥ.

The most important feature of Pesaḥ is the home service known as the *seder. Seder* means "order," and although the *seder* includes a festive dinner, it is much more than a banquet. The family and invited guests seated at the table participate in a religious service, using a special text called the *haggadah,* of which there are countless editions. Some editions of the *haggadah* include supplementary texts which highlight the significance of Pesaḥ for the contemporary Jew. There is a prescribed order for all of the text and rituals, which precede and follow the meal.

A basic function of the *seder* is to transmit the meaning of the Exodus and the theme of freedom to the next generation. Children are encouraged to participate actively in the *seder.* Usually one person leads the others in reading and chanting the *haggadah,* which includes a running narration whose focus is the story of the Exodus, with commentaries, prayers, and folk songs. Everyone is free to raise questions and to participate in suggesting answers, to explore the meaning of freedom in their own lives and in the lives of others.

In the synagogue service, the Torah readings and *haftarah* readings are related to the holiday, as they are during each festival. There are liturgical insertions which acknowledge and celebrate the festival. Psalms of praise *(Hallel)* are sung. It is also customary to read the Song of Songs during this holiday.

SHAVUOT

Shavuot, meaning "weeks," follows Pesaḥ by seven weeks. Shavuot celebrates the giving of the Torah on Mount Sinai. According to tradition, this took place seven weeks after the Exodus from Egypt. During the days between Pesaḥ and Shavuot, it is traditional to count each one of the forty-nine days. (This is called "the counting of the *omer*.") This links freedom from bondage (Pesaḥ) with the commitment to observe the Torah (Shavuot).

For obscure reasons, the days between Pesaḥ and Shavuot evolved into a period of semi-mourning. With the exception of Lag B'Omer (the thirty-third day of the *omer*), observant Jews refrain from celebrations during this period.

As with the other festivals, Shavuot begins with the lighting of candles and the recitation of *kiddush*. Paralleling the distinction of eating in the *sukkah* for the first time on the eve of Sukkot and celebrating a *seder* on the eve of Pesaḥ, Shavuot also has a special observance. In recent years, an increasing number of liberal Jews have been reclaiming the tradition of studying biblical and rabbinic texts throughout the first night of Shavuot, as a way of celebrating the Revelation of the Torah commemorated by the Festival. This special period of study is known as a *tikkun,* or *tikkun leil* Shavuot. The *tikkun* concludes at dawn with the recitation of the morning prayers.

Shavuot is also associated with the late spring harvest. In ancient times Israelites brought an offering of the first fruits from their harvest to the Temple in Jerusalem. During the centuries of exile from the Land of Israel, when Jews were rarely allowed to own land or to practice agriculture, this aspect of Shavuot remained only a memory. With the rise of Labor Zionism and its enthusiasm for Jews to return to the soil, however (see Chapter 14), Jews renewed their connection with the soil and agriculture and revived the ceremony of first fruits. Many *kibbutzim* (Jewish collective farms established by the Zionist movement), even the non-observant ones, came to commemorate Shavuot as an agricultural festival.

Unlike Pesaḥ, Shavuot has no specific home ritual associated with it, although it is customary to eat dairy foods on *Shavuot.* (The origin of this custom is unknown.) Synagogue services are similar to those of the other two festivals.

The biblical book associated with Shavuot is the Book of Ruth. Ruth, born a Moabite, chose to become part of the Jewish people and to accept their way of life as her own, just as the Jews had accepted the Torah at Mount Sinai. In stirring words, Ruth declared to her mother-in-law, Naomi:

> Entreat me not to leave you, to turn away from joining you. For wherever you go will I go, and wherever you lodge will I lodge. Your people will be my people and your God my God. Where you die will I die and there will I be buried. I vow before God that nothing but death could part me from you.
>
> (1:16–17)

Because Ruth is such a powerful role model for those choosing to become Jews, Shavuot is often an occasion chosen by new converts to Judaism to participate publicly in services.

Other Special Days

ḤANUKKAH

The holiday of Ḥanukkah follows Sukkot by eight and a half weeks, usually in the month of December. In the middle of the second pre-Christian century, the Greek ruler of Judea (King Antiochus of Syria) sought to impose the Greek religion and the Greek way of life upon the Jews. His troops converted the Temple in Jerusalem into a Temple of Zeus.

In 167 B.C.E., a small group of Jews rose in revolt. They were led by members of the Hasmonean family, whose distinguished leader was Judah the Maccabee. After three years of guerrilla warfare they overcame the more numerous and powerful foe. In 164 B.C.E., they recaptured Jerusalem, cleansed the Temple, relit the *menorah* (candelabrum) with ritually pure oil, and rededicated the Temple. The Hebrew word for dedication is *ḥanukkah*. The Maccabean revolt was understood by some to be a battle for religious freedom and their victory is celebrated as a triumph of the spirit. It should be noted though, that Ḥanukkah also celebrates the victory of traditional Jews within the Jewish community, over others, the so-called Hellenists, who had adopted Greek attitudes and customs, and sought to assimilate within the greater Greek world.

Ḥanukkah is celebrated much more at home than in the synagogue. Each evening, we light candles which are placed in a Ḥanukkah *menorah* (also called a *ḥanukkiah*). On the first night, one candle is lit with the help of a "servant" candle, called a *"shamash"* and appropriate *berakhot* are recited. One candle is added each night, leading to a total of eight candles on the eighth night. Songs, games, and the exchange of gifts may follow the candlelighting. Some people emphasize the gift giving, while other families de-emphasize the gifts. Ḥanukkah is a wonderful occasion for parties. Potato pancakes, or latkes, are featured on the menu, as are jelly doughnuts known as *"sufganiyot,"* popular in Israel. A favorite game involves spinning a special top called a *dreidl*. Traditionally, the *menorah* is placed in a window, so that the light of the candles will publicly proclaim the celebration of the miracle.

TU B'SHVAT

About a month and a half after Ḥanukkah, we observe Tu B'shvat ("the fifteenth day in the month of *Shvat*"). This is Jewish Arbor Day, the time when spring begins in the Land of Israel with the first blossoming of trees. Tu B'shvat is known as the New Year for trees.

Because of their intense connection with Zion, Jews have marked this day wherever they have lived by eating fruits associated with Israel (citrus fruits, almonds or other nuts, figs, and carob.) Kabbalists developed a ritual for the day (a Tu B'shvat *seder*). With the birth of Zionism and the remarkable reforestation of the denuded Land of Israel, Tu B'shvat has also become a day for encouraging the planting of trees in Israel. People can purchase trees to honor someone through the Jewish National Fund. They make a special effort to do so on Tu B'shvat.

PURIM

Purim falls in the middle of the month of *Adar,* just before Spring. Like Ḥanukkah, it celebrates a victory over a powerful ruler who sought to destroy Jews and their way of life. The biblical Book of Esther records the story of an arch anti-Semite, Haman, prime minister of the Persian Empire, who planned to kill all the Jews in the empire. Resourceful Queen Esther and her wise cousin Mordecai outwitted Haman. The king ordered that the Jews be protected and that Haman be hanged on the very day he had designated for their massacre.

Having experienced many Hamans throughout history, Jews have always taken courage from this story. Though anti-Semites have caused unimaginable pain, they have never succeeded in accomplishing their goal. Each of them has disappeared while the Jewish people continues to live.

Purim is among the happiest of Jewish holidays. The synagogue celebration features a festive reading of the Book of Esther from a special scroll, called a *megillah.* Whenever the reader of the *megillah* pronounces the name of Haman, everyone responds with his or her favorite noisemaker *(grogger)* to drown out the name of one who sought to destroy us.

Purim is celebrated at home and in the community. Children and adults make fanciful costumes to wear at Purim parties as well as at the synagogue service. In Israel, gala parades with floats fill the streets. The menu for Purim features three-cornered pastries filled with sweetened poppy seeds or with fruit. These pastries are known as hamentaschen (Haman's hats). (In Hebrew, they are called *"oznei haman,"* meaning, "Haman's ears.") It is traditional to deliver small packages of sweets, baked goods, and fruit *(mishloaḥ manot)* to friends and neighbors. Purim is also a traditional time for collecting and distributing charity. The gifts we give to the poor on Purim are called *matanot la-evyonim* after a phrase in the *megillah* (Esther 9:22).

YOM HA-SHOAH (HOLOCAUST REMEMBRANCE DAY)

This day (which falls less than a week after Passover) is set aside for remembering those whose lives were destroyed by Hitler and his followers. The anniversary of the final destruction of the Warsaw Ghetto in 1943, five days after Passover (the twenty-seventh of *Nisan*), has been chosen as the day when Jews the world over mourn and remember. Communal observances at synagogues or at Holocaust memorials usually take place on or around this day.

YOM HA-ZIKARON (ISRAEL MEMORIAL DAY)
YOM HA-ATZMAUT (ISRAEL INDEPENDENCE DAY)
YOM YERUSHALAYIM (JERUSALEM DAY)

Since 1948, two new special days, Yom ha-Zikaron (Israel Memorial Day) and Yom ha-Atzmaut (Israel Independence Day) fall in the week after Yom ha-Shoah. For centuries Jews prayed daily for the restoration of Zion, when they would again be a free people in their own land. Whatever the establishment of Israel may have meant as a haven of refuge, whatever its political significance may have been, it was also a triumph of a religious faith maintained throughout more than 1,900 years of suffering and persecution. Therefore, whatever their citizenship and their political loyalties, many Jews regard Israel's birth as a great religious miracle.

Yom ha-Atzmaut is marked in many synagogues by the recitation of *Hallel,* the psalms of praise which are recited on *yom tov.* The Conservative movement has introduced an appropriate liturgical passage in the *Amidah* and in the *birkat ha-mazon* (Grace after Meals). In Israel, the religious *kibbutz* movement has added a similar prayer. A Torah reading and a *haftarah* have also been designated for Yom ha-Atzmaut. Many Jewish communities hold communal celebrations on or around Israel Independence Day.

As the number of Israelis living in North America continues to increase, some local Jewish communities have also begun to observe Yom ha-Zikaron, Israel Memorial Day, which occurs on the day immediately prior to Yom ha-Atzmaut. On this day, those who gave their lives in defense of the Jewish state, whether in the course of military service or as a result of acts of terror, are honored. Memorial services, featuring the lighting of candles and special readings and prayers, are held in most major American cities.

Since the Six Day War of 1967, yet another holiday has been added to the calendar: Yom Yerushalayim (Jerusalem Day). Yom Yerushalayim, which falls on the 28th day of *Iyar*, celebrates the unification of Jerusalem which took place in June 1967, when Israeli forces liberated the city and, for the first time since 1948, Jews were permitted to worship at the Jewish holy sites in the Old City. Some Jews recite *Hallel* and other special prayers on Yom Yerushalayim.

TISHA B'AV

Tisha B'Av is the ninth day in the Hebrew month of *Av*, occurring in the middle of the summer. Many calamities are said to have befallen the Jewish people on this date throughout history. It is the anniversary of the destruction of both Temples in ancient Jerusalem (in 586 B.C.E. and 70 C.E.), and on this date we note as well the destruction of other Jewish communities, and the expulsion of the Jews from Spain (in 1492). This sad anniversary is marked by a fast. Jews gather in the synagogue to listen to the reading of the Book of Lamentations *(Eikhah)* and to chant sorrow-filled liturgical poems *(kinot)*.

CHAPTER 10

The Jewish Life Cycle

L IFE cycle events, such as a birth, a wedding, or a death can be powerful moments for experiencing religious insights. Such events transcend the individual or the family; they are part of life itself. If noted and elevated, they can inspire awe and raise religious consciousness. For this reason, Jewish rituals have evolved to mark significant life events. Such ceremonies can help us to become aware of the holiness of these occasions.

Not all life cycle events have traditional rituals associated with them. For this reason, many new rituals are being created today.

Birth

The most basic ceremony for infant Jewish males has become such a common contemporary practice that many may have forgotten its religious purpose. The circumcision ceremony is known in Hebrew as a *brit*, which means covenant. Technically, it is called *brit milah,* "covenant of circumcision." Many people know it as a *bris.* Through this ritual act each infant boy becomes linked to the covenant between God and the Jewish people.

As a religious ceremony, the *brit* must be carried out by a Jew trained in religious law, who performs the act as the conscious fulfillment of a religious commandment *(mitzvah).* This person, called a *mohel* (feminine: "*mohelet*"), is often certified by medical authorities as well. In some communities, Jewish physicians serve as *mohalim.*

Circumcision must take place on the eighth day after birth. We read in the Book of Genesis that Isaac was circumcised on the eighth day. So must it be with all the children of Abraham. In the event of illness or other disability, the child is circumcised when the physician declares him to be physically ready. If the baby is born without a foreskin or for some reason has been circumcised prior to the eighth day, the ritual of circumcision is completed by drawing a drop of blood from the corona of skin that surrounds the head (or glans) of the penis. This ceremony (called *hatafat dam brit*) is also required for an adult male convert who was circumcised prior to his conversion.

At the *brit milah* ceremony, certain individuals are honored. (Although the English term "godparents" is sometimes used for these people, they are not godparents in the Christian sense of the term.) The *kvaterin* brings the infant forward and hands him to the *kvater.* The *kvater* places the infant on the knees of the *sandek* who is already seated. The *sandek* holds the infant while the *mohel* performs the circumcision.

As the circumcision is performed, the *mohel* recites a *berakhah* declaring that his act is in fulfillment of a *mitzvah.* The parents then recite a *berakhah* acknowledging that their child has thereby entered into the covenant between God and the Jewish People. The child's Hebrew name is then formally bestowed.

There are no laws regarding names. Parents often spend many hours in choosing a name for their child. The general practice among Ashkenazi families (Jews of Central or Eastern

European background) is to give the child Hebrew and English names that bear some relationship to the name of a deceased relative whom members of the family wish to remember. Sephardim (Jews who trace their ancestry to Spain, Portugal or North Africa) may name children for living relatives. Sometimes, the Hebrew name declared at the ceremony is identical to that of the relative; sometimes it is related by sound or meaning. Sometimes the child's Hebrew name is simply the Hebrew form of his English name (for example, *Yosef* for Joseph; or *Shmuel* for Samuel); at other times parents choose a Hebrew name with the same first initial as the English name. Many people choose their children's Hebrew names from the Bible or from rabbinic literature or from the growing collection of modern Israeli names.

The birth of a daughter is marked in another fashion. Traditionally, there was no ceremony for a girl parallel to a *brit*. Girls were named soon after birth in the synagogue at a service at which the Torah was read. Neither the child nor her mother needed to be present at the naming ceremony in the synagogue. The father would be honored by being called to the Torah, a prayer would be recited conveying the child's Hebrew name and wishing her a long and healthy life of fulfillment, and all present would wish the father and his family *mazal tov*. This modest ceremony for girls is still practiced in many communities today.

Some Jews today, not satisfied with this practice, have been developing additional ceremonies to celebrate the birth of a daughter. These ceremonies go by several names, one of which is *"simḥat bat"* ("a celebration of [the birth of] a daughter"). Usually, the *simḥah* (celebration) is held at a convenient time (not necessarily on the eighth day after birth) when both parents and other relatives can be present. Often, the baby formally receives her Hebrew name and parents and other relatives participate by reading selections from the liturgy or sharing reflections. Sometimes, families arrange for their child to be named in synagogue as well, so that she can be welcomed by the entire community.

Another ritual takes place when a woman's firstborn child is a boy. The ceremony is called *pidyon haben* (literally, "redemption of the [firstborn] son"). The practice goes back to ancient Temple times. The Torah states that all firstborn males are to be consecrated to the service of God. Later, when the Priests *(kohanim)* and Levites *(levi'im)* became responsible for Temple worship, the practice arose to formally "redeem" one's firstborn son from these duties by handing over five shekels of silver to a *kohen*. (The money is customarily given to *tzedakah*.) Through this ritual, parents express their gratitude at the birth of their firstborn son and recall the the ancient communal obligations of the firstborn.

Since the Priests and Levites were part of the Temple establishment, their children did not need to be "redeemed." Therefore, no *pidyon haben* is held for the firstborn of a *kohen* or *levi*.

Bar Mitzvah and Bat Mitzvah

The new teenager, not quite an adult yet no longer a child, is maturing intellectually as well as physically. The terms *bar mitzvah* and *bat mitzvah* refer to the boy and girl who are obligated to fulfill religious duties *(mitzvot)* once they have attained their religious majority. Boys at age 13 and girls at age 12 are considered old enough to assume these responsibilities. Among the privileges of a *bar* or *bat mitzvah* in egalitarian congregations is to be included as one of the adults who constitute a *minyan* (a quorum of ten which is necessary in order to hold a public worship service). It is marked at a worship service generally close to the celebrant's thirteenth birthday. (Some communities celebrate a girl's coming-of-age following her twelfth birthday).

Attaining the status of *bar mitzvah* or *bat mitzvah* is an important milestone in a person's life. One is officially recognized as *bar* or *bat mitzvah* by being called to the Torah for an *aliyah*. The ceremony usually takes place on Shabbat mornings, but it may be held at any service when the Torah is read. In most congregations, when the celebration takes place on Shabbat or a festival, the *bar* or *bat mitzvah* is honored by being called to recite the blessings for the *maftir* portion, and then to chant the *haftarah*. They thus show that they are able to participate in services as full members of the congregation. Sometimes they also lead in chanting parts of the prayer service, or read part or all of the Torah portion.

There are Orthodox congregations which strive to mark a girl's coming-of-age despite the fact that in these communities women do not participate in leading public worship in the presence of men and do not receive *aliyot*. In such congregations, the *bat mitzvah* ceremony usually takes place after services or at a worship service attended only by women. Sometimes the young woman chants or reads passages from books of the Bible other than the Torah. She may also present a brief lesson which she has prepared.

It must be remembered that a *bar* or *bat mitzvah* celebration is not a private birthday party but a ceremony signifying one's willingness and ability to become a responsible member of the Jewish community. Many adults who never formally became a *bat* or *bar mitzvah* find it very meaningful to have an official ceremony after they have pursued a course of study and learned to read the Torah or to chant the *haftarah*. Such a ceremony is sometimes referred to as an "adult" *bar* or *bat mitzvah*.

Marriage

The Hebrew word for marriage is *kiddushin,* which means sanctification. That word reflects the Jewish view of marriage. During the wedding ceremony, God is praised for enabling a man and a woman to find fulfillment through marriage. As the Book of Genesis declares, "It is not good for a human being to dwell alone" (Genesis 2:8).

The wedding ceremony is held under a canopy called a *ḥuppah,* which symbolizes the couple's new home. According to Jewish law, two witnesses who are not relatives of the bride or groom must formally witness the ceremony and sign the marriage contract *(ketubah)*.

The ceremony consists of two parts. The first is called *erusin* (betrothal). In ancient times, a man and a woman were legally bound to one another at betrothal. After that ceremony, they returned to their parental homes to prepare for the wedding, which could take place several months later. In later years, however, the betrothal and the wedding ceremonies were combined into one ceremony under the *ḥuppah*. The *erusin* blessing praises God for the institution of marriage.

The groom places a ring on the bride's right forefinger (the most prominent finger, on which brides wore their wedding ring in ancient times). As he does so, he says in Hebrew (and sometimes in English as well): "Behold you are consecrated to me with this ring according to the law of Moses and the people Israel." Many contemporary brides place a ring on the groom's finger and recite another passage, chosen in consultation with the rabbi, to reflect a similar sense of consecration.

The ring ceremony is followed by the reading of the marriage contract *(ketubah)*. Traditionally, the *ketubah* states the basic obligations undertaken by the husband for his wife. Today many couples request that the *ketubah* be accompanied by statements describing mutual obligations and responsibilities. The rabbi may read all or part of the *ketubah* aloud.

The service continues with blessings called *birkhot nesuin* (the last word means "wedding"). Seven celebratory blessings *(sheva berakhot)* are chanted, praising God for creating human beings with the capacity to experience happiness with one another. The sixth blessing captures this spirit: "Grant perfect joy to these loving companions, as You did to the first man and woman in the Garden of Eden. Praised are You, Adonai, who grants the joy of bride and groom."

At the conclusion of the service the groom steps on a glass and breaks it. Even at the moment of their greatest joy, the newly married couple thus remember that they are part of the

Jewish people, not isolated individuals. The breaking of the glass recalls the destruction of the ancient Temple in Jerusalem.

It is customary for a rabbi to speak to the bride and groom at some point during this ceremony. There is no uniform practice in this matter.

Divorce

For those marriages that are not successful, divorce is accepted in Judaism. The Talmud, in fact, concludes that specific grounds, such as adultery or abuse, need not be alleged; incompatibility is sufficient. Couples who are mismatched need not remain bound to each other, although rabbis encourage them to seek counseling with the goal of working out their problems together. Divorce may be the only solution for frustrated lives and an unhappy home.

When a husband and wife reach a parting of the ways, Jewish law requires that they seek a religious divorce (in addition to any civil decree that may be required by the law of the land). Just as the marriage begins with a religious document, so must it end.

The early Rabbis found the precedent for divorce in Deuteronomy (24:1): "He writes her a bill of divorcement, hands it to her, and sends her away from his house." They decided, based on this verse, that Jewish religious procedure should require the husband to initiate the divorce proceedings. The rabbi, two witnesses, and the husband (or his agent) must be present as the divorce document—called a *get*—is begun and completed. The *get* must be written by a scribe for the specific man and woman involved; it cannot be a printed form with blanks for names to be inserted. After the document is signed and witnessed, it must be put into the hands of the wife or her agent.

The Reform movement has waived the requirement for a *get* and accepts a civil divorce as sufficient. The Orthodox and Conservative movements follow the traditional ruling that a husband and wife remain legally bound to one another unless they have a Jewish divorce. They cannot remarry in the Jewish tradition without having obtained a *get*.

In the days when Jews lived in self-contained communities, a clearly unfit husband could be forced to give his wife a *get*. Social pressure was strong enough to ensure compliance with a rabbinic decision. In an open society, however, it is difficult to force a recalcitrant husband to comply. In some instances, men have used the Jewish divorce as a means of extortion, refusing to give the *get* until a substantial sum has been paid. The Orthodox rabbinate has been looking for a way in Jewish law to overcome this problem. Some rabbis insist that couples execute a pre-nuptial agreement which obligates the husband, in the event of divorce, to give a *get* to his wife. The Conservative rabbinate has addressed the problem by inserting in the *ketubah* a passage stating that in the event of marital difficulties, the couple agrees to abide by the decision of a court convened by the Rabbinical Assembly and the Jewish Theological Seminary. As this is signed and witnessed, it is a legal document which could be enforced in a civil court. There are those who plead with the contemporary rabbinate to give a woman the right to divorce her husband just as the tradition gives a man the right to divorce his wife. However, those responsible for interpreting Jewish law have thus far not found a way to do so.

Death and Mourning

Jewish tradition helps mourners to confront death with a sense of reality and dignity. The sages who drew up the laws of mourning recognized that mourners need a time when they can grieve unrestrainedly. Before the burial, mourners need time to be alone with their grief, as well as to focus on making arrangements for the funeral and burial. Jewish tradition does not provide for or encourage anything similar to a wake. It is not considered helpful or proper for mourners to be at a funeral home or anywhere else the evening before a burial for the purpose of receiving visitors. Visits to comfort mourners should be made only after the funeral, when such visits are the fulfillment of a religious obligation.

The funeral is held as soon as possible after death, generally within twenty-four hours, unless a delay is necessary to give relatives time to travel great distances. Funerals do not take place on Shabbat or festivals.

The body is never left alone. It is ritually washed (in a procedure called *taharah*) and guarded *(shmirah)* before the funeral. Sometimes the washing and guarding are arranged for by the funeral home, sometimes by members of a congregational or community burial society *(ḥevrah kadisha)* who regard caring for the dead as an extremely important *mitzvah*. The body is dressed in a white linen shroud and placed in a plain wooden coffin. Rituals involving the funeral and burial are similar for all Jews regardless of social or economic status.

It is traditional at Jewish funerals not to adorn the coffin with flowers. It is appropriate to honor the dead by contributing to a cause which was meaningful to him or her and which will help the living.

Jewish law forbids cremation. The Rabbis who formulated the law took the verse, "for you are dust and unto dust shall you return" (Genesis 3:19) literally as a natural process. Jews have long regarded cremation as an abhorrent practice; this rejection of cremation has only become more pronounced in the post-Holocaust era.

Funerals in the past were generally conducted at the cemetery. In North America today, most funerals take place in funeral parlors. Funerals for rabbis, scholars, or other prominent members of the congregation may be held in a synagogue.

There is no fixed procedure for the funeral service. The rabbi, or other leader, recites various psalms and other appropriate passages from biblical and rabbinic sources. In the past, eulogies were delivered only for the learned; today they are a part of most funerals. The funeral concludes with a prayer *(El malei*

raḥamim) that the departed be granted complete peace in God's sheltering Presence, that the soul of the departed be bound up in the bond of life, and that the departed rest in peace.

According to Jewish law, one is obliged to mourn for a father, mother, son, daughter, brother, sister, husband, or wife. At the funeral, mourners tear their garments as a sign of sorrow. This is called *keriah* (tearing). As this may ruin expensive garments, some people first remove the stitches in a seam. Others pin a black ribbon to their clothing, after which the ribbon is cut to symbolize their grief.

At the cemetery, psalms and other passages as well as a prayer may be read at graveside. Interment follows. In the Jewish tradition it is considered a great *mitzvah,* a *mitzvah* of *ḥesed shel emet* ("true lovingkindness") to participate in the act of burial. The rabbis explain that when this *mitzvah* is performed, it is for its own sake, for one cannot reasonably expect a reward. Relatives and friends are therefore encouraged to participate in placing dirt into the grave to commence, if not to conclude, the act of burial. It is appropriate that they, rather than strangers, initiate this final step on behalf of their loved one. This may be acutely painful, but many find it enormously meaningful. Before leaving the cemetery, the mourners recite the Mourner's *Kaddish* (the special form known as the Burial *Kaddish*) for the first time.

The mourners return home to begin observing a seven-day period of mourning known as *shivah* (which means seven). They do not leave the house during this week, except to attend synagogue services on Shabbat, when public mourning is suspended. In many homes, all mirrors are covered during the *shivah* period. Although probably rooted in superstition, this practice today is a statement that vanity is not appropriate at a time of such grief. Mourners sit on low stools rather than on regular chairs. They do not wear leather shoes—another sign of mourning—or shave.

In the Jewish tradition the *mitzvah* of *niḥum aveilim* ("comforting the mourners") is highly esteemed. It is traditional for friends to prepare the first meal after the funeral and to bring

food for the mourners and their visitors during the rest of the week when members of the community and other friends come to express their sympathy. Visitors come to the home when morning, afternoon, and evening services are held, to constitute a *minyan,* enabling the mourners to recite the Mourner's *Kaddish* in the home. Out of respect for the feelings of the mourners, it is customary not to initiate conversations with them but rather to wait until the mourners feel like talking. It is appropriate, in conversation with the mourners, to recall the life of the person who died.

Shivah homes do not always reflect the tone described here. Many Jews are unfamiliar with traditional Jewish practices and are uncertain what to do in a house of mourning. Sometimes, the confusion and the natural discomfort surrounding death can cause a paradoxical reaction: the *shivah* home may begin to sound like a party is taking place, and people may find themselves talking about anything but the loss which turned the home into a house of mourning. In the past several years, more and more Jewish communities have striven to increase understanding of traditional Jewish practices, and this problem is diminishing.

After *shivah,* mourners enter a stage of transition from deep bereavement to resuming their normal routine. This is called *shloshim* (meaning thirty) and consists of the days until the thirtieth day after the funeral. During *shloshim* people may go back to work, but they do not attend parties, plays, movies, or concerts and generally do not participate in joyous occasions, although they may fulfill the *mitzvah* of attending certain religious ceremonies, such as a wedding ceremony.

Following the loss of a parent, mourning continues for a full year. Generally, the prohibitions of *shloshim* are extended for the entire year. Mourner's *Kaddish* is recited every morning and evening for eleven months. On the anniversary (the *yahrzeit*) of the death, mourners light a memorial candle in the person's

memory, contribute to *tzedakah,* and attend services to recite *Kaddish* in the presence of a *minyan.*

In subsequent years, mourners continue to recite *Kaddish* every year on the *yahrzeit* and at *yizkor* (memorial) services on Yom Kippur and on the three Pilgrimage Festivals (Pesah, Shavuot, and Sukkot).

What happens after death is a mystery that human beings can never fathom. There is no single definitive Jewish teaching about life after death. Jews have always held a variety of views. Many have believed that the dead will be resurrected, but there always have been those who do not take this teaching literally. (For some additional thoughts on this subject, consult Chapter 5, under "Teachings on the Afterlife.")

"Is death nothing but an obliteration, an absolute negation?" The question was posed by Rabbi Abraham Joshua Heschel, who then stated that our view of death:

> . . . is affected by our understanding of life. If life is sensed as a surprise, as a gift, defying explanation, then death ceases to be a radical, absolute negation of what life stands for. For both life and death are aspects of a greater mystery, the mystery of being, the mystery of creation. . . [1]

[1] Abraham Joshua Heschel, "Death as Homecoming" in *Moral Grandeur and Spiritual Audacity,* ed. Susannah Heschel (New York: Farrar Straus & Giroux, 1996), p. 366.

CHAPTER 11

History: Ancient and Medieval

THE Jews are an ancient people with a keen sense of history. History is not only a matter of the past for Jews. A striking imperative in Jewish tradition is *zakhor*—"Remember!" The obligation to remember the past, to understand it, and to learn from it is central to Judaism. Hence, the past (or, more accurately, a collective memory of the past) continues to function in every generation. Heroes and events of the past become almost contemporary; spiritual and moral insights from ancient times continue to guide the conduct and inform the decisions of subsequent generations. Jews of any one period do not, of course, think and live precisely as their ancestors did, but through the teaching of the Jewish people's collective memory from generation to generation, their thoughts and lives become very much rooted in those of the Jews who preceded them.

Since Jewish thought, practice, and faith regard past and present as parts of a continuous whole, it is imperative to gain familiarity with the history of the Jews and the history of Judaism. That is the purpose of this brief outline.

The Biblical Narrative

The pre-history and the early history of the Jewish people is embedded in the Torah and other books of the Hebrew Bible. These are literary works with theological premises. They are therefore much more reliable when we seek to learn from them Jewish beliefs and values than when we seek a chronological account of the history of the Jews. Verifiable information is less prominent than reflections on fundamental religious questions.

But the Bible is crucial for learning about Judaism. It is the Jewish people's story of its origins, organizing legend, law, and history into a coherent text. And in fact, archaeologists have confirmed the antiquity and general outlines of many of its narratives.

Significantly, the Torah begins not with an account of the origins of the Jewish people but with the creation of the universe. This reflects the long-held Jewish belief that God is not the exclusive sovereign of the Jews but rather Master of the entire world and Lord of all. As opposed to other, contemporaneous accounts of the creation of the world, Genesis asserts that the universe is not an accident, not the result of purposeless chance or divine caprice. It was created by God who so willed it and who is involved in its history.

Genesis states that God created human beings as well, and endowed them with divine potential. The Torah insists that human life is not determined by blind fate. Choices are put before Adam and Eve in the Garden of Eden (and thus, by extension, before each of us every day). We have the ability to transcend our instincts and impulses, because we possess spiritual qualities.

This was a radical assertion in the ancient world (if not today, as well). Other peoples firmly believed that human beings had little control over their destiny, that the universe is controlled by fate. The gods themselves were subject to it, and were not free to act as they wished. The Torah, in contrast, stresses that God endowed men and women with the ability to choose between good and evil, making them responsible for the consequences of their choices.

Genesis introduces us to Abram, living in highly civilized Mesopotamia. We are told that God calls out to Abram, and commands him to go to a land which God will show him. Abram immediately and unequivocally responds. He leaves the society of his birth and upbringing and proceeds to the land of Canaan, which God wills to him and his descendants. There he learns that God is not only the all-powerful Lord of the Universe, but is a just and righteous God who cares about the innocent. As an acknowledgment of Abram's willingness to follow God's will, God bestows a new name on him: henceforth, he is to be called "Abraham." The Hebrew letter ה (pronounced *"hay"*) which is added to his name becomes an eternal reminder of his willingness to follow God and of God's promise to bless him with numerous descendants.

Abraham's new religion is a family or tribal matter at first. He passes it on to his son Isaac who transmits it to his son Jacob (whose name is also later changed—to Israel, "the one who strives with God"). The children of the third patriarch, confronted by a severe famine in Canaan, move to Egypt temporarily but become trapped by a change of regimes. A new dynasty comes to power and enslaves them, and they endure a long, harsh bondage. According to midrashic sources, throughout their enslavement they retain their sense of kinship and remember their ancestors' teachings.

Moses, the man depicted as leading the slaves out of Egypt, is a remarkable figure. Under his leadership, the Israelites are transformed from a mass of frightened slaves into a nation. Moses leads them across the Sea of Reeds (known as the Red Sea) and then to Mount Sinai, where they participate in an awesome event. They gather at the foot of the mountain, collectively experience the presence of God, and come to understand that Moses is transmitting a set of laws that God expects them to observe. God's charge is for them to become a "kingdom of priests and a holy nation" (Exodus 19:6).

Though they are close to the Promised Land, they are not deemed ready to enter. Their faith is too weak, their vision too limited. Over the next forty years, as they wander in the wilderness, they face hunger, thirst, discord and despair. They learn to organize and govern themselves. Finally, they are ready to enter the Promised Land and live on their own soil. They bid farewell to Moses, who ascends Mount Nebo and dies within sight of the land he is not privileged to enter.

In the Book of Joshua, which immediately follows the Torah in the Hebrew Bible, Joshua succeeds Moses and leads the people in conquering and settling the land. As is true of the earlier stories, this is told in several ways, from different perspectives. According to the Book of Judges, which follows the Book of Joshua, Joshua apparently does not take all of Canaan, but he does succeed in settling each of the twelve tribes in its own territory. For a while, these tribes maintain a separate existence without forming a united kingdom, but they band together when threatened by an outside force and turn to talented individuals for leadership. These leaders are referred to as *shoftim,* usually translated "judges" or "chieftains." The names of the most prominent judges are Gideon, Deborah, and Samson.

In time, the need to stand up to threatening enemies requires greater unity, and the people demand a king. The last of the judges, the prophet Samuel, prefers to retain the existing system, but eventually acquiesces, and a promising young man named Saul is chosen as the first king.

Saul is described differently from other rulers of his day. Indeed, the Hebrew Bible describes kingship in Israel from its very inception as different from that of other nations. The king was not considered a divine figure in human form; he was not a potentate whose every word was obeyed unhesitatingly. Like all his subjects, the king was understood to be bound by the word of

God as conveyed and interpreted by the prophets and could never proclaim his will to be identical with God's. He was not the divine incarnate nor could he claim to be God's exclusive representative on earth. He shared power with other societal leaders: the priest *(kohen)*, who conducted religious rituals, and the prophet *(navi)*, who boldly spoke out in the name of God against injustice.

The First Commonwealth

The story continues: Saul fails to fulfill the promise of his youth. Samuel is deeply disappointed in him, and consecrates David, a young shephard, to take his place. After Saul falls in battle, David ascends to the throne. David's reign is filled with splendid achievements. He expands the borders of Israel, and establishes a viable, powerful state. He captures the city of Jerusalem and makes it the political and religious capital of his people. Generations later, as a sign of their idealization of this period, the sages come to believe that the Messiah (the anointed redeemer of the Jewish people) would be a descendant of King David *(Mashiah ben David)*.

David's successor is his son Solomon, who builds upon the brilliant achievements of his father. He introduces a new administrative organization that brings peace and prosperity to the kingdom. He builds a central sanctuary in Jerusalem, a Temple which becomes the national center for the worship of God. Moreover, Solomon encourages writers who produce great literature. Some of the books of the Bible are later attributed to Solomon or to his father. In later generations, Solomon becomes characterized as the wisest of all men.

Solomon's accomplishments, which include an intensive building program, take their toll. They are described as having been achieved at the expense of burdensome taxes which the people found unbearably oppressive. As a result, an insurrection takes place upon Solomon's death, and the united kingdom separates into two separate entities. The Israelites to the north of

Jerusalem, descendants of ten of the twelve tribes, set up a kingdom known as Israel. The two remaining tribes in the south constitute the kingdom of Judah.

Although the northern kingdom is larger and wealthier, its government is less stable. Dynasties do not remain in power very long. Established individuals take the crown for a short time only, since they or their offspring are assassinated and replaced by rivals. Israel enters into alliances with various neighbors from time to time, but these do not produce long-lasting benefits.

The great literary prophets first make their appearance in the eighth century B.C.E. These were sensitive, articulate and courageous individuals who were convinced that God had commissioned them to proclaim the divine will. They spared no one, whether monarch, priest, or fellow-citizen, who committed immoral or unjust acts. They insisted that justice and righteousness must prevail throughout all of society. They taught that the Master of the Universe is concerned with what people do, and that God punishes those who deceive, cheat, or exploit others. They proclaimed morality rather than power as the decisive factor in world history; they demanded that spiritual love operate in human affairs. They called on their people to repent and turn aside from their evil ways, foretelling doom for those deaf to the message. They foresaw inevitable catastrophe as the divine punishment for wickedness. Yet, with all their fury and woeful warnings, they also promised future redemption and the ultimate return of the faithful remnant to an idealized Zion.

As had been feared, the kingdom of Israel was eventually conquered by the great empire of the day, Assyria. (Through extra-biblical sources, this can be dated to the year 721 B.C.E.) Some of the people must have escaped to the south or to neighboring lands. A few remained in the destroyed homeland. The majority, however, were carried off and dispersed throughout the Assyrian Empire, where they assimilated or died out. There are many legends about these "Ten Lost Tribes" but no one knows precisely what happened to them.

Judah was smaller, less affluent, and less prominent in international affairs. Ruled by the Davidic dynasty, the Judeans did not experience the frequent changes of regimes of their northern brethren. However, they could not withstand the onslaught of the Babylonians who succeeded the Assyrians as world conquerors, and to whom they lost their capital, Jerusalem, and sanctuary (the Temple) in 586 B.C.E. Many national leaders were killed and many Judeans were taken into captivity. The people could have suffered the fate—assimilation and eventual extinction—of their northern brethren. But this did not occur. Unlike the Israelites, the Judeans were able to preserve their identity and did not disappear. They remained loyal to their national identity as Judeans even on alien soil. What was the source of their success? It appears to be their commitment never to forget what had happened to them:

> By the rivers of Babylon,
> There we sat,
> Sat and wept,
> As we remembered Zion.
> . . .
> If I forget thee, O Jerusalem,
> Let my right hand wither!
> Let my tongue stick to my palate
> If I cease to think of you,
> If I fail to elevate Jerusalem
> Above my foremost joy!
>
> (Psalm 137)

The fall of Jerusalem and the destruction of the Temple did not have the same result as similar catastrophes among other ancient peoples. Others who lost independence and central sanctuaries soon ceased to exist. They accepted the superiority of their conquerors and assimilated. The Judeans, however, did not regard their disaster as a sign that the enemy possessed a stronger deity, but rather as a sign of God's displeasure. Moreover, they believed that Babylonia's arrogance and failure to recognize its shortcomings would eventually lead to the downfall of its empire.

The exiled community was a religious-national body the likes of which the ancient world had never seen. It remained loyal to its national/religious traditions without cult, land, sacrifice, or temple and developed means to preserve these traditions.

The exiles never gave up yearning for Zion and praying for its restoration. The prophet Isaiah taught his people that though they were derided and abused by the nations, they would ultimately be vindicated by a glorious redemption in which the glory of God would be revealed to all humanity.

When the Persian Empire conquered the Babylonian Empire after fifty years and King Cyrus granted the Jews permission to return, many returned. Many, though, did not. The transformed faith and identity of the Judean exiles was apparently strong enough to sustain them even once the possibility of return became real. The Babylonian Jewish community, the first of many diaspora Jewish communities, continued to thrive for over 1,500 years.

The Second Commonwealth

In 515 B.C.E., the Judeans who returned to Judea rebuilt their Temple and proceeded to rebuild their religious-national lives. It was most difficult, and some became indifferent or discouraged. The scholar Ezra, along with Nehemiah, a gifted administrator (whose efforts are recorded in the biblical books bearing their names), returned from Babylonia in the fifth century B.C.E. and unified the Judeans as a community pledged to the Torah. Ezra trained scribes to copy the sacred scrolls and to visit towns and villages to instruct the people and to explain the contents of the scrolls. Some scholars regard Ezra as the editor of the Torah. In any event, the careers of Ezra and Nehemiah are among the latest historical events described in the Hebrew Bible.

In the fourth century B.C.E., a new power arose on the

world scene: the Greeks, led by Alexander the Great. Hellenism, the Greek way of life, spread throughout the Near East, including the Judean state. Tens of thousands of Greeks and Macedonians migrated throughout the conquered lands and Greek cities were established everywhere. The Greek tongue became the international language of culture and diplomacy and Greek culture and religion spread throughout the Near East. Over time, Hellenism was to have great influence on Jews and Judaism.

Hellenism engendered a broad range of responses. Some Jews were attracted to it; others repelled by it. In some diaspora communities, such as Alexandria (named for the emperor) in Egypt, Jews writing in Greek attempted to synthesize Jewish and Greek thought. The Alexandrian community produced an extensive body of writings in the Greek language, including a translation of the Bible into Greek, known as the Septuagint. An exemplar of this effort to integrate Greek thinking with traditional Jewish teaching was the Alexandrian philosopher Philo Judaeus, who lived several centuries after Alexander's conquest.

Elsewhere, especially in Judea, the challenge Hellenism posed to traditional Jewish belief and practice was felt more acutely. When Alexander the Great died, his empire was divided among his generals. Ptolemy became master of Egypt, while Seleucus became lord of Syria and the eastern territories. Both claimed Judea. As they fought each other, the rulers of the Jewish land often changed. The Ptolemid dynasty controlled Judea for about a century, during which they did not interfere in Jewish affairs, but in 198 B.C.E., the region came under Seleucid rule.

At first, the dominance of the Syrian Hellenists made little difference in the internal life of the Jews. They lived as they had before, without undue pressure to change their way of life. The High Priest served as their leader and was responsible to the government for order and taxes; teachers instructed students in Torah and met to deliberate religious matters. But this situation did not continue long. During the reign of Antiochus IV Epiphanes

(175–163 B.C.E.), relations disintegrated. With the help of some Judean aristocrats—including members of the priesthood—who embraced Hellenism, Antiochus decided to force Hellenization upon the Jews. As part of this process, Torah scrolls were destroyed, and Jewish ritual practices (such as circumcision and Sabbath observance) were outlawed. Pagan altars were constructed, and Jews were compelled to demonstrate their obedience to the new cult by eating pork. Finally, when the Jerusalem Temple was converted into a pagan shrine and a sacrifice of pork offered on the altar, a revolt erupted.

The banner of rebellion was raised by an elderly priest named Mattathias and his five sons, who came to be known as "the Maccabees." His son Judah led his rebel followers in successful attacks upon the better-trained imperial soldiers. After three years, Judah the Maccabee and his men routed the Syrians and proceeded to cleanse the Temple so that the worship of God could be resumed there. The dedication (in Hebrew, *ḥanukkah*) and the cleansing ritual took eight days.

The Maccabean struggle was, on the one hand, a battle for religious freedom against the Greek rulers, and for this reason Jews celebrate Ḥanukkah as a festival marking the triumph of right over might, of the righteous over the oppressors. But the revolt was also a civil war between traditionalists and assimilationists, and the conclusion of the war marked the victory of Jewish tradition over Hellenism within the Jewish community.

Four of the five Maccabean brothers were killed during the war. Simon was the only one to survive. He presided over the peace and laid the foundations of what became known as the Hasmonean dynasty (*Hasmon* was the name of one of the ruling family's ancestors). Simon was assassinated in 135 B.C.E. and was succeeded by his son. Thus the children of the Maccabees became royalty seeking to establish and maintain national grandeur. They embarked on wars of conquest and soon came to resemble in many ways those whom their grandparents had defeated. They adopted Greek names, pursued power, and became estranged from the masses and from Torah. Within less than a century, they lost their vigor and purpose—and eventually their crown.

By the middle of the first century B.C.E., the Romans controlled the region. When the great-grandson of Simon was deposed, the Romans installed a man named Herod on the throne. Although some historians speak of him as "Herod the Great," he is known in Jewish history as "Herod the Wicked." He was a brilliant administrator who built magnificent buildings and cities and headed an efficient army. Among his accomplishments was the expansion and reconstruction of the Temple in Jerusalem. Herod, however, was also a power-hungry tyrant. He was consumed by suspicion of those nearest to him, continually fearful of plots. Thus he put to death in-laws and friends, and even his own wife and sons. He died in 4 B.C.E., leaving Judea completely at the mercy of Rome. Upon his death, the Romans divided his realm among three of his surviving sons, but they proved so incompetent that Rome removed them within a decade.

Instead of appointing a new king, Rome ruled Judea directly, appointing governors over the province. These governors represented the worst features of imperialism. They were interested only in enriching their own coffers and were utterly insensitive to the needs, desires, and sensitivities of the people whom they ruled. They flouted Jewish religious law and cruelly enforced their will upon the populace. They crucified tens of thousands of anti-Roman activists. It was during the rule of one of the worst of the Roman governors, Pontius Pilate, that Jesus of Nazareth was put to death as a political offender.

The Jews, yearning for freedom and eager to break the foreign yoke, were increasingly irritated and outraged by the Romans. In the year 66, the Jews finally revolted. Despite inner dissensions, the Jews withstood the force of Rome for nearly four years. Rome, however, was a far superior military power. In the summer of the year 70, the Romans captured Jerusalem and destroyed the Temple. The day on which the Temple fell, the ninth day of the Hebrew month of *Av* (Tisha B'Av), the very same date observed as the anniversary of the destruction of the first Temple, has remained a day of fasting and mourning.

About sixty-three years after the destruction of the Temple, another revolt against Rome broke out. This one, led by a charismatic leader known as Bar Kokhba, drew widespread support, but the Judeans were again defeated (in 135 C.E.). This time, the Romans devastated the country and did their best to efface its Jewish identity. They changed the name of the province from Judea to Syria-Palestina and deported vast numbers of Jews. Jerusalem was turned into a pagan city, and Jews were prohibited from entering it. The practice of Judaism was outlawed and those who defied the Romans were brutally tortured and killed.

Just as one might have expected the fall of Jerusalem and the destruction of the Temple in 586 B.C.E. to have brought an end to the Jewish people, so one might have expected the great catastrophes of 70 and 135 to have brought Jewish history to a close. Other peoples who suffered a similar fate soon ceased to exist. The Jews, however, did not disappear. Their leaders were able to transform Judaism into a powerful, sustaining way of life that did not depend on a central sanctuary or even national sovereignty for national continuity. Subsequent Jewish vitality and creativity were rooted in the undertakings of those who supervised the shaping of Jewish life and thought following the tragedy: the Rabbis (the Jewish scholars and sages of late antiquity).

A story told in rabbinic literature presents the Rabbis' understanding of the basis for their success. According to the story, one of the most distinguished Rabbis, Yoḥanan Ben Zakkai, managed to escape besieged Jerusalem before it fell. He sought out the Roman general Vespasian, whom he greeted as "Caesar" ("Emperor"). Shortly afterward, the Roman Senate elected Vespasian as emperor, thereby entitling him to be referred to by that title. Out of respect for his prescience, the new sovereign informed Ben Zakkai that he would be granted a gift of his choice. The sage asked for permission to establish a school in the small coastal town of Yavneh to teach and to preserve the traditions of Judaism.

In fact, following the fall of Zion, Yavneh did become an important national cultural center. There and in other cities, the Rabbis developed the theology and the practices which would enable Judaism to survive the loss of their national sovereignty and cultic center. There they laid the foundation of what came to be known as rabbinic Judaism.

The Rabbinic Era

The Rabbis set themselves the task of interpreting the Torah and applying it to daily life in a world in which the Jews lacked both national sovereignty and a central shrine—a world in which they would live for almost two thousand years. They developed a set of beliefs and values, a system of ethics and morality for Jews to live by. Their work is reflected in the many volumes of the Talmud which became the foundation of later Jewish thinking and living. The Talmud, a vast literary work, records thoughts, convictions, debates, and decisions of Jewish spiritual leaders regarding all aspects of life: family relations, business affairs, ethics and morality, worship, and ritual. Two collections, edited over several centuries, were produced—one in Babylonia and one in the Land of Israel (see Chapter 3).

In the absence of a physical, geographical, national center, the Rabbis sought other means for uniting a people dispersed far from the borders of Palestine, throughout the Roman Empire and Babylonia. They developed regular Jewish worship services and a standard liturgy. These services required neither a priest nor an altar; they could be conducted anywhere in the world by ordinary Jews. The synagogue became an important Jewish institution, where Jews would gather for worship, study, and fellowship. So did the home, which became the focus of Jewish practices, such as the Pesaḥ *seder* and the weekly observance of Shabbat.

Rabbinic Judaism was portable. It could thrive wherever the Torah and its interpretations could be studied and Jewish law put into practice. It did not ignore the loss of Jewish national sovereignty or the destruction of the Jerusalem Temple. Indeed, these were mentioned, and lamented, by Jews at every worship service. The Jews thus never stopped dreaming of their *ge'ulah* (redemption). But Jews could live religiously fulfilling lives consistent with Jewish law (as generations did) without much hope of themselves witnessing the return to Zion.

The Gaonic Age

By the time the Talmud was completed, great academies existed where scholars sought to apply its teachings to life. The leaders of these schools were recognized as the religious authorities of all Jewry. Because each bore the title of *Gaon* (*gaon* means "excellency"), the period between the seventh and eleventh centuries is known as the Gaonic Age.

This period was one of great transformation in the outside world, which presented challenges that demanded responses. A dynamic new religion, Islam, arose in the seventh century and quickly spread throughout the Mediterranean region. The Arab empire of the eighth and ninth centuries brought together the Persian, Hellenistic, Arabic, and Jewish cultures. An era of astonishing cultural and intellectual creativity ensued. In the midst of this attractive and open Islamic culture, many young Jews began to question their own religious heritage. It became necessary to present Judaism in a way that made sense to the intellectuals of the era.

The one who did this most admirably was the most renowned of all the *geonim,* Saadia (882–942). A first-rate scholar, Saadia Gaon was a master of the Islamic tradition, as well as his own. His book *Beliefs and Doctrines* was the first major philosophical treatise on Judaism, the earliest systematic presentation of Jewish beliefs and teachings. Saadia felt the need to prove that science and philosophy do not conflict with Judaism and that, to the contrary, they validate it. He argued that there is one truth, though there are different sources of that truth. One source is reason, the other is the Jewish tradition. Therefore, true reason must lead to truths of revelation. For Saadia, the Torah is revealed reason. Saadia presented proofs for the existence of God and arguments for the observance of Jewish commandments, thereby exerting a profound influence on the Jewish thinkers of the day and those who followed. He pointed a way to find meaning in Judaism while being part of a changing world.

The *geonim* did not abruptly cease to function at the end of the first millennium, but their influence gradually waned. This was due partly to the lack of outstanding personalities and partly to the fact that the center of Jewish life was shifting from Babylonia to Europe.

The Golden Age of Spain

In the eleventh and twelfth centuries, Spain became one of the great dynamic centers of Jewish life. Jews had lived there long before that, indeed as early as pre-Christian days, but they reached the peak of their creativity as their culture came into contact with Islamic culture after the Muslims conquered Spain in the eighth century. The Muslims of this period were relatively liberal. They allowed non-Muslim communities considerable legal and religious freedom and permitted them to share in the flowering of science, philosophy, and poetry.

A remarkable period of creativity ensued. It is usually referred to as "The Golden Age of Spain." Many Jews were completely at home in Arabic as well as in Jewish culture. They wrote commentaries on biblical books and rabbinic works as well as philosophical treatises, poetry, and linguistic studies. In addition to rabbis, the leaders of the Jewish community were physicians, astronomers, and statesmen. A few were even generals.

Among these giants, two were towering. One was the greatest Hebrew poet since biblical days, Yehudah ha-Levi (c. 1075–1141). Ha-Levi, a physician, wrote poetry in Hebrew and philosophy in Arabic. His secular poetry is delightful, his religious poems are magnificent. Ha-Levi was the great Singer of Zion who expressed the deepest yearnings and undying love of his people for the Land of Israel. Some of his religious poems have been incorporated into the liturgy. Ha-Levi's philosophical masterpiece, *The Kuzari,* expresses ideas and emotions basic to the Jewish people, together with the presentation of his own mystical experiences.

The other giant produced by Spanish Jewry was Maimonides (1135–1204), also known by the initials of his name, *R*abbi *M*oses *b*en *M*aimon: Rambam. The Rambam was the greatest medieval philosopher of the Jewish people. He was a noted physician and a master of Jewish law whose legal works (especially the compilation entitled *Mishneh Torah*) are still studied widely.

Maimonides was a distinguished rationalist whose philosophic work, *A Guide for the Perplexed (Moreh Nevukhim),* was written to answer questions about Judaism raised by young intellectuals. Maimonides, like his tenth century predecessor Saadia, was convinced not only that religion and reason do not conflict, but that they corroborate each other. What appears to be irrational is simply misunderstood. He therefore devoted part of his book to explaining the meanings of specific words and concepts in the Bible. Maimonides deeply believed in God but did not attempt to define God, pointing out that we can assert only what God is *not*. Yet Maimonides also presented arguments to prove the existence of God. The *Guide* is one of the greatest Jewish philosophical works of all time. A classic of the medieval world, it carefully and methodically addresses the age-old challenges that reason poses to faith.

After Maimonides, the "Golden Age" began to fade. In the first half of the thirteenth century, in what became known as the "Reconquest" of the Iberian peninsula, the Christians drove the Muslims out of Spain, and would not tolerate other non-Catholic minorities. The flourishing cultural life of the Jewish community was harshly stifled.

It was during this period that Jewish mysticism, which is as old as the Bible, flourished. The mystical tradition known as the *Kabbalah* ("[esoteric] tradition") was explored and developed by scholars in Spain and Provence such as Moses ben Naḥman (Naḥmanides), Isaac the Blind, and Abraham Abulafia. The *Zohar* (the "Book of Splendor") was published during this period. (Even though it was attributed to a second century rabbinic sage, Rabbi Simeon bar Yoḥai, scholars believe that the bulk of the work was composed by a Castillian kabbalist, Moses de Leon, in the 1280s.) The rise of *Kabbalah* may have been a reaction to the rationalism of medieval Jewish philosophy. Instead of seeking through the intellect to reconcile Judaism with philosophical principles as Maimonides and his followers had done, the kabbalists perceived ostensibly irrational notions in the Bible or other Jewish writings as hints of hidden, inexpressible mysteries, and were not perturbed by contradictions. They sought, through their transmission of mystical, esoteric knowledge, to help Jews transcend the gap between the human and divine. The Jewish mystical tradition developed a "potential for consolidation in times of great trouble"[1] and thus became very important in this and subsequent periods of Jewish history.

[1] Robert Seltzer, *Jewish People, Jewish Thought* (New York: Macmillan, 1980), p. 450.

During the fourteenth and early fifteenth centuries, the Jews became subject to increasing discrimination and repression. They continually were pressured to convert and were often threatened with exile when they refused. Those who succumbed were watched constantly, suspected of living secretly as Jews. Many converts did preserve their Jewish identity secretly. Known by their oppressors as *marranos* (meaning "swine"), in some cases they retained Jewish loyalty for many generations. The Spanish Inquisition was established to target those who had renounced their Judaism, who were suspected of practicing Judaism in secret. Its instruments were terror, torture, and forced confessions.

Finally, the Jews were expelled from Spain in 1492. From that time on, no Jew could openly practice Judaism in Spain until the middle of the twentieth century.

European Jewish Communities in the Middle Ages

As Jews from Babylonia had migrated to Spain, so Jews from the Land of Israel went to Italy, France, and Germany. From France, some Jews followed William the Conqueror into England.

The Italian Jewish community, one of the oldest in Europe, produced a number of scholars and other authors, but it never reached the heights of Spanish Jewry. Jews lived in England from 1066 until being expelled in 1290. Legally, they were not permitted to return to England for four centuries. Jews were expelled from France in the fourteenth century and were not re-established there until the eighteenth. At times in these communities, great scholars arose who left an indelible imprint upon all of subsequent Jewish learning.

French Jewry produced one of the greatest Jewish thinkers, Rabbi Shlomo Yitzḥaki, better known as Rashi (1040–1105), the commentator *par excellence* on the Bible and the Talmud. Ever since his day, these sacred texts are rarely studied without his commentaries. His straightforward, brilliant explanations clarify the most difficult passages. There is hardly an equal to Rashi. Moreover, he trained disciples, known as the Tosafists, who supplemented his commentaries, not merely explaining words and passages but also developing Jewish law to meet contemporary needs while continuing the traditions of the past.

Rashi and his students lived through the terrible days of the Crusades. Communities along the crusaders' path were offered the choice of forced baptism or death. Many chose the latter. Violent Crusaders ruthlessly attacked the Jews in France and Germany, massacring entire Jewish communities and leaving many survivors destitute.

In twelfth century Europe, Jews were accused of deliberately beating or stabbing the wafer used in Communion, causing it to bleed. This ludicrous charge of "Desecrating the Host" served as the justification for further attacks, murders, and agony. Another preposterous canard with the same horrible results was the Blood Libel, the accusation that Jews annually killed a Christian, whose blood was then purportedly used in the baking of matzah. These two libels spread throughout medieval France and Germany, causing unimaginable sorrow and torture. In the middle of the fourteenth century, Jews were blamed for causing the Black Plague, and were persecuted once more.

Life in Central Europe became so unbearable that great numbers of Jews decided to leave. Many settled further East, where there was promise of relative calm and tranquility. They were welcomed in Poland and Lithuania, which had been undeveloped before the thirteenth century. The leaders of those areas thought that the Jews, with their talent and experience, could help to develop their lands. The Jews lived up to the royal expectations. For a few generations they were granted many privileges and lived without undue harassment.

Toward the end of the fourteenth century, however, the situation changed. Fanatic clergy began to preach virulent hatred of Jews, and German Christian merchants who had followed the Jews to Eastern Europe now regarded them as undesirable competitors. The Jews were soon denied the right to live where they pleased and in the early fifteenth century, they were confined to very limited quarters. Privileges earlier granted to them were often rescinded.

A new phase of Jewish history with a distinctive form of oppression began in 1515, when the Jewish community of Venice was forced to live in a segregated area of the city surrounded on all sides by high walls and canals. Because the area chosen had served as a foundry (Italian: *ghetto*), the word "ghetto" came to refer to the other exclusively Jewish quarters that were subsequently established. In 1555, Pope Paul IV ordered that all Jews in Rome be segregated in a ghetto. The establishment of ghettos in other cities in Christendom, the public burning of Hebrew books, and other oppressive measures soon followed.

Despite these measures, the Jews of Europe survived. They managed to cope with the anti-Judaism of both Church and government. They created strong communal organizations and enjoyed a remarkable degree of self-government, with their own courts, their own educational system, and their own administrative institutions. Local communities elected representatives to regional bodies and these bodies elected representatives to meet with those of other regional councils. Thus, the "Council of the Four Lands" came into being in Poland in the middle of the sixteenth century, constituting a virtual Jewish parliament. The council enacted laws governing taxation and business life, regulated social affairs, acted as a court of appeals, and supervised education and religious life.

The intellectual life of East European Jewry was on a remarkably high plane. Since the intellectual life of the general society was not open to them, the Jews concentrated on the Jewish classics. Their educational system centered on the Bible,

Talmud, commentaries on these documents and other religious works, and the intense study of Jewish law. The reverence for learning within the Jewish communities of Poland and Lithuania created an intense spiritual and intellectual life and the great academies produced many distinguished rabbis and scholars.

CHAPTER 12

History: Modern Times

*M*ODERNITY had a dramatic impact on Jews and Judaism. Because the Jewish experience in Eastern Europe was so different from that of Central and Western Europe, and Judaism in the two regions likewise developed so differently, we will discuss these two areas separately.

The Early Modern Period in Eastern Europe

Calamity struck the Jews of the southern part of Eastern Europe in the middle of the seventeenth century. A Cossack leader named Chmielnitzki led a revolt in 1648 against his people's Polish landlords and ruthlessly struck out against the Jews as well. In that year, and in the following year, Chmielnitzki's men brutally tortured and killed thousands of Jews. Women were raped, babies were dashed against walls, and men were put to the sword. Many Jews were sold into slavery, and all underwent terrorizing experiences. Those who survived were physically and emotionally exhausted and financially ruined. The atrocities initiated by Chmielnitzki continued for a decade. In some parts of the Ukraine, entire Jewish communities completely disappeared; in others, only one-tenth of the Jewish population survived. Refugees spread throughout Europe bearing terrible tales of woe and martyrdom. Neither the Church nor the government extended protection or evinced concern. The blow was so severe that the Jews of the southern part of Eastern Europe were never able to regain their former economic and intellectual eminence.

In the 1660s thousands of Jews throughout Europe were aroused from despair by a Turkish Jew, a mystic named Shabbatai Zevi, who claimed to be the Messiah. People who believed that the hour of redemption had arrived stopped doing business, in the expectation of being transported miraculously to the Land of Israel. Many questioned the need to continue religious practices. Representatives from Jewish communities all over Europe made their way to his court and treated him as royalty. The excitement and agitation, the disruption of economic life, the talk of an end to this world, all led the Sultan of Turkey to order Shabbatai Zevi to cease his activities. The Sultan gave the self-styled Messiah the choice of death or conversion to Islam. When Shabbatai Zevi chose to convert, masses of Jews were plunged into despair. They were able to find consolation only in mysticism. Reason and logic could neither explain their plight nor assuage their distress.

Soon after, a powerful movement arose, which brought spiritual comfort and inspiration to the despondent, impoverished Jews of Eastern Europe. It was called Hasidism (the word is derived from the Hebrew *ḥasid,* pious one). Rabbi Israel ben Eliezer, better known as the *Baal Shem Tov* (c. 1700–1760) founded this radical new movement.

Many legends are told about the *Baal Shem Tov,* all reflecting a man of great spiritual depth. He taught the masses that they matter to God. He preached the intrinsic value of every human being. He held that God is to be worshiped in joy and enthusiasm, that prayer is as precious as study.

The disciples of the *Baal Shem Tov* were remarkable spiritual personalities who spread their versions of the master's doctrines throughout Eastern Europe. Those who followed them as disciples took the name of *ḥasidim*. They lived with an intense, passionate faith. At times, the faith in the power of the *tzaddik* (a Ḥasidic spiritual leader) became all-encompassing. On one hand, Ḥasidism seemed radically at odds with normative Jewish practice; and yet, its mystical approach addressed a real need among its adherents for a transcendent religious experience. It has continued to be an important and dynamic movement within Judaism to our own day.

Not all Jews viewed the rise of Ḥasidism with favor. Particularly those in Lithuania, who had not suffered from the catastrophe that had struck southern Poland and were therefore able to pursue their studies with ardor, fought the new movement. These people were called Mitnagdim (derived from the Hebrew word *mitnaged,* an opponent). Their foremost spokesman in the eighteenth century was the phenomenal scholar Rabbi Elijah of Vilna, better known as the Gaon of Vilna (1720–1797). The Vilna Gaon's life was completely devoted to learning. He not only knew the Bible and the Talmud by heart; he also studied philosophy, anatomy, and astronomy. He emphasized the rabbinic notion that study is a way of worship; that an important way to serve God is through study. And he became the personification of rabbinic Judaism in his time. He could not accept a movement which stressed the emotions and minimized the intellect. The Gaon regarded Ḥasidism as a departure from the traditional emphasis upon learning, as an unbecoming emotional outburst which could easily lead its followers from strict observance of the law. His followers continued his opposition to Ḥasidism. The bitterness between the two camps eased only toward the end of the nineteenth century, when both joined hands to combat non-Orthodoxy and assimilation.

At the end of the eighteenth century, the Kingdom of Poland was too weak to maintain itself. It was partitioned by

Russia, Prussia, and Austria, with the area most heavily populated by Jews coming under the Russian crown. Russia did not want the Jews from the new area infiltrating Russia proper and therefore restricted them to the areas in which they had lived before the partition. This territory, known as "The Pale of Settlement," was further reduced in the nineteenth century. Since Jews were forbidden to move outside the Pale, they were forced into an economic straitjacket.

Eastern Europe in the 19th and Early 20th Centuries

As the years passed, the suffering of the Jews increased. Each succeeding Czar enacted laws that made life for the Jews ever more unbearable. The limited avenues for earning a living were constantly narrowed. Jews were frequently expelled from their villages and forced into the overcrowded cities of the Pale. In the middle of the nineteenth century, Russians drafted Jewish boys for a twenty-five year period of military service. Recruiters who did not fill their quotas would kidnap young boys from their homes. The autocratic rulers resorted to various ruses to convert Jews and reacted with anger when their attempts were frustrated. In the latter part of the century, Jews were victims of vicious attacks called "pogroms" (orchestrated outbursts of communal rioting) usually staged with the government's approval if not actually organized by the authorities. Until the end of the Czarist regime, the Jews were treated with contempt and barbaric cruelty.

The Jews responded to the economic, political, and social oppression in Eastern Europe in a variety of ways. Throughout the nineteenth century, there were efforts by Jewish *maskilim* ("enlightened" ones) to revive the use of the Hebrew language and to restore Jewish national pride. Many *maskilim,* although educated in *yeshivot,* rejected Jewish religiosity altogether, striving to create a secular Jewish national identity. As emancipation swept Western Europe (see below), some Eastern European Jews hoped that they would one day be liberated as well. Channelling the traditional Jewish duty to pursue justice, some Jews worked actively for the liberation of Jews and other oppressed peoples in the Eastern European lands.

For many Jews, hopes of a better future in Eastern Europe were dashed by the Russian pogroms of 1881 and thereafter. Soon after the assassination of Tsar Alexander II by revolutionaries, pogroms broke out and spread to over one hundred and fifty towns and villages. Many peasants participated actively in the looting and killing of Jews or, at best, were indifferent. Many Jews concluded that Russia held no future for the Jews.

Thus began a huge wave of immigration of Jews from Eastern Europe. Hundreds of thousands emigrated to the West, particularly to the United States. A smaller group concluded that Jews must forge their own destiny in their own land, and participated in efforts by the Zionist movement to build Jewish settlements in the Land of Israel (see Chapter 14). Many Jews remained in Eastern Europe. Some became revolutionaries and fought to overthrow the Tsarist regime, hoping that a socialist Russia would award equal rights to Jews.

Some Jews welcomed the Communist Revolution. But the Jewish condition was not improved under the new regime. Anti-Semitism was finally officially declared illegal, but it persisted nonetheless in the government and among the people. Although in theory the Communists deprived all religious groups of freedom, some groups were permitted to maintain contact with their coreligionists outside the Soviet Union. But not the Jews. The Jews officially were considered a national minority, but they were deprived of the rights granted other minorities. Jewish institutions were closed and the communal structures which had served the community were forbidden. Jews and Judaism would remain suppressed until the collapse of the Soviet Union in 1994.

Central and Western European Jewry: Enlightenment, Emancipation, Assimilation

As we saw in Chapter 11, the ghetto is an apt symbol of the vulnerability, isolation, and powerlessness Jews experienced during the Middle Ages. Even when they were treated with decency, the Jews of Central and Western Europe were outsiders. They lived and worked at the sufferance of the political and religious leaders of the lands in which they resided.

This began to change in the eighteenth and nineteenth centuries. The Enlightenment—an intellectual movement which stood for the supremacy of human reason and which promoted the extension of human freedom—spread through Europe. Some philosophers (even those who did not have much respect for Judaism) argued that Jews should be integrated into the European nations in which they lived. Among the early Jewish champions of the Enlightenment was Moses Mendelssohn (1729–1786). Mendelssohn was a broadly educated observant Jew. This was an anomaly at the time. He wrote many essays in felicitous German prose advocating the acceptance of Jews in society. He defended the Jewish religion against those who claimed it was a "backward" faith. He asserted that Judaism was rational, moral, and noble, and argued that Jews should not have to jettison their Judaism to be full and worthy participants of society. To help his fellow Jews acculturate, he translated the Torah into German. (It was printed in Hebrew characters.) In many ways, Mendelssohn paved the way for later generations of Jews to enter European society.

Shortly after Mendelssohn's death, European Jews began to acquire political rights. The French Revolution is often considered the event which triggered the evolution of the status of Jews throughout Central and Western Europe from members of a tolerated minority to citizens of a state. In 1791, the Jews of France were "emancipated"; that is, they were accorded legal protections and granted French citizenship in exchange for giving up their identity as members of a distinct people. This did not come without opposition. For two years the French Parliament debated the question of equal rights for Jews before deciding to grant them, and not long afterward, Napoleon limited the emancipation by issuing the "Infamous Decree" in 1808, restricting the Jews' economic activity and freedom of movement and requiring Jews to take French surnames.

During the decades which followed, Jews throughout Central and Western Europe were admitted into citizenship and began to participate in the general culture. Indeed, many Jews gained distinction and eminence in cultural, academic, and political spheres. Nonetheless, although many rights long denied them were granted, complete political equality and complete social acceptance remained elusive. To some this was unbearable. Frustrated by a persistent anti-Jewish animus (which, as we'll see, continued well into the twentieth century), some Jews chose to convert to Christianity in order to eliminate the remaining obstacle to their full acceptance into the dominant national culture. As Heinrich Heine, a German Jewish writer who himself converted, put it somewhat wistfully, "a baptismal certificate [was] the ticket of admission to European culture."[1] Among those who paid that price were, ironically, four of the six children of Moses Mendelssohn, including Abraham, father of the composer Felix Mendelssohn.

Even in France, the first of the European nations to emancipate its Jews, the successful assimilation of French Jews into the national culture did not inhibit discrimination or prejudice against Jews. In 1895, few Frenchmen objected when Captain Alfred Dreyfus was disgraced and imprisoned on the trumped-up charge of selling state secrets to the Germans. Anti-Jewish sentiment undoubtedly played a role in his condemnation.

As Jews experienced emancipation and began to enter Euro-

---

[1] Quoted in *Heinrich Heine: A Biographical Anthology,* edited by Hugo Bieber, trans. M. Hadas (Philadelphia: Jewish Publication Society, 1956), p. 196.

pean society, they changed. They became educated in European languages, culture, and mores. They began to live among gentiles and began to see themselves and their way of life as others did. Consequently, their understanding of Judaism changed as well. A variety of factors encouraged Jews to reconceive Judaism as more harmonious with their new status and new sense of self. Some made efforts to reform Judaism. By negating the national and folk aspects of Judaism which would tend to distinguish Jews from their neighbors, reformers hoped that Judaism would be seen as yet another religious denomination on the national scene and therefore more easily accepted. Others adhered ever more firmly to traditional practice and thought, but developed the means to defend those choices in terms which could be understood and appreciated by other Europeans. Still others embraced Jewish peoplehood, and so rejected radical reforms such as the elimination of Hebrew from the liturgy, yet were willing to consider a gradual evolution in Jewish law. These responses were the forerunners of the religious movements we today call Reform, Orthodox, and Conservative Judaism (see Chapter 4) and contributed to a dynamic, pluralistic, and intellectually sophisticated Jewish environment in Central Europe in the nineteenth century.

In the early twentieth century, German Jewry produced seminal thinkers who exerted a profound influence upon modern Jews. The writings of Hermann Cohen, Franz Rosenzweig, Martin Buber, and Leo Baeck sparked a renewed positive identification with Jewish values and the Jewish people. Tragically and cruelly, the advent of Hitler spelled doom for what was a thriving German Jewish community.

British Jewry was also part of the West, but its development was unlike that of its counterparts on the continent. Equal rights and citizenship were not suddenly thrust upon the Jews of England; they were enjoyed long before they became legal. Jews began returning to the British Isles in the late seventeenth century and quickly became part of English life without surrendering their heritage. Not until the middle of the nineteenth century was the last vestige of legal discrimination removed, allowing the first Jew, Lionel Rothschild (who had been elected nine years before), to take his seat in Parliament. But British Jews had been free of the kind of stress and strain characteristic of the French and German struggles for acceptance. To be sure, there were anti-Semites in England as elsewhere, but they were never powerful enough to endanger Jewish life and well-being.

Anti-Semitism

Unfortunately, no survey of Jewish life in Europe would be complete without at least a brief discussion of anti-Semitism. The dictionary definition of anti-Semitism is: "hostility toward or prejudice against Jews or Judaism." It is ironic that the term was created in the late nineteenth century by Wilhelm Marr, who was seeking a better, more scientific and rational-sounding word than *Judenhass* (Jew-hatred) to justify his own antipathy to Jews and Judaism.

Throughout the centuries, Jews have been scorned and oppressed in every country in which they have lived. There is no one cause of anti-Semitism. It is a complex phenomenon rooted in religious, social, political, economic, psychological, and cultural factors. Analyzing them is not completely satisfying, but it can help us understand it and may point to ways of combating it.

The fundamental point to recognize is that anti-Semitism is indifferent to truth and facts. Jews have been accused of grossly contradictory behaviors: Jews have been labeled ruthless capitalists and radical socialists, rootless internationalists and rabid nationalists, culturally sterile and dominating the creative arts. Although Jews have not had enough power even to save their own lives, they have been charged with plotting international conspiracies to overthrow governments.

Probably the most powerful source of anti-Semitism for the past two thousand years has been the Christian denunciation of Jews and Judaism. There was some religious distrust and dislike of Judaism among pagans even before the birth of Christianity, but as the new religion grew, it quickly became the fount of the most persistent anti-Jewish animus. Because Jews refused to accept the divinity of Jesus and other new doctrines, Christian leaders increasingly turned against them and accused them of the worst of evils, including, as conveyed explicitly in the gospel narratives of the New Testament, responsibility for the death of Jesus. Leaders of the Catholic Church, including popes and bishops, and Protestants like Martin Luther, insisted that the Jews should be punished for their ancestors' rejection of Christian teachings.

Only in our day, in the wake of the Holocaust (see below), have some Christian religious leaders denounced the cruelties and agonies caused by teachings of the past and urged their fellow Christians to repent. Pope John XXIII was one such leader. Under his direction (1958–1964), Vatican Council II officially declared that neither the Jews in Jesus' day nor their descendants are to be held accountable for his death. Other Catholic spokesmen, such as Cardinal Spellman of New York and Cardinal Cushing of Boston, vigorously denounced anti-Semitism as sinful and un-Christian. The renowned Protestant theologian Reinhold Niebuhr affirmed the legitimacy of Jewish existence and called for an end to all attempts to convert Jews. Some Protestant bodies have also declared anti-Semitism as a sin and are seeking ways to remove vestiges of it. Lutheran leaders in 1983 and 1994 denounced Martin Luther's anti-Semitism.

Not all anti-Semitism has stemmed from specifically religious teachings. Jews were often disliked because of their role in economic life. Anti-Semites projected the image of the Jew as a Shylock, a crafty money-lover who could not be trusted. In medieval Europe, agriculture and non-commercial avenues of earning a living were forbidden to Jews, who then were accused of failing to enter those very occupations. Non-Jewish merchants were more hostile to their Jewish competitors than to those who were not Jewish. When there was prosperity, they tolerated Jews; when conditions were difficult, they sought to be rid of them.

At times Jews have been selected as objects of derision because of their minority status in the lands in which they lived.

The awareness that this lack of status engendered fear and degradation led many Jews in the first half of the twentieth century to embrace Zionism. They concluded that anti-Semitism could never wane until the Jewish people ended their exile to become once again a people with a national home (see Chapter 14).

Racial anti-Semitism arose in the early modern period. This later became the basis for the murderous policies of the Nazis. German anti-Semites insisted that the Jews have a defect in their blood, that the Jews are an inferior, degenerate race of sub-humans (in German, *"Untermenschen"*) capable of "contaminating" or "infecting" others. This theory implies two things: First, that if other, presumably pure, people are to be protected from Jews, the Jews must, at the very least, be isolated, and that such isolation is scientifically justified and proper. Deeming Jews to be sub-human, though, also ominously implies that if it should be necessary to kill Jews to achieve this goal of preserving the purity of other "races," it wouldn't be morally equivalent to killing other human beings.

These racial theories were reflected in the national policy of the Third Reich when the Nazi regime embarked upon a program of exterminating those whom it declared to be genetically inferior.

The Holocaust: The War Against the Jews; The Destruction of Central and Eastern European Jewry

The rise of Hitler in Germany in the 1930s meant that anti-Semitism was now the guiding ideology of a police state that used every means at its disposal to carry out its discriminatory and ultimately murderous aims. Jews were forced to wear a yellow star of David with the German word *"Jude"* ("Jew") inscribed on it. Jewish-owned shops and stores were similarly distinguished. In 1935, the Nuremberg Laws were passed, which deprived German Jews of their citizenship and prohibited many contacts between Jews and non-Jews. German Jews began to emigrate; between 1933 and 1939, almost two-thirds of the German Jewish community emigrated.

On November 9, 1938, in response to the assassination of a low-level Nazi diplomat in Paris, a massive pogrom took place in Germany. On that night, later known as *Kristallnacht* (the night of broken glass), most German synagogues were vandalized, their glass windows shattered. Almost one hundred Jews were murdered and tens of thousands were arrested and sent to concentration camps. It became clear that Jewish life in Germany had reached a terrible turning point.

For the Jews of Eastern Europe, the worst was yet to come. Hitler invaded Poland in 1939, initiating World War II. Millions of Jews suddenly came under Nazi occupation. These Jews were concentrated into ghettos and exploited as slave laborers. With the Nazi invasion of Russia in 1941, a new phase began. Accompanying the invading German troops were groups of special Nazi police forces known as *Einsatzgruppen,* whose mission was to murder Jews. Once the German army had secured a village or town, the *Einsatzgruppen* would round up all of the Jews, escort them to an isolated area, and slaughter them.

Also in the early 1940s, camps were created, primarily in Eastern Europe. Commonly called concentration camps, most were actually death camps, whose sole purpose was the efficient extermination of massive numbers of men, women, and children. Throughout Nazi-occupied Eastern and Western Europe, ghettos and other communities were "liquidated" (i.e., their Jewish inhabitants deported). The Jews were put on trains and transported to the camps. They were often told that they were being taken to work camps. Upon arrival, most were told to strip and to enter large "shower rooms" for de-licing. These were actually gas chambers in which many Jews could be killed relatively quickly. Crematoria were also built in these camps, where the bodies could be burnt. In some camps, the crematoria were kept burning night and day. The most famous of the death camps is Auschwitz, where one and a half million Jews were exterminated.

Those Jews who could, rebelled against Nazi rule. There

are records of uprisings in the ghettos and in the camps. When the Nazis attempted to liquidate the ghetto in Warsaw, Poland, on the first night of Passover in 1943, they met with armed resistance, and it took almost a month to complete the task. In the Sobibor concentration camp, a desperate, unsuccessful revolt by several hundred poorly armed inmates took place in 1943.

For the most part, though, physical resistance was futile. The Nazis were single-mindedly determined to achieve their goal, which was none other than the complete annihilation of Jews throughout the world. They were well-armed and ruthless and freely employed starvation, torture, and mass murder as instruments of their cruel aims. Moreover, they kept their designs a secret from their victims. Millions of Jews went to their deaths unsuspectingly.

In all, six million Jews were murdered. Two terms are commonly used to describe this gruesome, painful episode in Jewish history. The first is "the Holocaust." A holocaust is a sacrificial offering that is consumed entirely by flames. The other term is "the *shoah*." *Shoah* is a Hebrew word meaning catastrophe or disaster.

Europe's Jews in the Aftermath of the Holocaust

The Holocaust left most Central and Eastern European Jewish communities decimated. Certainly the great centers of prewar European Jewish life never regained their strength. America became an important center of Jewish life as many refugees sought to start their lives anew in the New World. What little hope there was in Poland that a postwar Jewish community might thrive was dashed in the late 1940s when pogroms broke out, as Jews who had survived and been liberated from the camps sought to return to their homes. Many Jewish refugees throughout Europe sought to emigrate to Palestine. This was virtually impossible until the creation of the State of Israel in 1948.

Throughout the 1950s and 1960s, small numbers of Jews settled in Germany and elsewhere in Central Europe. Only recently has there been a revival of Jewish life in Germany, sparked in part by the influx of immigrants from the former Soviet Union.

In the Soviet Union, which had suffered huge losses in World War II, the government refused to acknowledge the unique tragedy of the Jews. After World War II, the Soviets did not destroy Jews in pogroms as their Tsarist predecessors had done, but continued to forbid them to have relationships with Jews outside the Soviet Union and continued to suppress the practice of Judaism. Although other religious groups suffered, the Jews were singled out for particularly harsh treatment. In the immediate postwar years—the "black years" of Soviet Jewry—many Jews were purged by Stalin. In the 1960s and 1970s some Jews were able to leave for Israel or the United States, but the possibilities for emigration were again limited in the 1980s. It was not until the early 1990s and the collapse of the Soviet Union that Jews were finally permitted to leave Eastern Europe en masse. During the first half of the 1990s, over 500,000 Jews emigrated from the lands of the former Soviet Union, most moving to Israel.

Notwithstanding this massive exodus, some Jews have chosen to remain in Eastern Europe, and Judaism there is today experiencing a renaissance: Jewish day schools, summer camps, and other institutions are proliferating. Anti-Semitism does persist, but several international Jewish organizations are assisting Jews who have chosen to remain in the states of the former Soviet Union to regain long-lost freedoms and to develop Jewish culture.

Sephardi and Oriental Jews

The history sketched in these pages has been primarily that of the Jews in Europe. The vast number of North American Jews are, in fact, descendents of immigrants from Central and Eastern Europe. Jews, however, have lived all over the globe, and in fact many early Jewish immigrants to this country (and a not insubstantial number of recent ones) have traced their ancestry to Spanish and

North African Jewish communities. Such Jews are called Sephardim (*Sepharad* is the medieval Hebrew name for the Iberian peninsula) and have preserved their own unique customs and traditions.

Jewish communities have existed in North Africa and in the Middle and the Far East for millennia. They are mentioned in biblical sources, and their numbers increased after the fall of both Temples (the First in 586 B.C.E. and the Second in 70 C.E.). Ethiopian Jews (who call themselves *"Beta Yisrael,"* House of Israel) trace the origin of their community to pre-exilic times. These Jews adapted to the cultures of the people among whom they dwelt, yet they maintained their own identity, were loyal to their own religion, and remained loyal to their homeland.

Particularly after the First Arab Conquest in the seventh century C.E. in Egypt and in the rest of North Africa, the Jews were usually considered legal and social inferiors. Yet they produced outstanding sages and scholars for many centuries. For example, Saadia Gaon was born and reared in Egypt, and Moses Maimonides practiced medicine in Cairo. First-rate scholars lived in what is today Morocco, Tunisia, and Algeria. These communities declined in the Middle Ages, but they did not disappear. The Jews lived in their own quarters (known in Morocco as *mellahs*), usually in squalor and poverty. They followed and maintained their traditions faithfully into the twentieth century. After the birth of the State of Israel, most of them emigrated there.

When the Second Temple fell, some Jews undoubtedly fled south to Arabia. For a time, Judaism became the religion of a Yemenite kingdom. When Muhammed started his new religion in the seventh century, he appealed to the Jews to join him. Some did, but the majority refused to do so. Small Jewish communities were able to maintain themselves in the peninsula for hundreds of years. The largest of these communities was in Yemen, where Jews were treated with contempt and harshness, but nevertheless maintained schools and produced scholars. After 1948, most members of the community were transported to the newly established Jewish State.

Syria was home to some Jews even before the beginnings of Christianity. Foreign conquerors came and went without putting an end to the Jewish community. Despite their deprivations and sufferings, these Jewish communities produced poets and scholars. In the present century, persecution intensified and most left Syria for Israel. Those who have remained have no rights and are subject to cruel discrimination.

The area known today as Iraq and Iran was called "Babylonia" in ancient times. Until the eleventh century, Babylonia was the center of amazing creativity. As discussed in Chapters 3 and 11, the Talmud was completed there in the sixth century. For nearly five hundred years, the *geonim* [plural of *"gaon,"* meaning "excellency"] flourished as leaders and scholars in rabbinic studies, philosophy, biblical commentary, and other fields of learning. The center of Jewish life gradually passed to Europe after the year 1000 but the Jews of Babylonia enjoyed long periods of tranquility. The situation changed with the coming of the Mongols in 1258, followed by the Jalayirids and later the Turks. Academies of learning continued to exist but they did not compare with those of former days. With the passage of time, Jewish life deteriorated, especially after Iraq became independent in 1932. Those who could leave after 1948 did so.

Although Iran is a Muslim country, its inhabitants are not Arabs. The majority of the population belongs to the Shiite branch of Islam, less tolerant of differences than the Sunnis. Under their rule, Jews often experienced persecutions, expulsions, and forced conversions. Still, the literary output of Iran's Jews was rich and their Jewish loyalties strong. In the nineteenth century, their condition grew worse and they suffered from ignorance and poverty. Their situation improved somewhat under the last shah, but it became more precarious than ever under the Ayatollah Khomeini and his successors. Many Jews have emigrated to Israel and the United States.

There have long been Jews in India. Many years ago, some Jews of Iran ventured further east to do business in India, where they found Jews who maintained that their ancestors had arrived in biblical times, claiming descent from the Ten Lost Tribes. They called themselves the *"Bene Israel,"* the "Children of Israel." All that is definitely known about their origin is that they have lived in or near Bombay since the Middles Ages. These Jews had accepted the idea of caste from the general environment. They had forgotten Hebrew and used the native Marathi language instead. Although they had had no contact with other Jews, they observed some religious practices (circumcision, dietary laws, and the Sabbath). They did not intermarry with other Jews and maintained their own communal life. After 1948, many went to Israel where they encountered problems in being accepted as full Jews. It was not until 1964 that the Chief Rabbis of Israel ruled that the Bene Israel from India are legally Jewish.

There was a Jewish community on the southwest coast of India, in and near Cochin. These Jews had no contact with the rest of world Jewry for centuries. The local rulers generally treated them with tolerance; in 1957, the rajah gave them a site near the palace for a synagogue. The Cochin Jews wore native dress and spoke the native tongue, but they prayed in Hebrew and zealously followed Jewish law. After 1948, most of them emigrated to Israel.

A third group of Indian Jews consists of Jews who came to India from Iraq in the early nineteenth century. They established their own synagogues and schools, and had little to do with their co-religionists who had long been in India. Many of this community also moved to Israel and, for many years, maintained their own distinct identity *vis-à-vis* the Bene Israel and Cochin Jews.

Jewish traders of Iran also traveled to China, and some settled there. When Turks stopped the trading in the sixteenth century and old caravan routes fell into disrepair, Jews living in China became isolated. There is little reliable information about Chinese Jews, although there are stone tablets from Kaifeng, capital of the Chinese Empire in the tenth through the thirteenth centuries, as well as later inscriptions. In 1461, flood waters from the Yellow River destroyed Torah scrolls and most of the Kaifeng synagogue. The Jews of the city then obtained

Torah scrolls from other communities in China (a tablet erected in 1663 mentions thirteen Torah scrolls). Over the course of time, knowledge of Jewish history was forgotten and intermarriage increased, yet some traditions were maintained. A Protestant missionary in 1866 found only a few thousand Jews there, and they soon assimilated.

In the 1840s, a number of British Jews settled in Shanghai. Not long afterward, a number of Russian Jews settled in some Chinese cities. During World War II, many Jewish refugees from Poland and Eastern Europe were able to reach Shanghai. Most of these refugees, however, left after the war.

Jews did not come to Japan until it was opened to European trade in the nineteenth century. Those engaged in business were restricted to a few cities (as were all foreigners) and made no effort to establish a Japanese Jewish community. The only Japanese Jews today are the few who have converted and married Western Jews. The small Jewish community in Japan, centered in Tokyo, is made up mainly of Western Jews.

The Jewish people have been scattered in many countries, but even small groups of Jews separated from the mainstream have usually tenaciously held on to their faith and identity. There even have been groups, such as the Jews of Ethiopia, who were cut off from the main Jewish body for centuries, to be reunited only in our day.

Despite profound ethnic and cultural distinctions among these groups, a sense of Jewish unity has prevailed. Despite distinguishing labels like "Ashkenazi," "Sephardi," or "Oriental," Jews have considered themselves, fundamentally, to be one people. Since 1948, the State of Israel has been a crucible for testing this unity. All of these communities have been forced to come together and work together at the formidable tasks of nation and state building.

CHAPTER 13

American Jewish History

*T*HE New World, particularly that part of the North American continent which became the United States of America, was developed by people of various national and religious backgrounds. Although a particular group may have become a majority in a certain area, none was exclusive; minorities and ethnic differences always have been a fundamental part of American culture. In such a society, Jews were able to achieve a political, economic and social status long denied them in Europe. Although in every generation there have been those who disliked Jews or Judaism intensely, they have been looked upon with disfavor by the government. In any event, they could not and did not prevent Jews from sharing the freedom and other American blessings enjoyed by all. Indeed the Jews have always been an important thread of the many-colored tapestry that has constituted American life.

Jews crossed the ocean to the New World with other European immigrants. They had problems in all areas controlled by

Spain, for the Spanish had exported the Inquisition and the intolerance of non-Catholics wherever they went. Some Jews sought to hide their origins, for those who openly practiced their religion were declared heretics. Some were even burned at the stake. In 1630, the Dutch captured Brazil and allowed Jews the same freedoms offered to others. In 1654, however, when Portugal wrested Brazil from Holland, approximately 5,000 Jews had to flee. Many recrossed the ocean to find a home in Holland or England; some settled in British colonies (such as Jamaica). One group of twenty-three Jews made their way to New Amsterdam (which ten years later fell into British hands and was renamed New York).

Although Peter Stuyvesant, governor of New Amsterdam, was not very cordial to the refugees, he obeyed the orders of his employers, the Dutch West Indies Company, and allowed them to settle. Thus, the first Jewish community in what is now the United States was established. The numbers gradually increased and they were granted certain rights, which were extended by the British. In 1706, the first Jewish congregation in New York, Shearith Israel, was established.

The second Jewish settlement was in Newport, Rhode Island. The other New England colonies, not hospitable to dissidents, extended freedom only to members of the established church. Pennsylvania was more liberal, and Jewish congregations existed there by the late eighteenth century. They were also established in Georgia and South Carolina, but other colonies in the south were not yet prepared to tolerate minorities.

The situation improved with the American Revolution and the Constitutional guarantee of equality for all. Although a few states did not agree to the separation of Church and State when they became part of the Republic, that principle was guaranteed by the American Constitution. Many Jews sided with those who broke their ties with England and supported those who fought for independence. Haym Solomon, a Polish Jew who settled in Philadelphia and became a stockbroker, was known as the "financier of the American Revolution." At great personal sacrifice, he provided the desperately needed funds required by George Washington to maintain his army and the new government.

Some states continued to discriminate against Jews well into the nineteenth century. For example, Jews continued to be disqualified from holding public office in Maryland until 1826; in New Hampshire, it was not until 1877 that the state constitutional requirement that the governor and members of the state legislature be Protestant was stricken. Social discrimination continued long thereafter; for example, quotas for Jews at Ivy League colleges persisted well into the twentieth century. But impediments to Jewish advancement gradually disappeared and legal protections for Jews and other minorities gradually increased.

There was no large Jewish immigration in the early years of the Republic. The Jews in the country were citizens, and met with little overt discrimination; indeed, many assimilated. The majority of them were Sephardim, i.e., of Spanish ancestry. Many were descended from those Jews who had been expelled from Spain and Portugal toward the end of the fifteenth century. German Jews began coming in the third and fourth decades of the nineteenth century, many fleeing after 1848, when an attempt at revolution failed in Germany. These Jews were Ashkenazim, i.e., descended from those who had settled in the German lands in the Middle Ages. The American Jewish population, which numbered only 4,000 in 1820, grew to 50,000 in about twenty years and to 250,000 in 1880. The German Jewish immigrants who arrived during the nineteenth century were poor, hardworking people who had left everything for a new land that offered freedom to work and freedom to worship God in their own way. Whereas Jews who came earlier had settled in the East, many of these newcomers went inland, helping to settle the Midwest. Some went further, even as far as California. Many were pioneers who traded with Native Americans or provided other pioneers with supplies. Many were plucky peddlers who eventually settled and opened stores, thereby quickening the economic development of the country. A few founded establishments that grew into huge department stores (such as Macy's and Gimbel's, which for a time were the premier retail clothing stores in New York City). As these Jews found fellow religionists, they established congregations. The first synagogue in Cincinnati was founded in 1824 and a second in 1841; St. Louis' first congregation was established in 1836, Louisville's in 1824; by 1847, Chicago had one and it was not long before there were others in many towns and cities. As these pioneers prospered they remembered the less fortunate and created organizations to help new immigrants and to take care of Jewish welfare needs. They also founded hospitals, free loan societies, and fraternal orders such as B'nai B'rith.

By the time of the Civil War, Jews lived in both the South and the North, sharing the loyalties of their fellow citizens in those regions. Judah P. Benjamin was secretary of state for the Confederacy; other Jews were ardent Union supporters. One source has identified 6,000 Jews in the Union armies and 2,000 in the Confederate.[1]

The Growth of American Judaism

The post-Civil War era was a time of building many of the institutions and movements that were to serve American Jews in the years to follow. This was the era in which Reform Judaism took hold. The principal organizer of Reform Judaism was Rabbi Isaac Mayer Wise (1819–1900) who, after a stay in Albany, New York, settled in Cincinnati, Ohio. His goal of organizing all Reform congregations became a reality in 1873 when the Union of American Hebrew Congregations was formed. In 1875, the Hebrew Union College, a seminary for training rabbis, opened

---

[1] Harry L. Golden and Martin Rywell, *Jews in American History* (Charleston, NC: Martin Co., 1950), p. 159.

its doors in Cincinnati with Rabbi Wise as president. In 1889, Rabbi Wise succeeded in organizing the Central Conference of American Rabbis, the professional organization of Reform rabbis.

Forerunners of the Conservative movement opened the Jewish Theological Seminary in 1886 to train rabbis according to their principles. In 1902 the renowned scholar Solomon Schechter (1850–1915) was invited to come from England to head that seminary. He began to develop instititutions which have shaped the Conservative movement. In 1913, Schechter organized Conservative congregations into the United Synagogue of America, now known as the United Synagogue of Conservative Judaism. The alumni of the Jewish Theological Seminary organized the Rabbinical Assembly in 1901 to represent the Conservative rabbinate. In later years it accepted into membership qualified graduates of other rabbinical schools.

The Orthodox created national institutions when their numbers swelled with the large immigration of East European Jews between 1881 and 1914. Although there was no single personality who served as a central figure, and more than one rabbinical seminary, rabbinical organization, and congregational union emerged, Yeshiva University, which was established in 1886, became a prominent institution of what became known as Modern Orthodoxy. The Union of Orthodox Jewish Congregations of America (1898) followed soon thereafter, as did the professional organization of Orthodox rabbis, the Rabbinical Council of America (1923).

Following the terrible Russian pogroms of 1881 and 1882, many Jews left Eastern Europe. Although a handful went to Palestine and some went to Argentina or to Western Europe, the majority came to the United States. Until immigration to the United States was stopped during World War I, hundreds of thousands came annually. By the time they arrived, both the Sephardim and the German Jews had become fully Americanized and looked on their East European brethren as "greenhorns." Yet, with all their feelings of superiority, they helped the newcomers adjust to their new environment. In the 1880s, the Hebrew Immigrant Aid Society (HIAS) was formed to assist immigrants in getting a start in the new land. In some communities, settlement houses, the forerunner of our contemporary Jewish Community Centers, were developed. As the number of Jewish organizations grew, leaders decided to cooperate in fundraising and in serving the entire community; they created Jewish Federations wherever there was a sizable Jewish population. To help Jews overseas, the Joint Distribution Committee was established early in the twentieth century.

The Jews from Eastern Europe came from a cultural environment that was more insulated from the non-Jewish world than the earlier immigrants from Central and Western Europe. Though eager to become part of America, many held on to the Yiddish language and did not readily surrender their distinctive culture. True, some cast aside all traces of their previous lives, but many strived to retain their traditions and their way of life. Consequently, a Yiddish press and theater prospered.

As these Eastern European Jews built synagogues to perpetuate and transmit their Judaism, Orthodoxy grew and several Orthodox *yeshivot* were founded. In addition, many of the new immigrants were drawn to Conservative Judaism. They sought rabbinic leadership in graduates of the Jewish Theological Seminary to help them foster an American Judaism that was both traditional and yet responsive to the changes brought on by their own dislocation from their native lands and the pressures of modernity.

After World War II, Orthodoxy in America was strengthened by the immigration of European refugees fleeing Hitler. Leaders of several Hasidic groups (the most prominent of which are the Satmar and Lubavitch communities) managed to escape the Holocaust and settle in New York. Small numbers of other non-Hasidic Orthodox communities also managed to find a haven in America. Unlike earlier waves of immigration, these groups were not attracted by the American promise of economic opportunity nor by the appeal of American culture. They sought an environment safe from persecution, where they could transplant Eastern European traditionalist Jewish culture. Both Hasidic and non-Hasidic Orthodox *yeshivot* soon sprang up, and in the past fifty years have helped create a strong network of Orthodox institutions.

Not all Jewish immigrants to America were religious, however. Many, particularly those who came from Eastern Europe in the early years of the twentieth century, were secular, having thrown off the yoke of traditionalist religion in Eastern Europe. Many Jews went to work in factories, often suffering under depressing and inhumane conditions. Even those who were ostensibly not religious sought to understand and confront this reality by drawing on their cultural legacy. Influenced by the prophetic tradition of fighting social injustice and by the ideals of socialism, they became pioneers in trade unionism and the labor movement.

As the first generation American offspring of these immigrants entered American society, they played important roles in the general American culture as well as in the Jewish community. Some pursued the theater and became among the foremost actors, entertainers and writers of their day; some entered the academic world and became renowned scientists and scholars; some entered government service and occupied important posts; some became noted financiers or labor leaders. Within a generation, the children of the East European Jews were indeed at home in American society.

This did not happen without a struggle. The immigrants had to overcome extreme poverty and want. Those who wished to remain observant had to cope with the problem of observing *mitzvot* (Jewish religious obligations) in an inhospitable environment. They had to face great intellectual and spiritual challenges. And they had to face anti-Semitism. Although it never erupted into the pogroms and massacres that were so characteristic of its European counterpart, it was blatant at times of stress and depression. Even in times of general prosperity, such as the post-World War II era, it did not disappear from the land of opportunity and freedom.

Throughout the history of Jews in America, some elements in the community have focused upon what could be done to counter anti-Semitism and weaken its potency. Organizations were founded as early as the nineteenth century to defend the Jews, to work for laws that prohibit legalized prejudices, and to educate. Besides the national religious bodies, the most prominent among these are the American Jewish Committee, the American Jewish Congress, and the Anti-Defamation League (founded by B'nai B'rith). Each originally emphasized a different aspect of the war against bias and prejudice; today their missions overlap. All are constituted to safeguard legal liberties and combat bigotry. Other organizations, such as the National Conference (formerly National Conference of Christians and Jews), endeavor to promote fellowship. Various religious groups, Jewish and non-Jewish, such as the National Council of Synagogues and the National Conference of Catholic Bishops, foster dialogue and ecumenical understanding as well as specific programs to counter prejudice.

Leaders from various Christian groups and representatives of the Jewish community meet regularly to explore the nature of both traditions, even though there are both Jews and Christians who disapprove of such dialogues. There are Christians who insist that Christianity is the sole path to God and that it is incumbent upon those who know the truth to bring others to that path. For example, in 1997, Southern Baptist leaders appointed a director for missionary activities among Jews. Many evangelical Christian groups have long supported the work of so-called "Messianic Jewish" groups such as the "Jews for Jesus" organization, whose goal is to proselytize among Jews and convince them to accept the divinity of Jesus. This is one reason that there are Jews who distrust all theological discussions with Christians and who are convinced that such meetings are masked attempts at conversion. Most Jewish and Christian spokespersons, however, are genuinely interested in mutual understanding and in sharing values without expecting others to convert to their faith.

While many national Jewish organizations in early twentieth-century America defended Jewish interests in the United States and abroad, others, such as the various Zionist organizations, strove to gain support from non-Jews as well as from Jews for a Jewish State. Still others engaged in activities to strengthen and deepen the religious, cultural and communal interests of American Jewry.

By the end of World War II, the distinctions between Sephardim and Ashkenazim and between German and East European Jews had all but faded; all had become American Jews. They had common leaders and institutions, common interests and needs, common problems and challenges. Together they accepted the responsibility of aiding and at times rescuing oppressed Jews in many parts of the world and together they sought to improve and intensify Jewish life in this country.

The Six Day War of 1967 (discussed in Chapter 14) had a profound effect on American Jewry. The fear that Israel might suddenly be destroyed reawakened Jewish identity and solidarity. Israel's lightning victory reinvigorated American Jews and strengthened their pride in their Jewishness. Jewish philanthropy and Jewish communal institutions flourished in its wake. However, this energy and renewed pride did not necessarily carry over into a commitment to Jewish study. During the 1980s and 1990s it became clear that a bi-product of Jews having "made it" in America was increasing acculturation and assimilation into the broader American society. As reported in the 1990 National Jewish Population Study, one oft-quoted sign of this was a higher (52 percent) rate of intermarriage among Jews marrying since 1985.

The 1990 study challenged the Jewish community. The message of the study appeared to be that the Jews of America no longer had to worry about physical survival, but they did have to worry about maintaining Jewish life. In response, Jewish federations have established commissions devoted to promoting "Jewish continuity" through education and the promotion of Jewish gateway institutions such as synagogues and Jewish community centers. Philanthropic dollars previously devoted to rescuing and sustaining Jews abroad (in the former Soviet Union, Arab countries, or in Israel) have begun to be diverted to the fashioning of an educated Jewish community worthy of the heritage transmitted from the past.

There are signs that these efforts are succeeding. Most American Jews feel that Judaism can continue to flourish and thrive, even as a minority faith and culture in an increasingly multicultural America.

CHAPTER **14**

Zionism and the State of Israel

*T*HE Jews have always viewed the Land of Israel as fundamentally different from all other places on earth. First, of
course, it was their birthplace, the land where, in the words of the
Israel Declaration of Independence, "their spiritual, religious and
political identity was shaped." But it has always represented more
than that. For Jews, throughout their many centuries of dispersion, it remained the object of their dreams. The Land of Israel
was associated with their ultimate redemption, the only place
where they might one day fully experience freedom. Throughout
their history, they "never ceased to pray and hope for their return
to it and for the restoration in it of their political freedom."

There has always been a Jewish community in the Land of
Israel, though it has been small at times. Since the Roman wars
in the first and second centuries of the Common Era, substantial
numbers of Jews have lived outside of Palestine, but wherever
Jews have lived they remembered their homeland. Regardless of
the climate of the places in which they have lived, they would
pray for rain when the rainy season was due in the Land of

Israel. Three times a day their prayers would repeat: "May our eyes behold Your return to Zion" and "Rebuild Jerusalem, Your holy city." After every meal, they would voice in the Grace After Meals their yearning to return to the Holy Land. Jewish poets and philosophers throughout the ages have been eloquent in expressing their deep love for *Eretz Yisrael* (the Land of Israel).

For centuries, however, the Jews did little about returning in great numbers, and there were no large-scale back-to-Israel movements. People relied on God to answer their prayers for the speedy realization of the messianic promise.

By the second half of the nineteenth century, social and political conditions in Europe created a climate that changed this passivity to activism. Italy and Germany, swept by strong nationalist movements, became unified states. The revolutionary ideas of Darwin and other scientists spurred the intelligentsia to reject the supernatural bases of religion that had encouraged passive resignation. The increased virulence of anti-Jewish sentiment and the persecution of Jews stimulated many young men and women to initiate activities that would radically alter the status of their people.

The first movement to direct the age-old yearnings for Zion into activities that would lead Jews back to *Eretz Yisrael* came into being after the pogroms of 1881–82. This Eastern European movement, called *Ḥibbat Tziyon* (Love of Zion), did not enroll many members but it did elicit widespread support. Moreover, it succeeded in starting the modern Jewish settlement of the historic Jewish homeland. The *Ḥibbat Tziyon* movement, considered dangerous by the Russian authorities, had to carry on its activities clandestinely. Chapters were formed; speakers traveled across the Pale of Settlement to deliver speeches; articles and pamphlets aroused Jews to seek a return to Zion. The members collected funds to support the courageous ones who actually left Russia to establish colonies in the ancestral homeland. They also established and supported schools and published journals, many of which became vehicles for the new idea.

The leaders of *Ḥibbat Tziyon* not only urged the colonization of Palestine, they also pioneered the revival of Hebrew. Although the national tongue had never died out, and in fact had continued to be employed as a language of scholarly writing and discourse, it had not developed much linguistically after the Middle Ages, and had ceased to be the living language of everyday Jewish life. Eliezer Ben-Yehuda (1858–1922) pioneered the revival of Hebrew as a spoken language. After moving to Palestine from his native Odessa, he established with his family the first entirely-Hebrew speaking Zionist home and created new words by the thousands to help Hebrew become a modern, living language.

Perhaps the best representative of *Ḥibbat Tziyon* goals was Asher Ginzberg, who is better known by his nationalist pen name, Ahad Ha-Am ("One of the People") (1856–1927). Ahad Ha-Am was a master Hebrew stylist who taught that the characteristic which binds all Jews, past and present, is ethical nationalism. (As the word "nationalism" now has a political connotation which it did not necessarily convey a century ago, we might well substitute the word "peoplehood.") He did not oppose the idea of a Jewish state, but did not regard it as an immediate, or even primary objective. Unlike others who sought Jewish autonomy, Ahad Ha-Am envisioned a Jewish community reborn in *Eretz Yisrael* as a *spiritual* center which would revitalize and influence all Jews wherever they lived, no matter what the size or population of the community in Israel. Because of his emphasis on this role of a Jewish national entity and his key role in reviving Hebrew literature, Ahad Ha-Am became known as "the Father of Cultural Zionism."

An even more popular nationalist philosophy at the end of the nineteenth and beginning of the twentieth centuries was "Political Zionism." The "father" of this movement was Theodor Herzl (1860–1904), a Viennese journalist who once had advocated assimilation as the answer to the so-called "Jewish problem" (persecution and anti-Semitism). In the aftermath of the Dreyfus trial (see p. 161), it was clear that anti-Jewish sentiment was virulent in French society and that assimilation was unlikely to be successful. To provide a refuge for the Jewish nation, Herzl proposed a Jewish state, to be granted political legitimacy by the great powers of Europe. He convened the first Zionist Congress in 1897 to launch the World Zionist Organization. Herzl's charismatic personality and the grandeur of his vision attracted Jews throughout the continent and elsewhere. Whereas *Ḥibbat Tziyon* was engaged in small-scale projects and did not embrace all of Jewry, political Zionism was all-embracing and placed the Jews on the international agenda. Land was purchased, colonies were established, and the growing Jewish community in Palestine (known in Hebrew as the "*yishuv*") became the core of a state in the making.

Herzl died young, at the age of 44, in 1904. Nonetheless, the movement he created persevered. Despite setbacks, indifference and even betrayal, it finally achieved its goal with the establishment of the State of Israel in 1948.

In addition to "Cultural Zionism" and "Political Zionism," there was a third type which exerted a great impact on many of those who personally engaged in the task of rebuilding. It was called "Labor Zionism" because it insisted that the new Jewish Commonwealth had to be built by the personal labor of Jews. It called for Jews to return to the soil from which they had so long been banished by their oppressors in the Diaspora. It represented a joining of Socialism and Zionism, an insistence upon a just and equitable society in which there would be no exploiters and no exploited. Some Labor Zionists were Marxists, and others advocated the kind of equality preached by the prophets, but all believed in the importance of manual labor and a return to agriculture.

The pioneers who resolved to put their theories into practice were not trained for their task. They had not been reared on physical labor; they were not familiar with the climate and diet of *Eretz Yisrael;* they knew little of the Arabs with whom they had to interact. Nevertheless, they proceeded, embued with passion and spirit. They dried up swamps, built roads, planted and weeded and cultivated. They revived a land which had been neglected and lain barren for ages. And, as they did so, they resolutely revived the Hebrew language and created a vibrant cultural life.

The three different aspects of Zionism remained distinct before World War I, but there were those who saw them as parts of a whole and spoke of "synthetic Zionism." The man who coined that term was Dr. Chaim Weizmann, a talented scientist who was a loyal disciple of Ahad Ha-Am, a friend of Labor Zionists, and president of the World Zionist Organization in the twenties and for much of the thirties. During World War I, Weizmann succeeded in convincing the British Government of the justice of the Zionist cause as well as the benefits which would be Britain's by being its sponsor. The British committed themselves in the Balfour Declaration of November 2, 1917, which stated that "His Majesty's Government views with favour the establishment in Palestine of a national home for the Jewish People." That promise received formal, legal authorization a few years later when the League of Nations entrusted Great Britain with the Mandate over Palestine.

The Mandatory Government was faced with the very difficult problem of reconciling Zionist interests with those of growing Arab nationalism. The Arabs living in Palestine were developing their own natural identity and were beginning to resist the British, whom they saw as yet another imperialistic regime. They resisted Jewish settlement and tried to put a stop to all Jewish immigration. British officials thought that they could curb Arab extremism by a policy of appeasement. London was concerned with imperial interests and sought to maintain the loyalty of the Arab world, even at the expense of promises which had been made to the Jews. Therefore, Arab rioters were neither suppressed nor punished. Whenever the Arab leadership fomented disturbances, restrictions were imposed upon the Jews. The British severely limited Jewish immigration. The Arab argument that the Jews were acquiring too much land led to restrictions on land purchases by Jews.

The Zionist enterprise succeeded despite the vitriolics of Arab spokesmen and despite the indifferent or inimical colonial officials in Great Britain. Zionist leaders had great faith in Britain's sense of honor, in its democratic traditions, in its general philo-Semitism. They were discouraged but not despondent as a result of the increasingly anti-Zionist positions it adopted. Reluctantly, they accepted the partition of Palestine in 1922, which established Arab rule in the section of Palestine east of the Jordan River (which ultimately became the country now known as Jordan). In the 1930s and 1940s, Dr. Weizmann and his colleagues were prepared to accept various plans to divide western Palestine (the region west of the Jordan River) as they felt that having any sovereign territory was better than being subject to the whims of outsiders. The Arabs, however, repeatedly refused to accept any partition plan.

Early in the Mandatory regime, the Jews learned that they could not rely on British troops to protect them against murderers and terrorists. They therefore established their own self-defense corps, the *Haganah*. The *Haganah* was a disciplined fighting force responsible to the Jewish authorities. It refrained from terrorist acts, even from reprisals, but defended Jewish life and property from attacks. Even when the British would not permit refugees fleeing from Hitler's horrors to enter Palestine, the *Haganah* refrained from taking the offensive against Arabs or Englishmen.

Continual provocation, however, led a minority to reject the *Haganah* philosophy in favor of a more activist policy. The Revisionists, led by Vladimir Jabotinsky (1880–1940), believed that only Jewish military action could stop Arab aggression and force the British to leave. They organized into a separate military organization, known as the *Irgun*.

Despite British resistance, the Jewish community of Palestine became larger and better established between the world wars. Despite immigration quotas, all kinds of Jews did come: religious and nonreligious, capitalists and socialists, farmers and city dwellers. The cities—Jerusalem, Tel Aviv, and Haifa—expanded, and small towns developed. The *kibbutz* movement, founded in pre-World War I days by Labor Zionists, established collective agricultural settlements. Other kinds of cooperative settlements emerged too. The Hebrew language became the vernacular. The Hebrew University in Jerusalem and the Haifa Technion, which had opened their doors in the mid-twenties, expanded. Hebrew dailies and journals reflected vibrant and creative thought. The theater, art, and the Palestine Symphony Orchestra were all part of a sophisticated cultural life.

During this period, the Jews developed their own democratic structure in order to govern themselves. They formed political parties reflecting their varied ideologies, and these parties elected delegates to an Assembly of Representatives. That Assembly and its executive, the National Committee *(Vaad Leumi)* conducted all the affairs of Palestinian Jewry. The parties also elected representatives to the World Zionist Organization, thereby sharing in the decision-making policies of their colleagues who were not in *Eretz Yisrael*. The Jews were well prepared for a smooth transition from running a semi-autonomous community to a national government.

The state came into being because Great Britain could no longer continue to exercise the Mandate. British rule was unpopular on both sides. On the one hand, Arab leaders grew increasingly frustrated as they demanded far more territory than what British leaders were prepared to give. On the other hand, the British resisted Zionist efforts to create a a Jewish national home.

During the 1940s, the terrible disclosures of the Nazi atrocities made the nations of the world keenly aware of their obligations to the Jewish people. The United Nations concluded that, despite Arab resistance and unwillingness to endorse partition, partitioning Palestine was the only solution to the thorny conflict. On November 29, 1947, the United Nations approved a partition plan to take effect at the conclusion of the mandate the following May. The decision was greeted with dancing in the streets of Tel Aviv and Jerusalem and a resolve by Palestinian Arabs and the leaders of neighboring Arab states to resist the creation of a Jewish state.

In the intervening months, pressure was put on the Zionists to refrain from proclaiming a state. The leader of Palestinian Jewry, David Ben Gurion, refused to acquiesce. On the day pre-

ceding the British withdrawal (May 14, 1948), he and his colleagues met to proclaim the birth of the State of Israel. With
Arab armies poised to attack, the provisional government of the
Yishuv gathered in a Tel Aviv hotel and broadcasted the Declaration of the State of Israel to an anxious nation:

> By virtue of our natural and historic right [we] hereby declare the
> establishment of a Jewish State in Eretz-Israel to be known as the
> State of Israel.

> We offer peace and unity to all the neighboring states and their
> peoples, and invite them to cooperate with the independent Jewish
> nation for the common good of all.

> Our call goes out to the Jewish people all over the world to rally to
> our side in the task of immigration and development and to stand
> by us in the great struggle for the fulfillment of the dream of gen-
> erations—the redemption of Israel.

Ben Gurion became prime minister, head of the government. Chaim Weizmann was elected president, an office that was
mainly symbolic, and a parliament *(Knesset)* of 120 members was
created. The new democracy began to function without delay.

Immediately, immigrants began pouring into Israel by the
hundreds of thousands. No one was turned away, even though
the infant state was embroiled in a war of survival. The Arab
states, although members of the United Nations, refused to
abide by the majority decision of the U.N.'s General Assembly
and declared a war of annihilation. They were vastly superior to
the Jews numerically, yet were unable to defeat Israeli determination. In 1949, a ceasefire was declared, with Israel firmly in
control of the area accorded the Jewish state by the 1947 partition plan and additional buffer areas as well. Under pressure
from the United States and the Soviet Union, and with the
United Nations' promises to safeguard the borders, Israel withdrew from several of these areas and hoped for peace.

On the other side of the border from the infant state were
camps filled with Palestinian Arab refugees. In many cases these

refugees were not absorbed into their host countries. They remained refugees and their fate remained a major factor inhibiting a peaceful resolution of the conflict.

Many Arab leaders declared their determination to throw the Israelis into the sea. Backed by Russia, they became increasingly aggressive, threatening the very existence of Israel. Periodically, Egypt threatened to block access to the Israeli port city of Eilat. In 1956, war with Egypt broke out, with England and France joining forces with Israel. The Sinai peninsula was occupied. Following American diplomatic pressure and assurances that United Nation soldiers would patrol the border, Israel withdrew from the Sinai. Nonetheless, throughout the 1950s and 1960s, border skirmishes repeatedly took place. Tensions continued to build. Finally, in June of 1967, following the massing of five Arab armies on Israel's borders and the blocking by Egypt of the Straits of Tiran, all-out war again broke out.

It was a perilous time. Many Jews in Israel and throughout the world were convinced that the State of Israel was doomed. There was grave concern that the Arab armies would overrun Israel and destroy the nineteen-year-old nation. Unexpectedly and seemingly miraculously, Israel achieved a lightning victory. In six days, the Israel Defence Forces pushed back the Arab armies on all fronts. They reunited the Old City of Jerusalem with the New; captured the Golan Heights from which Syrians had often fired at Jewish farmers and fishermen below, and took Sharm-el-Sheikh, the Egyptian fortress that controlled free passage into the Gulf of Aqaba and hence shipping to and from the port of Eilat. On the seventh day, in a state of relief and disbelief, the army and the nation rested.

The territorial gains had been substantial: The Israeli Army now occupied the Sinai peninsula, the Gaza Strip, the Golan Heights, and the so-called "West Bank" (the area west of the Jordan River that had been occupied by Jordan since 1948). But the victory still did not bring peace. The Arab leaders continued to vow eternal hatred and revenge. Terrorists were trained to infiltrate and to kill Israeli civilians. The 1960s and 1970s saw the rise of Palestinian terrorist organizations whose members hijacked airplanes and murdered Israeli civilians with impunity. The 1972 Summer Olympic Games in Munich, Germany, were marred by the murder of over twenty Israeli athletes. Soon thereafter, on Yom Kippur, in October of 1973, Egypt and Syria attacked again. Though caught by surprise, and paying a terrible price in loss of life and in psychological insecurity, the Israelis were able to win yet another military victory.

But they were unable to make any political progress. It was hoped that peace would emerge from the new situation, but the Arab countries persisted in looking upon Israel as their implacable foe. The United Nations was unable or unwilling to impose any restraint. On the contrary, The United Nations General Assembly passed a resolution in 1975 which declared that Zionism was a form of racism.

Among Arab leaders, only President Anwar Sadat of Egypt concluded that continued warfare was destructive for everyone. In defiance of the rest of the Arab world, he courageously went to Jerusalem in 1978 to initiate a peace process. This trip, which electrified the world and instilled hope in the hearts of many people, was soon followed by a meeting at Camp David with U.S. President Jimmy Carter and Israeli Prime Minister Menachem Begin, which concluded with a peace treaty between Egypt and Israel. The three statesmen were able to overcome what had seemed insurmountable problems and to inaugurate a period of peace between the largest, most important Arab country and the State of Israel. The other Arab governments condemned Sadat, expelled Egypt from their organizations and tried to isolate it economically and politically. Sadat's assassination by Islamic extremists several years later did not add to the popularity of pursuing peace with Israel. The Arab nations and the Palestinian nationalist organizations entered the 1980s without altering their basic positions, although some of them from time to time seemed to be more conciliatory.

In the late 1980s, Palestinian resistance to Israeli control of the West Bank and Gaza erupted into violence. The Palestinian

"Intifada" (struggle) produced almost daily skirmishes between rock-throwing Arab youths and Israeli security forces. The pressure, from both within and without, for Israel to withdraw from these areas increased. The Gulf War in 1991, during which Iraqi Scud missiles fell on Israel even though it was not a party to the conflict, reinforced a discouraging sense that Israel would long be plagued by intractable military conflict. (For many, the sight of Israeli families in gas masks huddled in sealed rooms evoked long-suppressed anxieties about Jewish vulnerability.)

A breakthrough occurred in 1993. Israeli and Palestinian negotiators, who had been meeting secretly for months in Oslo, Norway, reached agreement to pursue a "peace process." Under the leadership of Prime Minister Yitzhak Rabin and Foreign Minister Shimon Peres, Israel agreed to recognize the Palestine Liberation Organization and its chairman Yasser Arafat, as legitimate representatives of the Palestinian people. The Oslo Accords marked a turning point. For the first time since 1948, Palestinian nationalist aspirations were officially recognized by the Jewish state, and the PLO, in turn, officially recognized the State of Israel. At a White House ceremony hosted by U.S. President Bill Clinton, Rabin's obviously reluctant handshake with Arafat, sealing the agreement, symbolized the challenges ahead. Rabin, Peres, and Arafat were awarded the Nobel Peace Prize for their roles in this historic process.

In the wake of this diplomatic achievement, others soon followed. A peace treaty with Jordan was signed by King Hussein and Prime Minister Rabin. Over a hundred Arab, African and Asian nations established or re-established diplomatic relations with Israel.

Not all Israelis and Palestinians supported the peace process. Within Israel there were militant right-wing and rigorously Orthodox leaders who condemned Israel's government as traitorous for pursuing peace with the Palestinians by "abandoning" the age-old Jewish hinterland of Judea and Samaria (the biblical names for the area known as the West Bank) in which so much ancient Jewish history had taken place. In protest against the peace process, the fundamentalist Muslim organization known as Hamas carried out a series of suicide attacks against Israeli civilians which terrorized the population. It was clear that building trust was not going to be easy and that the peace process would be continually challenged.

Hopes for peace were dealt a severe blow in 1995 when Prime Minister Rabin was assassinated by a young Israeli student. This was a traumatic event for Israel which sent shock waves throughout the Jewish world. The assailant, an Orthodox Jewish student at a prestigious Israeli law school, defiantly defended his behavior by referring to Jewish law. It became clear that Israel's greatest assets throughout its history—its democracy and its unity in the face of external threats—could no longer be taken for granted. Nonetheless, democracy and democratic institutions continued to function and have withstood this grave assault.

The imminent dangers threatening Israel from its very first hour could easily have led to a totalitarian regime. Such changes occurred in many other states created after World War II, states that were much less threatened than Israel. Israel, however, has remained steadfastly democratic. With the exception of the Prime Minister who is now elected by popular vote, elected officials are responsible to the electorate through their parties (similar to the British rather than the American system). Freedom of speech and freedom of the press and other basic freedoms are part of the fiber of life for Israeli citizens.

There are, however, exceptions. An old joke has it that there is freedom of religion for everyone in Israel—except for Jews. The first part of the assertion is essentially correct: non-Jews living in Israel have the freedom to practice, or to refrain from practicing, any religion, even though religion does play a role that is absent in Western democracies, for each religious group has exclusive jurisdiction over the marriages and divorces of its adherents.

As far as Jews are concerned, the situation is more complicated. As Israel is the national home of the Jewish people, Judaism is accorded primary national status. Thus, all public institutions are closed on the Sabbath and festivals, and follow the Jewish dietary laws. Many stores and businesses are closed on Saturday and there is limited public transport on that day. But the builders of the state—whether from Eastern Europe or North Africa—did not know or care much about the nineteenth century efforts in Western and Central Europe to reconceptualize Jewish belief and practice in the light of Western culture, and they knew and cared little about the American Reform and Conservative movements. There was an Orthodox political party in the World Zionist Organization from the beginning of the century and it became part of the political arrangements when the state was born. It made demands in the area of religious life in return for its political support, which was needed to form a ruling coalition. Hence, in Israel, Orthodoxy became the officially recognized expression of the Jewish religion. The Orthodox parties became part of the political establishment in Israel and had their way in matters of concern to them. In recent years, additional religious parties have arisen, which have increased the level of *k'fiyah datit* (religious coercion) in Israeli society. The Reform and Conservative movements in Israel are still small and must struggle against those who would deny them legitimacy. Most synagogues are Orthodox, but Reform and Conservative congregations are slowly developing. The latter are not mere replicas of their American sister congregations, and will undoubtedly come to represent an indigenous non-Orthodox Judaism. Non-Orthodox rabbis are not permitted to officiate at marriages or to carry out the functions that are theirs in other countries, but they and their movements are struggling for the acceptance of religious pluralism in Israel.

The development of Israel would not have been possible without outside help. Since its birth, Jews throughout the world have been deeply conscious of their responsibility to guarantee the successful survival of the state. The United Jewish Communities annually collects and distributes millions of dollars; the Israel Bond Organization sells millions of dollars worth of bonds for investments; the Jewish National Fund collects large sums for reforestation, land reclamation, and development. Thus, a partnership has existed between the Jews in Israel and their brothers and sisters elsewhere. This partnership is more than financial. Whereas the Jews of the Diaspora contribute funds, they receive great psychological, cultural, and spiritual benefits in return. All Jews benefit from the existence of the State of Israel. Instead of the image of the Jew as a poor, oppressed refugee, there is now one of a proud, free, liberty-loving people. Literature and the visual and performing arts have flourished, vastly increasing Jewish creativity. In Israel, Jewish civilization is primary. The Land of the Bible is once again the land in which Jewish history is being made, and Israel continues to imbue Jews with new purpose and new life.

As we face the twenty-first century, many questions can be asked: What does it mean to be a Zionist today? Is there anything left to Ahad Ha'am's vision? To what extent is Israel a Jewish cultural center for world Jewry? What about Herzl's vision? Is Israel the refuge it was intended to be? Has it solved the problem of Jewish insecurity? Will peace ever be achieved? On what terms? Is Israel a state like any other? If not, how is it different? What makes it Jewish?

Prospective converts to Judaism must ask an additional set of questions: What is the relationship of a Jew by choice to the State of Israel? Can one adopt a distant nation, a distant "homeland," as well as a people? To what extent will Israel remain a foreign country instead of a second home? How does one come to terms with religious intolerance in the Jewish state—intolerance which might include the failure of various authorities to recognize the validity of one's conversion to Judaism? Can one love such a country?

The fundamental challenge for the North American Jew by choice is identical to that of the Jew by birth: to develop an honest, caring relationship with the State of Israel. This challenge can be met by visiting Israel, learning its language, contributing to its welfare, and advocating on its behalf.

Afterword

*A*ccording to Jewish tradition, the Torah was given to the Jewish people at the foot of Mt. Sinai. (A medieval depiction of this event appears on the cover of this volume.) The *Mekhilta*, a rabbinic midrashic commentary to the Book of Exodus, finds this curious: Why was the Torah given in the *wilderness*? What could possibly be the significance of this tradition? After all, the Jewish people have long been strongly and firmly connected to the Land of Israel. Wouldn't that have been a more suitable place to transmit the Torah? Why was it given in the midst of the Sinai desert, that "great and terrible wilderness" (Deuteronomy 1:19)?

The answer given in the *Mekhilta* is as follows:

> The Torah was given in the wilderness because the wilderness is public, open, and free. Had it been given in the Land of Israel, the Children of Israel could have said to the nations of the world: "You have no share in it!" But because it was given in the wilderness,

which is open, public, and free for all to enter, we learn that *all who wish to receive the Torah are welcome to do so.*[1]

This book has been written in the spirit of that invitation. However, this is but an *introduction* to Judaism. The message at the conclusion of the book remains, then, the same as that of the beginning, namely, the charge that the sage Hillel gave to the prospective convert in the talmudic story quoted in the Introduction: "Go and learn!" Even though this work may have been read from cover to cover, there is much, much more learning to be accomplished. Academic learning, to be sure, but experiential learning as well.

This book has outlined the contours of Judaism. Those wondering whether to become Jewish—as well as Jews seeking to live rich, fully intentional Jewish lives—are encouraged to explore the entire terrain of Jewish experience. We hope that this book has given the reader some guideposts for the journey.

[1] *Mekhilta de-R.Ishmael, ha-Hodesh 1* (Italics mine).

Bibliography

Chapter 2: Jews by Choice

Berkowitz, Allan and Patti Moskovitz, eds. *Embracing the Covenant: Converts to Judaism Talk About Why & How.* Woodstock, VT: Jewish Lights Publishing, 1996.

Diamant, Anita. *Choosing a Jewish Life.* New York: Schocken Books, 1997.

Epstein, Lawrence. *Conversion to Judaism: A Guidebook.* Northvale, NJ: Jason Aronson, 1994.

Fink, Nan. *Stranger in the Midst: A Memoir of Spiritual Discovery.* New York: Basic Books, 1997.

Forster, Brenda and Joseph Tabachnik. *Jews By Choice: A Story of Converts to Reform and Conservative Judaism.* New York: KTAV, 1991.

Hamolka, Walter Jacob and Esther Seidel, eds. *Not by Birth Alone: Conversion to Judaism.* Herndon, VA: Cassell, 1997.

Isaacs, Ronald H. *Becoming Jewish: A Handbook for Conversion.* New York: The Rabbinical Assembly, 1993.

Kukoff, Lydia. *Chooosing Judaism.* New York: UAHC Press, 1981.

Lamm, Maurice. *Becoming a Jew.* New York: Jonathan David Publishers, 1991.

Lester, Julius. *Lovesong: Becoming a Jew.* New York: Henry Holt, 1988.

Myrowitz, Catherine Hall, ed. *Finding a Home for the Soul: Interviews with Converts to Judaism.* Northvale, NJ: Jason Aronson, 1995.

Romanoff, Lena with Lisa Hostein. *Your People, My People: Finding Acceptance and Fulfillment as a Jew by Choice.* Philadelphia: Jewish Publication Society, 1990.

Rosenbloom, Joseph R. *Conversion to Judaism: From the Biblical Period to the Present.* Cincinnati: Hebrew Union College Press, 1978.

Chapter 3: Classical Jewish Sources

Adler, Morris. *The World of the Talmud.* New York: Schocken Books, 1958.

Bialik, Hayim Nahman and Yehoshua Hana Ravnitzky. *The Book of Legends: Sefer Ha-Aggadah.* New York: Schocken Books, 1992.

Ginzberg, Louis. *Legends of the Jews* (reprint edition, volumes 1–7). Baltimore: Johns Hopkins University Press, 1998.

Holtz, Barry W., ed. *Back to the Sources: Reading the Classical Jewish Texts.* New York: Summit Books, 1984.

Holtz, Barry W. *The Schocken Guide to Jewish Books: Where to Start Reading About Jewish History, Literature, Culture and Religion.* New York: Schocken Books, 1992.

Katz, Michael and Gershon Schwartz. *Swimming in the Sea of Talmud.* Philadelphia: Jewish Publication Society, 1998.

Kravitz, Leonard and Kerry Olitzky, eds. *Pirke Avot: A Modern Commentary on Jewish Ethics.* New York: UAHC Press, 1998.

Leibowitz, Nehama. *Studies in Bereshit (1981); Studies in Shemot (1981); Studies in Vayikra (1980); Studies in Bamidbar (1980); Studies in Devarim (1980).* Jerusalem: World Zionist Organization.

Matt, Daniel Chanan, ed. *The Essential Kabbalah: The Heart of Jewish Mysticism.* San Francisco: HarperSanFrancisco, 1996.

Millgram, Abraham E., ed. *An Anthology of Medieval Hebrew Literature.* London and New York: Abelard-Schuman, 1962.

Neusner, Jacob, ed. *The Mishnah: A New Translation.* New Haven: Yale University Press, 1988.

Neusner, Jacob. *Invitation to the Talmud: A Teaching Book.* San Francisco: Harper and Row, 1973.

Porton, Gary G. *Understanding Rabbinic Midrash: Text and Commentary.* Hoboken, NJ: KTAV, 1985.

Sarna, Nahum N., ed. *The JPS Torah Commentary* (volumes 1–5). Philadelphia: Jewish Publication Society, 1989–1996.

Stein, David E. Sulomm, ed. *The Hebrew-English TANAKH.* Philadelphia: Jewish Publication Society, 1999.

Steinsaltz, Adin. *The Essential Talmud.* New York: Basic Books, 1976.

Steinsaltz, Adin. *The Talmud: The Steinsaltz Edition.* New York: Random House, 1989– (ongoing publication; new volumes appear regularly).

Telushkin, Joseph. *Jewish Literacy: The Most Important Things to Know About the Jewish Religion, Its People and Its History.* New York: William Morrow, 1991.

Chapter 4: Religious Movements

Borowitz, Eugene. *Choices in Modern Jewish Thought: A Partisan Guide.* West Orange, NJ: Behrman House, 1983.

Borowitz, Eugene. *Explaining Reform Judaism.* West Orange, NJ: Behrman House, 1985.

Dorff, Elliot N. *Conservative Judaism: From Our Ancestors to Our Descendents.* New York: The United Synagogue, 1997.

Eisenstein, Ira. *Varieties of Religious Belief.* New York: Reconstructionst Press, 1966.

Gillman, Neil. *Conservative Judaism: The New Century.* New York: Behrman House, 1993.

Goldsmith, Emanuel S., ed. *Dynamic Judaism: The Essential Writings of Mordecai Kaplan.* New York: Schocken Books and Reconstructionist Press, 1985.

Gordis, Robert, ed. *Emet Ve-Emunah: Statement of Principles of Conservative Judaism.* New York: The United Synagogue, 1988.

Greenberg, Blu. *On Women and Judaism: A View from Tradition.* Philadelphia: Jewish Publication Society, 1981.

Hartman, David. *A Living Covenant.* New York: The Free Press, 1987.

Hartman, David. *A Heart of Many Rooms: Celebrating the Many Voices within Judaism.* Woodstock, VT: Jewish Lights Publishing, 1999.

Kaplan, Mordecai M. *Questions Jews Ask.* New York: Reconstructionist Press, 1966.

Kaufman, William. *Contemporary Jewish Philosophers.* New York: Reconstructionist Press and Behrman House, 1976.

Lamm, Norman. *Torah Umadda: The Encounter of Religious Learning and Wordly Knowledge in the Jewish Tradition.* Northvale, NJ: Jason Aronson, 1990.

Meyer, Michael A. *Response to Modernity: A History of the Reform Movement in Judaism.* New York: Oxford University Press, 1988.

Rosenthal, Gilbert. *Four Paths to One God.* New York: Bloch Publishing Company, 1973.

Schorsch, Ismar. *The Sacred Cluster: The Core Values of Conservative Judaism.* New York: The Jewish Theological Seminary, 1995.

Soloveitchik, Joseph B. *Halakhic Man.* Philadelphia: Jewish Publication Society, 1983.

Staub, Jacob J. and Rebecca T. Alpert. *Exploring Judaism: A Reconstructionist Approach.* New York: The Reconstructionist Press, 1985.

Wertheimer, Jack. *A Divided People: Judaism in Contemporary America.* New York: Basic Books, 1993.

Chapter 5: What Does Judaism Teach?

Ariel, David S. *Spiritual Judaism.* New York: Hyperion, 1998.

Borowitz, Eugene. *Renewing the Covenant: A Theology for the Postmodern Jew.* Philadelphia: Jewish Publication Society, 1991.

Cohen, Arthur Allen and Paul R. Mendes-Flohr. *Contemporary Jewish Religious Thought: Original Essays on Critical Concepts, Movements, and Beliefs.* New York: The Free Press, 1988.

Dorff, Elliot N. *Knowing God: Jewish Journeys to the Unknowable.* Northvale, NJ: Jason Aronson, 1996.

Editors of *Commentary Magazine,* compilers. *The Condition of Jewish Belief: A Symposium.* Northvale, NJ: Jason Aronson, 1995.

Feld, Edward. *The Spirit of Renewal: Finding Faith After the Holocaust.* Woodstock, VT: Jewish Lights Publishing, 1995.

Gillman, Neil. *The Death of Death: Resurrection and Immortality in Jewish Thought.* Woodstock, VT: Jewish Lights Publishing, 1997.

Gillman, Neil. *Sacred Fragments: Recovering Theology for the Modern Jew.* Philadelphia: Jewish Publication Society, 1990.

Gordis, Daniel. *God Was Not in the Fire: The Search for a Spiritual Judaism.* New York: Touchstone Books, 1997.

Green, Arthur. *Seek My Face, Speak My Name: A Contemporary Jewish*

Theology. Northvale, NJ: Jason Aronson, 1994.

Green, Arthur. *These are the Words: A Vocabulary of Jewish Spiritual Life.* Woodstock, VT: Jewish Lights Publishing, 1999.

Herberg, Will. *Judaism and Modern Man: An Interpretation of Jewish Religion.* Woodstock, VT: Jewish Lights Publishing, 1997.

Heschel, Abraham Joshua. *God in Search of Man.* New York: Noonday, 1997.

Jacobs, Louis. *The Book of Jewish Belief.* West Orange, NJ: Behrman House, 1984.

Jacobs, Louis. *The Jewish Religion: A Companion.* New York: Oxford University Press, 1995.

Jacobs, Louis. *We Have Reason to Believe: Some Aspects of Jewish Theology Examined in the Light of Modern Thought.* Portland, OR: Vallentine Mitchell, 1995.

Kertzer, Morris M. *What is a Jew?* New York: Touchstone Books, 1993.

Kugel, James. *On Being A Jew.* Baltimore and London: Johns Hopkins University Press, 1990.

Kushner. Harold S. *To Life: A Celebration of Jewish Being and Thinking.* New York: Warner Books, 1994.

Rubenstein, Richard. *After Auschwitz.* Baltimore: Johns Hopkins University Press, 1992.

Schulweis, Harold. *For Those Who Can't Believe: Overcoming the Obstacles to Faith.* New York: HarperCollins, 1994.

Sonsino, Rifat and Daniel Syme. *Finding God: Ten Jewish Responses.* New York: UAHC Press, 1986.

Steinberg, Milton. *As a Driven Leaf.* West Orange, NJ: Behrman House, 1996.

Steinberg, Milton. *Basic Judaism.* New York: Harcourt Brace, 1986.

Wolpe, David. *Why Be Jewish?* New York: Henry Holt, 1995.

Wouk, Herman. *This is My God: The Jewish Way of Life.* Boston: Little Brown & Co., 1992.

Chapter 6: A Way of Living

Artson, Bradley Shavit. *It's A Mitzvah!: Step-by-Step to Jewish Living.* West Orange, NJ and New York: Behrman House and The Rabbinical Assembly, 1995.

Diamant, Anita and Howard Cooper. *Living a Jewish Life: Jewish Tradi-*

tions, Customs, and Values for Today's Families. New York: Harper-Collins, 1996.

Dosick, Wayne D. *Living Judaism: The Complete Guide to Jewish Belief, Tradition and Practice.* San Francisco: HarperSanFrancisco, 1995.

Dresner, Samuel, Seymour Siegel and David Pollack. *The Jewish Dietary Laws.* New York: The Rabbinical Assembly and the United Synagogue Commission on Jewish Education, 1982.

Dorff, Elliot N. *Matters of Life and Death: A Jewish Approach to Modern Medical Ethics.* Philadelphia: Jewish Publication Society, 1998.

Dresner, Samuel. *The Sabbath.* New York: Burning Bush Press, 1970.

Greenberg, Blu. *How to Run a Traditional Jewish Household.* New York: Simon & Schuster, 1983.

Heschel, Abraham Joshua. *The Sabbath: Its Meaning for Modern Man.* New York: Farrar, Straus & Giroux, 1995.

Holtz, Barry. *Finding Our Way: Jewish Texts and the Lives We Live Today.* New York: Schocken Books, 1990.

Jacobs, Louis. *The Book of Jewish Practice.* West Orange, NJ: Behrman House, 1987.

Klein, Isaac. *A Guide to Jewish Religious Practice.* New York: The Jewish Theological Seminary, 1979.

Lebeau, James M. *The Jewish Dietary Laws: Sanctify Life.* New York: The United Synagogue, 1983.

Peli, Pinhas. *Shabbat Shalom: A Renewed Encounter with the Sabbath.* Washington, DC: B'nai B'rith Books, 1988.

Sandberg, Martin I. *Tefillin: And You Shall Bind Them.* New York: The United Synagogue, 1993.

Strassfeld, Michael and Sharon Strassfeld, eds. *The Jewish Catalogs.* Philadelphia: Jewish Publication Society, 1973, 1976, 1980.

Trepp, Leo. *The Complete Book of Jewish Observance.* New York: Behrman House/Summit Books, 1980.

Wolfson, Ron. *The Art of Jewish Living: The Shabbat Seder.* New York: Federation of Jewish Men's Clubs and the University of Judaism, 1985.

Chapter 7: An Introduction to Jewish Worship

Buxbaum, Yitz. *Real Davvening: Jewish Prayer as a Spiritual Practice and a Form of Meditation for Beginning and Experienced Davveners.* Flushing, NY: Jewish Spirit Publishing, 1996.

Donin, Haim Halevy. *To Pray as a Jew.* New York: Basic Books, 1980.

Elbogen, Ismar. *Jewish Liturgy: A Comprehensive History.* Philadelphia: Jewish Publication Society, 1993.

Grishaver, Joel Lurie. *And You Shall Be a Blessing: An Unfolding of the Six Words That Begin Every Brakhah.* Northvale, NJ: Jason Aronson, 1993.

Hammer, Reuven. *Entering Jewish Prayer: A Guide to Personal Devotion and the Worship Service.* New York: Schocken Books, 1994.

Heschel, Abraham Joshua. *Quest for God.* New York: Crossroads, 1990.

Hoffman, Lawrence A., ed. *The Sh'ma and Its Blessings.* Woodstock, VT: Jewish Lights Publishing, 1997.

Millgram, Abraham. *Jewish Worship: A Comprehensive History.* Philadelphia: Jewish Publication Society, 1973.

Petuchowski, Jacob, ed. *Understanding Jewish Prayer.* New York: KTAV, 1972.

Rosenberg, Arnold S. *Jewish Liturgy As a Spiritual System: A Prayer-By-Prayer Explanation of the Nature and Meaning of Jewish Worship.* Northvale, NJ: Jason Aronson, 1997.

Chapter 8: Congregations, Synagogues, and Ḥavurot

Eisen, Arnold. *Taking Hold of Torah: Jewish Commitment and Community in America.* Bloomington, IN: Indiana University Press, 1997.

Grossman, Susan and Rivka Haut, eds. *Daughters of the King: Women and the Synagogue.* Philadelphia: Jewish Publication Society, 1992.

Wagner, Jordan Lee. *The Synagogue Survival Kit.* Northvale, NJ: Jason Aronson, 1997.

Wertheimer, Jack, ed. *The American Synagogue: A Sanctuary Transformed.* New York: Cambridge University Press, 1987.

Chapter 9: Holy Days and Festivals

Agnon, S. Y., ed. *Days of Awe: A Treasury of Jewish Wisdom for Reflection, Repentence, and Renewal on the High Holy Days.* New York: Schocken Books, 1995.

Goodman, Philip. *JPS Holiday Anthologies* (7 volumes). Philadelphia: Jewish Publication Society, 1974–1976.

Greenberg, Irving. *The Jewish Way: Living the Holidays.* New York: Summit Books, 1988.

Reimer, Gail Twersky and Judith A. Kates, eds. *Beginning Anew: A Woman's Companion to the High Holy Days*. New York: Simon & Schuster, 1997.

Steingroot, Ira. *Keeping Passover*. San Francisco: HarperSanFrancisco, 1995.

Strassfeld, Michael. *The Jewish Holidays*. New York: Harper & Row, 1985.

Trepp, Leo. *The Complete Book of Jewish Observance*. New York: Behrman House/Summit Books, 1980.

Waskow, Arthur. *Seasons of Our Joy: A Modern Guide to the Jewish Holidays*. New York: Beacon Press, 1991.

Chapter 10: The Jewish Life Cycle

Diamant, Anita, *The New Jewish Baby Book*. Woodstock, VT: Jewish Lights Publishing, 1993.

Diamant, Anita. *The New Jewish Wedding*. New York: Summit Books, 1985.

Geffen, Rela M., ed. *Celebration and Renewal: Rites of Passage in Judaism*. Philadelphia: Jewish Publication Society, 1993.

Goodman, Philip and Hanna Goodman, eds. *The Jewish Marriage Anthology*. Philadelphia: Jewish Publication Society, 1968.

Isaacs, Ronald H. *Rites of Passage: A Guide to the Jewish Life Cycle*. Hoboken, NJ: KTAV, 1992.

Lamm, Maurice. *The Jewish Way in Love and Marriage*. New York: Harper & Row, 1980.

Lamm. Maurice. *The Jewish Way in Death and Mourning*. New York: Jonathan David Publishers, 1969.

Neusner, Jacob. *The Enchantments of Judaism: Rites of Transformation from Birth through Death*. New York: Basic Books, 1987.

Orenstein, Debra, ed. *Lifecycles: Jewish Women on Life Passages and Personal Milestones,* Vol. 1, Woodstock, VT: Jewish Lights Publishing, 1994.

Salkin, Jeffrey. *Putting God on the Guest List: How to Reclaim the Spiritual Meaning of Your Child's Bar or Bat Mitzvah*. Woodstock, VT: Jewish Lights Publishing, 1996.

Sonsino, Rifat and Daniel B. Syme. *What Happens After I Die?: Jewish Views of Life After Death*. New York: UAHC Press, 1990.

Wolfson, Ron. *A Time to Mourn, A Time to Comfort.* Woodstock, VT: Jewish Lights Publishing, 1993.

Chapter 11: History: Ancient and Medieval

Barnavi, Eli, ed. *A Historical Atlas of the Jewish People: From the Time of the Patriarchs to the Present.* New York: Schocken Books, 1995.

Baron, Salo. *Great Ages and Ideas of the Jewish People.* New York: Random House, 1956.

Bayme, Steven. *Understanding Jewish History: Texts and Commentaries.* New York: KTAV, 1997.

Ben-Sasson, H.H. *A History of the Jewish People.* Cambridge, MA: Harvard University Press, 1976.

deLange, Nicholas. *The Illustrated History of the Jewish People.* Toronto: Key Porter Books, 1997.

Eban, Abba. *My People.* New York: Behrman House and Random House, 1968.

Heschel, Abraham Joshua. *The Prophets.* New York: Harper & Row, 1962.

Johnson, Paul. *A History of the Jews.* New York: Harper & Row, 1987.

Katz, Jacob. *Tradition and Crisis: Jewish Society at the End of the Middle Ages.* New York: New York University Press, 1993.

Potok, Chaim. *Wanderings.* Philadelphia: Jewish Publication Society, 1978.

Robert Chazen. *In the Year 1096.* Philadelphia: Jewish Publication Society, 1996.

Scheindlin, Raymond P. *A Short History of the Jewish People: From Legendary Times to Modern Statehood.* New York: Macmillan, 1998.

Seltzer, Robert. *Jewish People, Jewish Thought.* New York: Macmillan, 1980.

Yerushalmi, Yosef Hayim. *Zakhor: Jewish History and Jewish Memory.* Seattle: University of Washington Press, 1982.

Chapter 12: History: Modern Times

Baron, Salo. *Great Ages and Ideas of the Jewish People.* New York: Random House, 1956.

Chazen, Robert and Marc Lee Raphael. *Modern Jewish History: A Source Reader.* New York: Schocken Books, 1974.

Dawidowicz, Lucy S. *The War Against the Jews*. Ardmore, PA: Seth Press, 1986.

Dawidowicz, Lucy, ed. *The Golden Tradition: Jewish Life and Thought in Eastern Europe*. New York: Holt, Rinehart and Winston, 1967.

Gubbay, Lucien and Abraham Levy. *The Sephardim: Their Glorious Tradition from the Babylonian Exile to the Present Day*. Philadelphia: Jewish Publication Society, 1992.

Heschel, Abraham Joshua. *The Earth is the Lord's: The Inner World of the Jew in Eastern Europe*. Woodstock, VT: Jewish Lights Publishing, 1995.

Hilberg, Raul. *The Destruction of the European Jews* (3 volumes). New York and London: Holmes and Meier, 1985.

Mendes-Flohr, Paul and Jehuda Reinharz. *The Jew in the Modern World: A Documentary History*. Oxford University Press, 1995.

Sachar, Howard M. *The Course of Modern Jewish History*. Cleveland and New York: Vintage Books, 1990.

Schorsch, Ismar. *From Text to Context: The Turn to History in Modern Judaism*. Waltham, MA: Brandeis University Press, 1994.

Chapter 13: American Jewish History

Farber, Roberta Rosenberg and Chaim Isaac Waxman, eds. *The Jews in America: A Contemporary Reader*. Waltham, MA: University Press of New England, 1999.

Feingold, Henry L., ed. *The Jewish People in America* (5 volumes). Baltimore: Johns Hopkins University Press, 1992.

Glazer, Nathan. *American Judaism*. Chicago: University of Chicago Press, 1989.

Gordis, Daniel. *Does the World Need the Jews?: Rethinking Chosenness and American Jewish Identity*. New York: Scribner's, 1997.

Hertzberg, Arthur. *The Jews in America: Four Centuries of an Uneasy Encounter*. New York: Columbia University Press, 1998.

Hertzberg, Arthur and Aron Hirt-Manheimer. *Jews: The Essence and Character of a People*. San Francisco: HarperSanFrancisco, 1998.

Howe, Irving. *World of Our Fathers*. New York and London: Harcourt Brace Jovanovich, 1976.

Hyman, Paula and Deborah Dash Moore, eds. *Jewish Women in America: An Historical Encyclopedia*. New York: Routledge, 1997.

Karp, Abraham. *Haven and Home: A History of the Jews in America*. New York: Schocken Books, 1985.

Sachar, Howard M. *A History of the Jews in America*. New York: Vintage Books, 1993.

Sarna, Jonathan D., ed. *The American Jewish Experience*. New York: Holmes & Meier, 1997.

Sklare, Marshall. *The Jewish Community in America*. New York: Behrman House, 1974.

Wertheimer, Jack. *A Divided People: Judaism in Contemporary America*. New York: Basic Books, 1993.

Chapter 14: Zionism and the State of Israel

Avnieri, Shlomo. *The Making of Modern Zionism: The Intellectual Origins of the Jewish State*. London: Weidenfeld & Nicolson, 1981.

Eban, Abba. *My Country: The Story of Modern Israel*. New York: Random House, 1972.

Elon, Amos. *The Israelis: Founders and Sons*. New York: Bantam, 1971.

Hertzberg, Arthur, ed. *The Zionist Idea: A Historical Analysis and Reader*. Philadelphia: Jewish Publication Society, 1997.

Heschel, Abraham Joshua. *Israel: An Echo of Eternity*. Woodstock,VT: Jewish Lights Publishing, 1997.

Horovitz, David and The Jerusalem Report staff. *Shalom, Friend: The Life and Legacy Yitzhak Rabin*. New York: New Market Press, 1996.

Laquer, Walter. *A History of Zionism*. New York: Schocken Books, 1989.

Ravitzky, Aviezer. *Messianism, Zionism, and Jewish Religious Radicalism*. Chicago: University of Chicago Press, 1996.

Sachar, Howard M. *A History of Israel from the Rise of Zionism to Our Time*. New York: Alfred A. Knopf, 1979.

Glossary

Adon Olam: lit. "Lord of Eternity"; liturgical hymn attributed to Solomon ibn Gabirol.

aggadah: lit. "legend or lore"; type of rabbinic literature.

Adonai: lit. "My Lord"; the Hebrew word used to refer to God.

Aleinu: lit. "It is our duty"; liturgical hymn.

aliyah (aliyot): lit. "ascent"; synagogue honor; emigration to Israel.

am: a people; as in *am Yisrael* (the Jewish people).

Amidah: lit. "standing"; the silent devotional prayer (see *Sh'moneh Esreh*).

Arba'a Turim: lit. "four rows"; code of Jewish law written by Jacob ben Asher (c. 1475).

aron ha-kodesh: ark in synagogue that contains Torah scrolls.

Arvit: see *Ma'ariv.*

Ashamnu: congregational confession recited during Yom Kippur services.

Ashkenaz: Medieval Hebrew name for Northern and Central Europe.

Ashkenazim (sing. Ashkenazi): Jews who trace their ancestry to Ashkenaz.

Ashrei: lit. "happy are they"; daily liturgical hymn.

atzei ḥayim (etz ḥayim): lit. "trees of life"; wooden staves holding Torah scroll.

avodah: lit. "worship"; passage in the *Amidah* prayer; portion of the Yom Kippur liturgy.

avot: lit. "fathers"; ancestors.

b'tzelem Elohim: lit. "in God's image."

ba'al korei: Torah reader.

bar mitzvah: a boy attains religious majority and is obligated to fulfill the *mitzvot.*

bar'khu: the formal call to prayer.

baraitot: early rabbinic teachings not found in the *Mishnah.*

bat mitzvah: a girl attains religious majority and is obligated to fulfill the *mitzvot.*

beit k'nesset: lit. "house of assembly"; synagogue.

beit midrash: lit. "house of study"; place devoted to Jewish study.

beit tefillah: lit. " house of worship."

Bene Israel: lit. "Children of Israel"; Jews of India.

berakhah (berakhot): blessing.

Bereshit Rabbah: rabbinic midrashic commentary on the Book of Genesis.

Beta Yisrael: lit. "House of Israel"; Ethiopian Jews.

besamim: spices used in *havdalah* ceremony.

bet din (batei din): Jewish legal tribunal.

bimah: lit. "raised platform."

birkat ha-mazon: blessings recited after a meal.

birkhot ha-shaḥar: lit. "morning blessings"; introductory portion of the morning service.

brit milah: covenantal ritual circumcision.

d'var Torah: discourse on the Torah portion.

Da Lifnei Mi Atah Omed: lit. "Know before Whom you stand."

daven: pray.

dreidl: spinning top associated with Ḥanukkah.

Eikhah: Book of Lamentations.

Ein Keloheinu: liturgical poem proclaiming God's uniqueness.

El Malei Raḥamim: Jewish memorial prayer.

erev: lit. "eve of" as in *"erev* Shabbat," the evening before the Sabbath day.

Eretz Yisrael: Land of Israel.

erusin: Jewish betrothal ceremony.

eruv: a halakhically-defined boundary within which carrying is permitted on Shabbat.

etrog: a citron ritually used on Sukkot; see *lulav.*

Etz Ḥayim Hi: lit. "it is a tree of life"; liturgical passage sung when Torah is returned to the ark.

Even Ha-Ezer: a section of the *Tur,* written by Rabbi Jacob ben Asher; also a section of the *Shulḥan Arukh.*

fleishig: food that contains meat or meat derivatives.

ga'al yisrael: lit. "Who has redeemed Israel"; name of blessing following recitation of *Shema.*

gaon (geonim): rabbinic leader following the talmudic age.

gefilte fish: chopped fish, served cold with horseradish.

Gehinnom: Gehenna.

Gemara: the explanation and expatiation of the *Mishnah;* see Talmud.

ger (gerim): lit. "stranger"; a convert to Judaism.

get: bill of divorce.

ge'ulah: redemption.

gevurot: lit. "powers"; second blessing of the *Amidah.*

goyim: lit. "nations"; offensive term used for gentiles.

grogger: noisemaker used on Purim.

ha-gollel: person who dresses the Torah after it is read.

ha-olam ha-ba: "the world to come."

ha-olam ha-zeh: "this world."

ha-motzi: blessing recited before eating bread.

ha-tefillah: lit. "the prayer"; *Amidah.*

haftarah: Prophetic passage recited after the Torah reading on Shabbat and festivals.

Haganah: Jewish self-defense militia in pre-State Palestine.

haggadah: lit. "the telling"; text containing the narrative of the Exodus from Egypt, read at the Pesaḥ *seder.*

halakhah: lit. "the way"; Jewish law.

ḥallah (ḥallot): braided loaf of bread eaten on Shabbat and holidays.

Hallel: collection of psalms of praise sung on festivals and holy days.

ha-magbiah: person who lifts the Torah scroll after it is read.

hamantaschen: lit. "Haman's hats"; triangle-shaped tarts served on Purim.

ḥametz: leavened food forbidden on Pesaḥ.

Ḥanukkah: lit. "dedication"; holiday celebrating rededication of the Temple.

ḥanukkiah: Nine-branched candlelabrum lit on the festival of Ḥanukkah.

ḥaredim: lit. "trembling"; rigorously Orthodox Jews.

Hashkiveinu: blessing following the evening *Shema.*

ḥasid: lit. "pious one"; sometimes refers to follower of East European Hasidic movement.

hatafat dam brit: covenantal symbolic circumcision for males previously circumcised.

havdalah: lit. "separation"; ceremony performed at the close of the Shabbat.

ḥavurah (ḥavurot): Jewish fellowship circle or informal community.

ḥazzan: cantor.

hekhsher: rabbinical certification of food products.

ḥesed: lovingkindness.

ḥesed shel emet: lit. "true lovingkindness."

ḥevrah kadishah: lit. "holy society"; Jewish communal burial society.

Ḥibbat Tziyon: lit. "Love of Zion"; early East European Zionist movement.

Hodayah: lit. "grateful acknowledgment"; one of the blessings in the *Amidah.*

ḥol ha-moed: intermediate days of Pesaḥ and Sukkot.

Hoshanot: ceremonial processionals during the festival of Sukkot.

Ḥoshen Mishpat: section of the *Tur,* written by Rabbi Jacob ben Asher; also a section of the *Shulḥan Arukh.*

ḥuppah: wedding canopy.

Irgun: a Jewish underground military organization in pre-State Palestine.

k'fiyah datit: religious coercion.

Kabbalah: Jewish mystical tradition.

Kabbalat Shabbat: lit. "welcoming Shabbat"; introductory service recited on *erev* Shabbat.

Kaddish: lit. "holy"; publicly recited prayer in praise of God.

kadosh: holy.

kahal kadosh: lit. "holy congregation"; Hebrew term for synagogue community.

kashrut: Jewish dietary practices.

Kedushah: lit. "holiness"; third blessing of the *Amidah.*

kehillah: Jewish community.

keriah: lit. "tearing"; mourning ritual in which an article of clothing is torn as a sign of grief.

kesil: fool.

ketubah: marriage contract.

kibbutz: Jewish collective settlement in Israel.

kiddush: lit. "sanctification"; prayer chanted over wine on Shabbat and holidays.

kiddushin: lit. "sanctification"; refers to a section of the Jewish wedding ceremony.

kinot: sorrowful liturgical poems read on Tisha B'Av.

kippah (kippot): Jewish skullcap.

knaidlakh: matzah balls.

Knesset: Israeli parliament.

Kohelet: Book of Ecclesiastes.

kohen: descendant of *kohanim,* ancient Jewish priestly caste.

Kol Nidrei: lit. "all vows"; solemn prayer commencing the service on the eve of Yom Kippur.

k'riat Shema: recitation of the *Shema*.

kvater (kvaterin): godparent.

latkes: fried potato pancakes served on Ḥanukkah.

l'tzaref et ha-briyot. lit: "to refine the human being" (given as a reason for the practice of *mitzvot*).

Lag B'Omer: thirty-third day of the *Omer;* a celebratory day between Pesaḥ and Shavuot.

Lekha Dodi: liturgical poem welcoming Shabbat, written by Shlomo ha-Levi Alkabez.

levi: descendant of *levi'im;* ancient Jewish priestly tribe.

lulav (lulavim): a cluster of palm, myrtle, and willow branches used on Sukkot.

Maariv (Arvit): evening worship service.

maftir: the concluding *aliyah* on Shabbat.

Maḥzor (maḥzorim): prayerbook for Rosh Hashanah and Yom Kippur.

maskil: intelligent and understanding.

Maskilim: lit. "enlightened ones"; Jewish proponents of Enlightenment in Eastern Europe.

matzah (matzot): unleavened bread eaten on Pesaḥ.

mazal tov: lit. "good fortune"; congratulatory expression.

megillah: lit. "scroll"; refers to the Book of Esther.

Mekhilta: rabbinic midrashic commentary on the Book of Exodus.

menorah: Nine-branched candelabrum used for Ḥanukkah (see *ḥanukkiah*); also refers to seven-branched candlelabrum.

mezuzah: lit. "doorpost"; refers to the case containing parchment inscribed with certain biblical verses, affixed to doorways in Jewish homes.

midrash (midrashim): legal or literary explication of a biblical text.

Mikra'ot G'dolot: classic edition of the Bible with Rashi's and other medieval commentaries.

mikveh (mikva'ot): pool or gathering of waters; used for ritual immersion.

milkhig: food that contains milk or dairy products.

Minḥah: lit. "gift"; afternoon worship service.

minyan: lit. "count"; quorum of ten traditionally required for public worship.

mishloaḥ manot: small packages of sweets distributed on Purim.

mishnah (mishnayot): lit. "teaching"; a passage offered by an early rabbinic sage.

Mishnah: Code of Jewish law compiled by Rabbi Yehuda ha-Nasi (c. 200).

Mishneh Torah: comprehensive legal code written by Maimonides (c. 1180).

Mitnagdim: opponents of the Hasidim in Eastern Europe.

mitzvot: commandments, religious practices.

mohel, mohelet (f): person who performs covenantal circumcisions.

Mashiaḥ ben David: anointed descendent of King David.

Musaf: Shabbat and festival additional service.

Neilah: lit. "closing"; concluding service on Yom Kippur.

ner tamid: lit. "eternal light"; a lamp generally found in synagogues in front of the ark.

nesuin: a portion of the Jewish marriage ceremony.

niḥum aveilim: the *mitzvah* of comforting mourners.

omer: lit. "sheaf"; the forty-nine days between Pesaḥ and Shavuot.

oneg: lit. "enjoyment"; informal social gatherings on Shabbat.

Oraḥ Ḥayim: lit. "way of life"; section of the *Tur,* written by Rabbi Jacob ben Asher; also a section of the *Shulḥan Arukh.*

parashah: weekly portion of the Torah.

pareve: food that is neither meat nor dairy.

parokhet: curtain before the Torah scrolls in the ark.

Pesaḥ: Passover.

pidyon haben: symbolic redemption of the firstborn son.

Pirkei Avot: tractate of the *Mishnah* containing ethical aphorims; referred to as Chapters or Ethics of the Fathers.

piyut (piyyutim): medieval liturgical hymn.

P'sikta Rabbati: midrashic collection containing sermons for different occasions of the year.

P'sukei D'zimra: a preliminary morning service.

rimmonim: lit. "pomegranates"; silver ornamental covers for Torah scroll handles.

Rosh Hashanah: lit. "head of the year"; Day of Judgment, the Jewish New Year.

Rosh Ḥodesh: the day on which a new moon is noted; refers to the semiholiday at the beginning of each Jewish month.

sandek: person who holds the baby boy during the *brit milah.*

seder: lit. "order"; Pesaḥ festive gathering at which the story of the Exodus from Egypt is retold.

Sepharad: medieval Hebrew name for the Iberian peninsula.

Sephardim (sing. Sephardi): Jews who trace their ancestry to Sepharad.

sefer Torah: Torah scroll.

Sefer Yetzirah: medieval Kabbalistic text.

Seliḥot: petitionary prayers.

seudah shlishit: the late afternoon "third meal" on Shabbat.

Shabbat shalom: lit. "a Sabbath of peace"; Shabbat greeting.

Shaddai: biblical name of God. Acronym for *Shomer D'latot Yisrael,* "guardian of the doorways of Israel."

Shaharit: morning worship service.

shalom: peace, well-being.

shalom bayit: family harmony.

shamash: lit. "servant"; candle used to light the other candles on the *ḥanukkiah.*

shavua tov: lit. "good week"; traditional greeting following *havdalah.*

Shavuot: lit. "weeks"; the pilgrimage festival occuring seven weeks after Pesaḥ.

she-heḥeyanu: lit. "Who has kept us in life . . . "; refers to the blessing said upon experiencing something new.

Shema: basic Jewish declaration consisting of three biblical passages; also refers to the first line of this declaration, beginning with the word "*shema.*"

Shemini Atzeret: "eighth day of assembly"; festival at end of Sukkot.

sheva berakhot: seven celebratory blessings recited at a Jewish wedding ceremony.

shiksa: derogatory term referring to a non-Jewish female.

shivah: seven-day period of mourning.

Shiviti Adonai l'negdi tamid: "I set Adonai before me always" (Psalm 16:8).

shloshim: lit. "thirty"; thirty-day period of mourning following burial.

Sh'moneh Esreh: lit. "eighteen"; see *Amidah*.

shmirah: the *mitzvah* of guarding a body between death and burial.

Shoah: refers to the Holocaust.

shofar: ram's horn sounded during the High Holy Day season.

Shoftim: "Judges"; Israelite tribal leaders prior to the establishment of the monarchy.

shohet: certified ritual slaughterer of kosher animals.

shul: lit. "school"; refers to synagogue.

Shulhan Arukh: lit. "set table"; encyclopedic law code written by Rabbi Joseph Karo (c. 1565).

siddur (siddurim): prayerbook.

sidrah: see *parashah*.

simhah: celebration.

simhat bat: ceremony celebrating the birth of a daughter.

Simhat Torah: "rejoicing over the Torah"; festival at the end of Sukkot.

sufganiyot: jelly donuts eaten on Hanukkah.

sukkah: lit. "shelter"; temporary structure built for the holiday of Sukkot.

Sukkot: Jewish harvest festival.

tahanun: private prayers of petition.

taharah: ritual washing of a body in preparation for burial.

tallit (tallitot): prayer shawl.

tallit katan: small garment with *tzitzit*, generally worn under the shirt.

Talmud: lit. "teaching"; refers to comprehensive collection of rabbinic teachings consisting of the *Mishnah* and the *Gemara*.

Talmud Torah: the *mitzvah* of Torah study.

Tanakh: acronym for the Hebrew Bible: *Torah, Nevi'im* (Prophets), *K'tuvim* (Writings).

taref, tereifah, treif: lit. "torn to pieces"; generally refers to non-kosher food.

Tashlikh: New Year ceremony of symbolically casting sins into a body of water.

tefillin: leather boxes containing passages of Torah, which are worn during weekday morning prayers in order to "bind" them upon one's hand and between one's eyes.

teshuvah: repentance.

tevilah: ritual immersion.

tikkun leil Shavuot: Torah study on the first night of Shavuot.

tikkun olam: lit. "perfecting the world"; social justice.

Tisha b'Av: lit. "the ninth of *Av*"; mid-summer fast day marking the destruction of the Temple in Jerusalem.

tohorat ha-mishpahah: lit. "family purity"; laws pertaining to the regulation of marital relations and immersion in a *mikveh.*

Tosafists: medieval Jewish commentators.

Torah: lit. "teaching"; refers to the Five Books of Moses and Jewish learning in general.

Torah she-b'al peh: Oral Torah.

Torah she-bikhtav: Written Torah; Five Books of Moses.

Tu B'Shvat: lit. "fifteenth day of *Shvat*"; Jewish Arbor Day.

Tur: see *Arba'a Turim.*

tzaddik: lit. "righteous one"; Hasidic spiritual leader.

tzedakah: lit. "righteousness"; refers to the *mitzvah* of distributing resources to the less fortunate.

tzitzit: fringes on the four corners of a *tallit* or *tallit katan,* worn as a reminder to fulfill *mitzvot.*

yad: lit: "hand"; ornamental pointer used while reading from the Torah scroll.

yahrzeit: annual commemoration on the Hebrew date of a person's death.

Yamim Noraim: Days of Awe.

yarmulke: see *kippah.*

yeshiva (yeshivot): talmudic academy of higher learning.

yetzer ha-ra: the inclination to do evil.

yetzer ha-tov: the inclination to do good.

Yigdal: liturgical hymn based on Maimonides' Thirteen Principles of Faith.

yirat shamayim: reverence for the sacred.

yishuv: Jewish community in pre-State Palestine.

Yisrael: refers to the Jewish people; also refers to the land or State of Israel.

Yizkor: memorial service.

Yom ha-Atzmaut: Israel Independence Day.

Yom ha-Shoah: Holocaust Remembrance Day.

Yom ha-Zikaron: Israel Memorial Day.

Yom Kippur: lit. "Day of Atonement."

yom tov: Hebrew term for holiday.

Yom Yerushalayim: Jerusalem Day.

Yoreh De'ah: section of the *Arba'a Turim;* also a section of the *Shulhan Arukh.*

zakhor: imperative term for "remember."

z'mirot: Shabbat songs.

Zohar: Book of Splendor; medieval kabbalistic work.

Names of the months: *Tishri, Ḥeshvan, Kislev, Tevet, Sh'vat, Adar, Nisan, Iyar, Sivan, Tammuz, Av, Elul*

Books of the Torah: *Bereshit, Sh'mot, Vayikra, Bemidbar, D'varim*

Index

Abraham, 13, 14–15, 22, 84–85, 123, 136
Adam and Eve, 66, 127, 135
Adon Olam, 97
Afterlife, 49–51, 58, 133
    See also Ha-olam ha-ba; Immortality
Aggadah, 27
Ahad Ha-am (Asher Ginzberg), 185, 196
Akedah, 109
Akiba, Rabbi, 13, 74–75
Aleinu, 57, 88, 90, 91, 92, 97
Alexander the Great, 142
Alfasi, Isaac, (*"the Rif"*), 31
Aliyah (*aliyot*), 95, 96, 114, 125, 126
Alkabez, Shlomo ha-Levi, 91
Amidah, 54, 84–88, 90, 91, 92, 93, 97, 120

Animals, 53, 65–66, 97; *See also Kashrut;* Sanctity of Life
Antiochus, 117, 142–143
Anti-Semitism, 7, 17
    and repression, 151, 159, 164
    Christian leaders against, 164
    in Europe, 155–156, 158–159, 161, 163–165, 168, 184, 185
    in the United States, 174, 175, 179–180
    sources of, 119, 151, 152–153, 161, 163–165, 170, 174, 175, 177, 179
    See also Prejudice and Discrimination
Arabs, 148–150, 169, 170, 182, 186–187, 190–194
    Palestinian Arab refugees, 190–193

Arabs *(cont.)*
  Palestine Liberation Organiza-
    tion (PLO), 193
Arafat, Yasser, 193
Arba'a Turim, 31
Ark (*aron ha-kodesh*), 93, 94, 96,
  104–105
Ashamnu, 111. *See* Yom Kippur
Ashkenazic Jews
  customs and practice, 31, 69,
    71, 100, 115, 123–124
  history of, 175, 177, 181
Ashrei, 97
Assimilation. *See* Judaism,
  Enlightenment; United
  States

Baal Shem Tov (Israel ben
  Eliezer), 156–157
Babylonia, 28–29, 94, 151, 170
Babylonian Exile, 11, 100,
  140–141, 146
Baeck, Leo, 162
Balfour Declaration, 187
Bar Kokhba, 13, 145
Bar mitzvah, vii, 44, 125–126
Bar'khu, 81,90
Bat mitzvah, vii, 38, 44, 126
Begin, Menahem, 192
Ben Asher, Jacob, Rabbi, 31
Ben Gurion, David, 189–190
Ben Yehuda, Eliezer, 185
Bene Israel, 170–171
Benjamin, Judah P., 176
Berakhot (Blessings), 92, 95, 98,
  107
  after meals, 64, 72, 120
  Amidah, 84–88, 90, 97, 120
  before meals, 63, 71
  brit milah, 123
  candlelighting, 1, 70, 118

children, 70–71
conversion with immersion
  (*tevilah*), 18
definition of, 79–80
k'riat Shema, 82–84, 90
priestly, 71
marriage, 127
structure, 80, 81–91, 107
See also Prayer; Synagogue Ser-
  vices; *individual blessings and
  prayers by name*
Bereshit Rabbah, 27
Beta Yisrael, 169, 172
Bet din (batei din), 5, 12, 17
Bialik, Hayim Nahman, 27
Birkat ha-mazon , 64, 72, 120
  See also Berakhot, after meals
Birkhot ha-shahar, 89–90
Birth, of daughter, 124
  of son. *See* Circumcision
Blessings. *See Berakhot*
Blood libel, 152
Boaz, 11
Brit milah. See Circumcision
Buber, Martin, viii, 162

Calendar, 94, 106–107
Canaan, 136, 137
Candlelighting, 1, 70, 72, 107,
  110, 116, 117–118, 132
  See also Berakhot; Hanukkah;
    Shabbat; *Yahrzeit*
Cantor. *See* Hazzan
Carrying, on Shabbat and holi-
  days, 73, 108
Carter, Jimmy, 192
Charity. *See* Philanthropy;
  Tzedakah
Children, blessing of, 70–71
China, Jews of. *See* Kaifeng
Chmielnitzki, 155–156

Christianity
  and Judaism, 47, 150,
    152–153, 156, 163–164,
    180–181
  conversion to, 33, 151, 161,
    180–181
  tenets of faith, 5, 25, 47, 164
Christmas, 1, 8, 21
Circumcision, 12, 14, 16, 18–19,
    35, 74, 122–123, 143
Clinton, Bill, 193
Clothing, 60–62. *See also* Head
    Coverings; *Kippah; Tallit*
Cochin, Jews of, 171
Cohen, Hermann, 162
Commandments. *See Mitzvot*
Committee on Jewish Law and
    Standards, 39, 73, 101
  See also Conservative Judaism
Community. *See* Jewish People-
    hood; Congregation; Syna-
    gogue
Confession. *See* Yom Kippur
Congregation, 39–40, 42, 99,
    101–103, 104, 105, 111,
    174; *See also* Synagogue
Conservative Judaism, ix, 5,
    41–42, 93, 94, 162
  concepts, 39–42, 101, 120
  conversion efforts, 16, 40
  definition of, 38–39, 40
  Get, 40, 128–129
  history in America, 38–41, 177,
    178
  in Israel, 195
  *Siddur Sim Shalom for Shabbat
    and Festivals,* 32, 48, 81, 85
Conversion
  to Christianity, 151, 156,
    180–181
  to Islam, 156, 170

  to Judaism, xiii–xiv, 4–5, 8, 11,
    17–22, 40, 84, 196
  early converts, 12–14
  ger, 12–13
  history of, 11–16
  prohibition of, 13–15
  process, 16–19, 21–22
  ritual of, 12, 17–18, 117
  See Study; United States; *also
    under individual movements*
Council of the Four Lands, 153
Covenant, 19, 25, 35, 45, 123
Creation. *See* Judaism; Torah
Cremation. *See* Death; Mourning;
    Judaism, Holocaust
Crusades, 14, 152
Cyrus, 141

Daniel, Book of, 49, 104
David (King), 11, 53, 138
Death, 9, 51, 53, 156
  customs and practice, 129–133
  See also Mourning
Dietary Laws. *See Kashrut*
Divorce, 26, 128–129
Dresner, Samuel, 65
Dreyfus, Alfred, 161, 185

Ecclesiastes, Book of (*Kohelet*),
    113
Education, 21–22, 74–76,
    153–154, 182
  See also Study; *Talmud Torah;*
    Torah, study of
Egalitarian. *See under* Synagogue
    Services; *individual move-
    ments*
Egypt, 53, 169, 191, 192
Ein Keloheinu, 97
El Malei Raḥamim. See Death;
    Mourning

Electricity, on Shabbat and holidays, 39, 73
Emancipation. *See* Judaism, Enlightenment
Emet Ve-Emunah, 40
England, 151, 162–163, 187–190, 194
Erev, 70, 107
Erusin. *See* Marriage
Eruv, 73
Esther, Book of, 119–120
Ethiopian Jews. *See Beta Yisrael*
Etrog, 113
Even Ha-Ezer, 31
Evil, 49–50, 109, 136
Exodus (from Egypt), 12, 69, 84, 92, 112–116, 136
Ezra and Nehemiah, 141

Faith, 41, 42, 45, 62, 82, 149–150, 157
Fasting, 4, 72, 110, 112, 121, 145
Finkelstein, Louis, 23
Flood, 66
Food and meals, 63–68, 71–72, 92, 97–98, 108, 112, 115, 117, 119
    See also Berakhot; Ḥametz; Kashrut; Shabbat
France, 151–152; *See also* Judaism, Enlightenment
Free Choice, 51–52, 135–136

Gaon (pl. *Geonim*), 30–31, 147–148, 170
Gaon of Vilna (Elijah of Vilna), 157
Garden of Eden, 66, 127, 135
Gays and Lesbians, 36
Gemara, 28, 46; *See also Mishnah;* Talmud

Germany. *See* Anti-Semitism; Hitler; Judaism, Enlightenment, Holocaust
Get, See Divorce *See also under individual movements*
Ghetto, 33, 153, 160, 166
God, 54, 55
    attributes and principles, 41–42, 45, 47–49, 57
    belief, 2, 9, 23, 37, 40, 58, 60–65, 149–150, 156
    oneness of, 47, 49, 82–83, 98
    historical aspects, 11, 22, 45, 66, 71, 125, 140–141
    holiness, 52, 59–60
    liturgy, 77, 80–91, 92, 108, 109, 111, 127
    names of, 63, 81
    theology, xiv, 19–20, 41–42, 51–53, 57–58, 123, 135–139, 148–150
    See also references to God in individual prayers
Golden Age of Spain, 148–150
Gordis, Robert, 51
Guide for the Perplexed, 149–150

Ha-Levi, Yehudah, 149
Ha-olam ha-ba, 50–51; *See also* Afterlife; Immortality
Ha-motzi, 63, 71, 72, 80, 108, 110
Haftarah, 96, 99, 111, 115, 120, 126
Haganah, 188
Haggadah, 115
Hai Gaon, 30–31
Halakhah, 40, 41–42, 43, 46, 58, 73
    definition of, 26, 39, 45

See also Jewish Law; *individual movements*

Ḥallah, 1, 71, 72, 110

Hallel, 98, 113, 115, 120, 121

Haman, 119

Ḥamas. *See* Terrorism

Ḥanukkah, 1, 8, 21, 54, 99, 117–118, 119, 143

Ḥaredim, 37

Hashkiveinu, 84

Ḥasidism, 156–157, 178–179

Hasmonean Dynasty. *See* Maccabees

Hatafat dam brit, 18, 123
  See also Circumcision

Havdalah, 72–73, 98, 112

Ḥavurah (*ḥavurot*), 3, 4, 42, 43, 105
  See also Reconstructionist Judaism

Ḥazzan (cantor), 102–103

Head coverings, 38, 61–62

Hebrew language
  in liturgy, 20, 34, 38, 78–79, 162
  relationship to people, ix, 10, 40, 41, 160, 171, 185, 186, 188

Heine, Heinrich, 34, 161

Hellenism, 53, 100, 117–118, 141–144

Herod, 144

Herzl, Theodor, 185–186, 196

Heschel, Abraham Joshua, viii, xiv, 69–70, 73–74, 76, 133

Hesed, 20, 56–57

Ḥevrah Kadisha. *See* Death; Mourning

Ḥibbat Tziyon, 184–185, 186

Hillel, xiv, 28, 50, 99, 198

Hirsch, Samson Raphael, 37

Hitler, Adolf, 35, 162, 165, 166, 178, 188

Holiness, 52, 60, 64, 65, 70, 86, 92; *See also* God; *Kedushah*

Holocaust (*Shoah*). *See* Judaism

Holy Days, 4, 32, 52, 73, 106–112
  pilgrimage festivals, 61, 97, 98, 112–117, 126, 130
  See also individual holidays by name

Hoshanot, 113

Ḥoshen Mishpat, 31

Idolatry, 48

Immortality, 46, 49–51

Inquisition, 151, 174

Intermarriage, 11, 36, 181–182

Intifada, 192–193

Irgun, 188

Isaac, 14, 84–85, 109, 123, 136

Isaiah, 11–12, 54

Islam, 147, 149–150, 156, 170, 173–174, 194

Israel (kingdom)
  leadership of, 137–141, 142–143, 145

Israel, land of
  living in, 11, 27, 91, 116, 159, 170
  relationship to, ix, 104, 107, 147, 156, 183–184

Israel, State of, 170, 174, 181, 182, 196
  Declaration of Independence, 183, 190
  history of, 54, 159, 167, 184–194
  relationship to 3, 4, 10, 35, 40, 181, 182,196

Israel, State of *(cont.)*
  religion in, 94, 100, 107, 114,
    116, 118, 119, 120–121,
    194–195
Isserles, Moses, Rabbi ("the
    Rama"), 31
Italy, 151,184

Jabotinsky, Vladamir, 188
Jacob, 14, 84–85, 136
Jacobs, Louis, 40
Jerusalem
  ancient history, 88, 104, 107,
    117, 124–125, 138, 140, 145
  modern history, 188, 191, 192
Jesus, 14, 144, 164, 180
Jew, definition of, 16, 36, 42–43,
    44–45, 46, 60, 68
Jew by choice, ix, 8, 16, 20–21,
    22, 44, 60, 196
  See also Conversion
Jewish History. *See* Judaism;
    Torah, books of; *and under
    individual topics*
Jewish Law, 26, 34–35, 37, 38,
    39, 40, 42–43, 45, 46, 55,
    66, 103, 126, 131, 151, 166,
    177, 178
  *See also Halakhah; Mishnah;
    Gemara;* Talmud
Jewish Peoplehood (*am*), ix, 3,
    10–11, 15, 19, 24, 35, 36,
    40,
  community, 3, 22, 36, 41, 58,
    76, 99, 101, 127–128, 170,
    172, 181–182, 185, 194
  historical aspects, 10–11, 15,
    24, 35, 46, 114, 134, 135,
    158–159
  relationship to God, 19, 88,
    162

Jewish Theological Seminary, 40,
    41, 129,177, 178
Jonah, Book of, 111; *See also* Yom
    Kippur
Judah (kingdom), 143–144
Judah ha-Nasi, Rabbi, 27–28
Judah the Maccabee, 54, 117,
    143
Joshua, 137
Judaism
  and Christianity, 47, 150,
    152–153, 156, 163–164,
    180–181
  and Islam, 147–148, 169
  beliefs, xiv, 34, 44–46, 49,
    51–58, 59, 135–136, 157
  definition of, 10–11, 21, 23,
    41, 44–46, 56, 135, 160
  in Europe, 33–35, 160–163
    Eastern Europe, 37–38,
    155–158, 159–163, 170,
    172
    Enlightenment, 16, 158,
    160–163
    Holocaust, 165–167, 178
    Middle Ages, 99, 151–154,
    175
  in Israel, 94, 100, 107, 114,
    118, 119, 120–121, 159,
    187–188, 194–195
  in the United States, 33,
    35–36, 38–39, 41, 92–93,
    101–103, 121, 130, 159,
    173–182
  modern movements, 16, 33–43,
    176–180
  values in, 9–10, 19–20, 40,
    64–68, 74, 161–162
  See Torah, books of; *also names
    of individual movements*
Judea, 140–141, 142, 144, 193

Judges, Book of, 137
Justice. *See Tzedakah*

Kabbalah, 4, 32, 150–154
   kabbalists, names of, 150
Kabbalat Shabbat, 70, 91, 92; *See
      also* Shabbat; Synagogue Ser-
      vices
Kaddish (Mourner's), 90, 91, 92,
      93, 97, 104, 131, 132, 133
   definition and translation,
      88–89
Kaifeng, 171–172
Kaplan, Mordecai M., 41–42
Karo, Joseph, 31
Kashrut, 5, 36, 46, 171
   definition of, 64–65
   kosher home, 67–68
   laws of, 66–67
   milk and meat, separation of,
      67–68
Kelman, Wolfe, 6
Kedushah, 86, 90
Keriah. See Death; Mourning
Ketubah. See Marriage
Kibbutzim, 116, 188
Kiddush, 71, 72, 92, 97, 107, 113,
      116
Kippah (kippot), 36, 62; *See also*
      Head coverings
Knesset, 190
Kol Nidrei, 111
K'riat Shema, 6, 81, 83, 84, 90
Kristallnacht, 166

Lag B'Omer, 116
Lamentations, Book of (*Eikhah*),
      121
Leah, 71, 85
Lekha Dodi, 91
Leviticus, Book of, 60, 66

Life. *See* Sanctity of Life
Liturgy. *See Siddur*
Lubavitch, 178; *See also* Hasidism
Lulav, 113
Luria, Solomon, 15
Luther, Martin, 164

Maariv (Arvit), 80–89, 90, 92,
      98, 111
   See also Synagogue Services
Maccabees, 118, 143–144; *See
      also* Ḥanukkah
Maftir, 96, 126
Maḥazor (maḥzorim), 32
Maimonides (Rabbi Moses ben
      Maimon), viii, 14–15, 22,
      31, 45, 48, 51, 84, 109–110,
      113, 149–150, 169
Marranos, 151
Marriage (*Kiddushin*), 18, 26, 126
   ceremony, 126–128
Maskilim, 158
Mattathias. *See* Maccabees
Matriarchs, 70, 85
Matzah, 114, 152
Megillah, 119
Meir, Rabbi, 13, 80
Mekhilta, 197
Mendelssohn, Moses, 160
Menorah, 1, 3, 104, 109,
      117–118
   See also Candlelighting
Messiah (Messianic Age), 46, 53,
      57, 88, 109, 138, 156, 180
Mezuzah, 62–63, 83
Micah, Book of, 25, 110
Midrash (midrashim), 27, 32,
      145; *See also books by individ-
      ual names*
Mikra'ot G'dolot, 25; *See also*
      Torah

Mikveh, 6, 16, 17–19
Minḥah, 90–91, 92, 97
Minyan, 40, 43, 90, 101–102,
    107, 129, 132
    women counted in, 101, 129
Mishnah, 27–28, 29, 46, 52–53,
    54
    See also Talmud
Mishneh Torah, 31, 149
Mitnagdim, 157
Mitzvot
    brit milah, 122–123
    death, 130–133
    kashrut, 64–69
    number of, 104
    observance of, 20, 41 ,46, 53,
        61–62, 70, 83–84, 101,
        136–137
    people, relationship to, ix, 22,
        24, 45, 49, 60
    types, 59–62
    See also individual ones by name
Muhammed, 76, 169
Modern Orthodox Judaism,
    37–38, 39, 105
Mohel, mohelet, 19, 123
    See also Circumcision; *Mikveh*
Monotheism. *See* God
Moses, xiv, 11, 47, 48, 75,
    136–137
Mount Sinai, xiv, 37, 109, 117,
    136, 197
Mourning, 9, 72, 90–91, 103,
    116, 129–133, 145
    See also Death; *Kaddish*
Musaf, 96–97
Music in synagogue, 34, 79, 99,
    103
    trope (cantillation), 95- 96, 97,
        103
Mysticism, 32, 58, 150–151, 157
Names, Hebrew, 19, 123–124

Naomi, 117
Napoleon, 161
National Jewish Population Study,
    181
Nationalism. *See* Jewish People-
    hood; Zionism
Nehemiah. *See* Ezra and
    Nehemiah
Neo- Orthodox Judaism. *See*
    Modern Orthodox Judaism
Nesuin. See Marriage
Noah, 66

Oraḥ Ḥayim, 31
Oriental Jews, 171–172
Original Sin, 51
Orthodox Judaism, 43, 61, 162,
    193, 194
    concepts, 5, 36–38, 40, 42, 101,
        102, 126
    conversion efforts, 16
    get, 128–129
    history in America, 177,
        178–179
Outreach, 8, 16, 36
    See also Conversion

Pale of Settlement, 159, 184
Palestine, 26, 28, 145, 167, 177,
    183, 185, 192–194
    See also Israel
Palestinian Arab refugees,
    190–193
Palestine Liberation Organization
    (PLO), 193
Parashah, 24, 95, 96–97
Passover. *See* Pesaḥ
Patriarchs. *See under individual
    names*
Peace (*shalom*), 54–55, 192,
    193–194; *See also Shalom*
Peres, Shimon, 193

Pesaḥ, 53, 107, 112, 113, 116, 117, 120, 133, 167
  preparations and practice, 114–115
Philanthropy
  in the United States, 56, 99–100, 178, 181–182
  toward Israel, 56, 122, 181, 195–196
  See also Tzedakah
Philo Judaeus, 142
Pidyon haben, 125
Pilgrimage Festivals. *See* Synagogue Services; Holy Days; *See also under individual names*
Pirkei Avot, xi, 28, 50, 58
Pogroms, 155–159, 177, 178
Poverty, 55–56, 169, 179
Prayer, 9, 46, 52, 55
  minyan, 101–102
  types of, 36, 40, 55
  women's *tefillot,* 38
  worship, 77–79, 99, 100, 103, 156
  See also Berakhot ; *Siddur;* Synagogue services ; *and under individual prayers*
Prayerbook. *See Siddur*
Prayer shawl. *See Tallit*
Prejudice and Discrimination, 1, 3, 8, 151, 161, 170, 173–174, 179–180, 185
  Jewish groups against, 180
  See also Anti-Semitism
Prophets, 137–138
Proselytizing, 12, 14–16
  See also Conversion
Psalms, Book of, 25, 45, 105, 115
P'sikta Rabbati, 27
P'sukei D'zimra, 90
Purim, 119–120

Rabbinate, rabbis, 5, 9, 22, 34, 44, 52, 102, 128, 130, 177
  women in, 36, 102
Rabbinical Assembly, the, 129, 177
Rabbis (Sages), 12, 13, 26, 46, 49, 50, 54, 73, 74, 128, 129, 146–148
  names of, 58, 113, 145
Rabin, Yitzhak, 54, 193, 194
Rachel, 71, 85
Racism. *See* Anti-Semitism; Prejudice and Discrimination
Rambam. *See* Maimonides
Rashi (Rabbi Shlomo Yitzhaki), 25, 151–152
Rav, 50, 79
Ravnitzky, Yehoshua Hana, 27
Rebecca, 71, 85
Reconstructionist Judaism, 41–42
  concepts, 41–42, 101, 102, 105, 107
Red Sea, 136
Redemption (*Ge'ulah*), 147
Reform Judaism, 39, 43, 92, 100, 107, 162, 195
  concepts, 34–37, 42, 84, 89, 101, 102, 104, 107
  conversion process, 16, 36–37
  get, 128
  history in America, 176–177
  in Israel, 195
Repentance (*teshuvah*), 52, 108, 111
  See also under Rosh Hashanah; Yom Kippur
Responsa, 22, 31, 39–40
  See also Conservative Judaism; Jewish Law; Talmud
Resurrection, 86, 133
Revelation, xiv, 24, 91, 116, 141
Reward and Punishment, 49

Roman oppression, 26, 74, 86,
    144–146, 183
Rosenzweig, Franz, 62
Rosh Hashanah, 4, 52, 108–110
    observance and customs, 110
Rosh Ḥodesh, 97
Russia. *See* Soviet Union
Ruth, Book of, 11, 117

Saadia Gaon, 47, 148, 149, 169
Sabbath. *See* Shabbat
Sacrifices, 96–97, 109, 143; *See
    also* Animals
Sadat, Anwar, 192
Sanctity of life, 51–54, 65–66
    See also Kashrut
Sarah, 22, 71, 85; *See also* Matri-
    archs
Satmar, 178. *See also* Ḥasidism
Saul (King), 137; *See also* Israel
    (kingdom)
Schechter, Solomon, 177
Schorsch, Ismar, 40
Seder (Pesaḥ), 3, 53, 115, 116,
    147
    Tu B'Shvat Seder, 118; *See also*
        Tu B'Shvat
Sefer Ha-Aggadah, 27
Sefer Torah (Torah scroll), 64, 93,
    96, 104, 114, 143, 171–172
    description, 94–95
    writing of, 95
    See also Torah
Sefer Yetzirah, 32
Seliḥot, 108
Sephardic Jews
    customs and practice of, 31,
        115, 121, 124
    history, 168–169, 175, 177,
        181
Septuagint, 142
Sermon, 34, 38, 96

Seudah shlishit, 72, 98
Shabbat, 5, 8, 20, 22, 39–40, 74,
    84, 87, 108, 143, 147
    definition, 69–70
    erev Shabbat, 70–72, 91
    Havdalah, 72–73, 98
    meals on, 71–72, 92, 98
    practice, 46, 69–73, 90, 91–94,
        97, 110, 125, 171
    prohibitions on, 26, 39–40, 61,
        73, 108, 194–195
    seudah shlishit, 72, 98
    Shabbat shalom, 69
    See also Synagogue services;
        individual movements
Shabbatai Zevi, 156
Shaddai. See God; *Mezuzah*
Shaḥarit, 55, 60, 89–90, 91
Shalom, 55, 87
    shalom bayit, 63
    See also Shabbat
Shammai, xiv, 50
Shavuot, 107, 112, 113, 116–117,
    133
    conversion practice, 117
    tikkun leil Shavuot, 116
Shema, 47, 81–84
    recitation of, 84
Shivah, 4, 131–132
    See also Death; Mourning
Shloshim. See Death; Mourning
Sh'moneh Esreh. See Amidah
Shemini Atzeret, 113, 114
Shrage, Barry, viii, 75
Shoah. See Judaism, Holocaust
Shofar, 109–110, 111
Shoftim (Judges), 137; *See* Israel
    (kingdom)
Shulḥan Arukh, 31
Siddur
    definition of, 32 , 78
    differences, 34 ,41, 81, 86, 97

liturgy, 13, 32, 34, 38, 41, 77, 87, 94, 98, 115, 120, 121, 146–147
    structure, 79–90
    versions, 32, 34, 41, 48, 81, 85, 97
    See also Berakhot; Prayer; Synagogue Services
Simeon ben Gamliel, Rabbi, 58
Simḥat bat, 124
Simḥat Torah, 24, 114
Sin, 51–52, 108, 111
Six Day War, 54, 125, 181, 195–196
Solomon (King), 11, 138; *See also* Israel (kingdom)
Solomon, Haym, 174
Song of Songs, Book of, 25, 115
Soviet Union (Russia), ix, 158–159, 168, 176, 182, 184–185, 191
Spirituality, 9, 21, 98, 101, 107, 108, 110, 139, 185
Steinberg, Milton, 51
Steinsaltz, Adin, 6–7, 29–30
Study, 41, 50, 72, 96, 116, 138, 153–154, 156
    for conversion, vii, 17, 21–22, 198
    Talmud Torah, 74–76
    See also Shavuot
Stuyvesant, Peter, 174
Sukkot, 107, 114, 117, 133
    Sukkah, 112–113, 116
Synagogue, 8, 35, 36, 43, 73, 78, 129, 135, 171, 176, 182
    architecture and design, 103–105
    definition of, 100, 147
    names of, 100–101
Synagogue services, 44, 45, 130, 146

daily prayer, 40, 54, 55, 60, 79
egalitarian, 36 ,40, 125
Ḥanukkah, 99, 119
    in Conservative Judaism, 39–40, 92–94, 103, 120
    in Orthodox Judaism, 38–39, 126
    in Reconstructionist Judaism, 42, 107
    in Reform Judaism, 34–36, 84, 89, 93, 96, 103, 107
    language, 36, 40, 78–79, 166
    musaf service, 96–97
    music, 34, 36, 79, 96, 97, 99, 103
    new observances, 120–121
    Pilgrimage Festivals, 40, 87, 96, 97, 98, 99, 112–117, 137
    Purim, 99, 119
    Rosh Hashanah, 4, 99,107, 109–110
    Rosh Ḥodesh, 98
    Shabbat, 35, 36, 38, 40, 87, 91–98, 141
    Tisha B'Av, 121
    Torah service, 90, 93–96, 97, 124, 125; *See also* Holy Days
    weekday, 80–91
    Yom Kippur, 4, 99, 111–112
Syria, 117, 142, 145, 170–171, 192

Tabernacle, 104
Tallit (tallitot), 36, 38, 94, 95
    tallit katan, 61
    wearing of, by women, 40, 61–62
Talmud, 32, 45–46, 50, 55, 56, 63, 78, 105, 128, 153–154
    conversion, 13
    codes, 30–31

Talmud *(cont.)*
  definition and format of, 28, 29
  study of, 29, 74, 157, 174
  versions *(Bavli, Yerushalmi),*
    28–30, 146, 170
Tarfon, Rabbi, 58
Tefillin, 61–62, 83
  wearing of, by women, 40, 62
Temple in Jerusalem, First
  in history, 11, 12, 24, 54, 71,
    100, 116, 117, 128, 140
  in liturgy, 90, 95, 97, 103, 104,
    125
Temple in Jerusalem, Second
  in history, 141, 143–145
  in liturgy, 34, 86, 112, 121
Ten Commandments, 26, 53, 69,
    105, 109
Ten Lost Tribes, 139, 171
Terrorism, 53, 191–192, 193–194
  See also Anti-Semitism; Preju-
    dice and Discrimination
Tevilah (ritual immersion), 12, 16,
    17–18; *See also Mikveh*
Thirteen Principles of Faith, 45
Theology. *See Berakhot;* God;
    Prayer
Tikkun olam, 36, 41, 56–58
Tisha B'Av, 121, 145
Tohorat ha-mishpaḥah, 17–18
Tosafists, 152
Torah, ix, 62–63, 78, 81, 82, 89
  books of, viii, 4, 14, 23–26, 45,
    135–141
  commentaries on, 25, 26–27,
    32, 150–152, 197–198
  definition of, 24, 64, 75
  giving of, xiv, 37, 116, 117,
    197; *See* Shavuot
  Oral Torah, *Torah she-b'al peh,*
    26

reading of, 24, 72, 90, 93,
    94–96, 97, 104, 105, 114,
    120, 125, 141
  study of, 25, 40, 42, 74–75,
    83, 96, 153–154, 157, 198;
    See also Study
  Tanakh, 24–26
  teachings, 12, 26, 47, 51, 57,
    65–67, 126, 128, 130
  translations of, 142, 160
  triennial cycle, 94
  trope, 95, 96, 97, 103
  Written Torah, *Torah she-
    b'khtav,* 26
  See also Sefer Torah; Synagogue
    services
Travel. *See* Shabbat, prohibitions
    on
Tu B'Shvat, 118–119; *See also
    Seder*
Tur. See Arba'a Turim
Tzedakah, 20, 55–56, 119, 120,
    125, 130, 133, 180
Tzitzit, 61, 83–84
  See also Tallit

United Nations, 189, 190
United States, 56, 92–93, 102,
    104, 105, 134–135, 164,
    170, 191
  American Jewish history, 33,
    35–36, 168, 173–180,
    181
  assimilation, 75, 157, 179,
    181–182
  conversion, 11, 16, 21
  demographics, 124–125,
    174–176, 182–183

Vegetarianism, 65–66, 68
Vespasian, 145–146

Washington, George, 175
Weizmann, Chaim, 187, 188, 190
West Bank, 191, 193
Wise, Isaac Mayer, 176–177
Women
  as rabbis, 102
  bat mitzvah, 38–39, 129–130
  birth of a daughter, 124
  candlelighting, 70
  counted in *minyan*, 40, 101, 129
  head covering, 38, 62
  in liturgy, 85
  participation in services, 5, 38–39, 40, 71
  simhat bat, 124
  tohorat ha-mishpahah, 17–18
  wearing of *tallit*, 40, 61–62
  wearing of *tefillin*, 40, 62
Work, prohibition of, 5, 26, 73, 108
World Zionist Organization, 189, 195
Worship. *See* Synagogue Services

Yahrzeit, 89, 114, 132
Yavneh, 146
Yeshiva (yeshivot), 37, 158, 178, 179
Yigdal, 45, 48
Yizkor, 111, 113, 133
Yohanan ben Zakkai (Rabbi), 145–146
Yom ha-Atzmaut, 120–121
Yom ha-Shoah, 120
Yom ha-Zikaron, Yom Yerushalayim, 120–121
Yom Kippur, 52, 72, 107, 108, 109, 110–112, 113, 133, 192
  observance, 4, 111–112
Yoreh De'ah, 31

Zionism, 35, 116, 118, 159, 165, 185, 186–189; *See also* Jewish Peoplehood
Zion. *See* Israel; Jerusalem; *Siddur*
Zohar, 32, 154

Rabbi Simcha Kling (1922-1991) was ordained at the Jewish Theological Seminary, where he also earned a master's degree in Hebrew literature and a doctorate in Hebrew letters. He was a pulpit rabbi for over forty years, serving congregations in St. Louis, Missouri; Greensboro, North Carolina; and Louisville, Kentucky.

Rabbi Carl M. Perkins is the spiritual leader of Temple Aliyah in Needham, Massachusetts. A graduate of Harvard Law School and the Wexner graduate fellowship program, he earned a master's degree in Talmud and Rabbinics and was ordained at the Jewish Theological Seminary in 1991.